Penguin Education

Sociology of Law

Penguin Modern Sociology Readings

General Editor
Tom Burns

Advisory Board

Fredrik Barth
Michel Crozier
Ralf Dahrendorf
Erving Goffman
Alvin Gouldner
Edmund Leach
David Lockwood
Gianfranco Poggi
Peter Worsley

Sociology of Law

Selected Readings

Edited by Vilhelm Aubert

Penguin Books
Baltimore, Maryland

Penguin Books Ltd, Harmondsworth,
Middlesex, England
Penguin Books Inc., 7110 Ambassador Road,
Baltimore, Md 21207, U.S.A.
Penguin Books Australia Ltd, Ringwood,
Victoria, Australia

First published 1969
This selection copyright © Vilhelm Aubert, 1969
Introduction and notes copyright © Vilhelm Aubert, 1969

Made and printed in Great Britain by
C. Nicholls & Company Ltd
Set in Monotype Times

Contents

Introduction

It is sometimes striking how much the vocabulary of sociology resembles the language of law. The emphasis upon rights, obligations and expectations, upon sanctions and predictability within sociology has its counterpart in the sophisticated analyses of these concepts in the tradition of legal scholarship. The same terms are, however, used for different purposes in law and in sociology. Where the lawyer or the legal scholar talks about rights and expectations he does so with normative intentions. He purports to give directives to clients or to legal functionaries, and he intends his analysis to form the basis of decisions, ultimately of action. The sociologist, on the other hand, uses the same terms without any directly normative purpose, in an attempt to describe, reveal and explain. Terms like rights and obligations are to him only convenient ways of summarizing observations of actual transactions between people or of depicting the normative convictions of the actors.

This juxtaposition presents sociology as less value-laden than would be warranted if a complete picture had been intended. Nevertheless, the contrast does express a basic tendency in the differences between the two disciplines, differences which are rooted in the different social functions of law and of sociology. Doctrinal legal research (*Rechtswissenschaft*) has had the practical purpose of providing lawyers, judges and others with the tools needed to reach decisions on an immense variety of problems, usually with very limited time at disposal. This task makes the question, for example, of how often a judicial decision on a specific point has been made, uninteresting as long as one or a few good precedents are available for analysis. Since the precedents are primarily to be found in High Court decisions, these judgements constitute the universe from which empirical materials are drawn, while the actual practices of the lower courts and of administrative agencies with semi-judicial functions are left unmapped. In so far as judges' opinions have been scrutinized, the normative purpose of the analysis has made it uninteresting

9

to trace the influence from factors outside the recognized sources of positive law.

What characterizes the sociology of law in relation to doctrinal law is the exemption of the former from the obligation to prepare for instant decision-making. Once this pressure is removed it becomes possible to investigate rates, to count, tabulate and correlate. Once the emphasis is put, not only upon what happens in court, but also upon how often it happens, attention is drawn to the lower courts and to agencies outside the judiciary which perform parallel tasks in the administration of justice and in the settlement of disputes. The response of the citizen to the law presents another interesting empirical problem, and is no mere matter of speculation for lawyers who include references to the sense of justice, and to public opinion, in their technique of arguing. Whether the behaviour of judges, of civil servants or of ordinary citizens is to be explained, it appears arbitrary to limit attention to those influences which are normatively respectable. The operation of interests, passions and prejudices becomes a legitimate concern for legal research.

Sociology of law is here viewed as a branch of general sociology, just like family sociology, industrial or medical sociology. It should not be overlooked, however, that sociology legitimately may also be viewed as an auxiliary of legal studies, an aid in executing the tasks of the legal profession. Sociological analyses of phenomena which are regulated by law, may aid legislators or even the courts in making decisions. Quite as important is the critical function of sociology of law, as an aid in enhancing the legal profession's awareness of its own function in society.

In this volume it seemed on balance advisable to exclude studies of so-called 'primitive law'. A distinction is thus drawn between the sociology of law and the ethnography of law. The one exception to this principle, the inclusion of Gluckman, illustrates that the borderline is, in some respects, an arbitrary one. The limitation to modern legal systems, characteristic of industrialized societies, is primarily based upon practical considerations, the need to avoid undue diversity in an already highly diversified subject-matter, as well as the previous availability of suitable selections on the ethnography of law (see Further Reading).

Sociology is concerned with values, with the preferences and evaluations that underlie basic structural arrangements in a society. Many of these values are embodied in law, in substantive rules as well as in the guiding procedural principles. Durkheim tried to make the most of this point of view, and overdid it in some respects. Part One is devoted to this aspect of the relationship between law and society. Law is used as a diagnostic tool to uncover structural preconditions which in other areas remain tacit and less readily observable. The description of value consensus is only one aspect of the task of sociology of law. Arnold has shown, in his highly satirical style, how legal precepts may serve more as 'symbols of government', to which everybody pays lip service, than as realistic indicators of the public's behaviour or attitudes. If this thought is carried one step further one arrives at the insight that beneath the veneer of consensus on legal principles, a struggle of interest is going on, and the law is seen as a weapon in the hands of those who possess the power to use it for their own ends. Thus, law is seen both as a cohesive force (Durkheim, Bredemeier) and as an instrument which maintains and confirms basic cleavages in a society. This latter point of view is most clearly held by the eminent representative of the Marxist tradition in legal studies, Renner.

In Part One law is more often than not seen as the dependant variable, causally determined by the societal structure. But law can, of course, also be viewed as a more active instrument for shaping future behaviour and social forms. With the emergence of legislation as a major legal institution in common-law countries as well as on the continent, in capitalist as well as in socialist states, it lies near at hand to view law as a vehicle of social engineering. The legislators, and those who carry out the precepts of the law, set a process of influence into motion. The aim is to modify and constrain the behaviour of the public, maybe even to mould their morals. The function of law, and most clearly of legislation, is seen as one of communicating with the public. The legal influence process is seen as one among several other processes of mass communication and influence in a modern society posing problems parallel to those of advertising, propaganda and mass entertainment. In law, maybe more than in other fields, the process is a two-way affair. Sumner claimed in his famous work on 'Folkways' that laws can never shape mores, and that whatever correspondence is found between laws and public attitudes and conduct is due to the fact that the law has been shaped by the mores. The modern interest in social engineering rests, of course, upon a different conception of the function of law in the development of a modern society. In Part Two we shall have occasion to observe different nuances in the conception of this two-way influence process between the law and the public to which it addresses its rules and decisions.

The field of law offers many opportunities for studying social mechanisms that also occur outside legal institutions. The pervasive problems of conflict and of conflict resolution are central in legal studies, as they are also in the study of racial tensions, industrial relations and international affairs. Due to the great systematizing and analytical efforts of previous generations of lawyers, this is an area where the sociologists meet the data in a more readily available form than is the case in many other areas. Part Three deals with conflict resolution in the courts and in other legal institutions, but contains, by way of contrast also, references to the settlement of disputes by non-legal means. Thus, Macaulay's paper deals less with legal techniques of dispute settlement than with the avoidance of legal formalities as a way of keeping up harmonious and profitable business relations. It is in this part, also, that the single reference to 'primitive law' has found its natural place. Above anything else, it is the common focus upon conflict resolution which connects the sociology of law with the ethnography of law.

Decision-making has become a catchword in modern social science, indicating an interest in revealing the processes through which those who wield power make their choices when faced with alternative paths towards a goal. The judge attracts attention as a decision-maker for several reasons. For one thing, he holds the power to release that ultimate use of naked force which society holds in store to keep order and control deviance. His decisions are, furthermore, open to public scrutiny and his reasons are explicitly stated. Because of the central place accorded the judge in the Anglo-Saxon legal systems, judicial behaviour was one of those areas where lawyers and philosophers of law early expressed a need for behavioural studies. A programme of empirical research followed as a logical consequence of the philosophically founded definitions of law proposed by the American school of legal realism. Part Four shows that when the sentencing of the courts is phrased as a problem of judicial behaviour or of decision-making it is unsatisfactory to accept the traditional legal explanations in terms of 'sources of law'. In the sociological approach to the courts there has been a 'debunking' aspect, an unwillingness to accept the judge's own claim that he based his decision upon nothing but precedent, statute or other recognized legal sources. A quest began for the latent grounds, the hidden motives, the group interests that might impinge upon the behaviour of the judge. In order to tease out these extra-legal sources of judicial decisions the most refined statistical techniques have recently been brought to bear upon the activities of the courts.

Probably no other term is in more ubiquitous, and sometimes indiscriminate, use in modern sociological writings than 'role' and its equivalents. Among the wide variety of roles in a modern society, the occupational roles are of great intrinsic interest, at the same time as they are often fairly well codified already in advance of the sociological analysis. The professions, in particular, have developed explicit ethical standards as well as a systematic theory as a basis for role performance. With medical doctors and others, lawyers have become the subjects of study as a part of a more general endeavour to map the world of the professions. Private practitioners, attorneys, barristers, and solicitors, have attracted most interest, but the problem of the professions involves all men of law, all those who have a training in law, and who make the claim that their activities and the decisions they render are, at least partly, based upon legal principles and techniques. Part Five deals with law as a task allotted to a group of trained experts, a profession.

This approach raises in a new form the question of the relationship between law and sociology, as a problem of the interrelationship between two professions. The relationship has not been very intimate, and when it becomes closer, a touchiness often arises because of a certain ambivalence in the foundation of the relationship. Lawyers are the subjects of sociologists, but they are simultaneously collaborators, or even teachers and mentors. Legal thinking and methods of decision-making are interesting subject matters for sociological analysis. In this respect the sociology of law could be construed as a branch of the sociology of knowledge, dealing with the social circumstances under which certain modes of thought are being applied to solve problems. In so far, however, as sociology is using legal analyses to improve upon its own analytical tools, the relationship shifts from one of observer/subject to one of partnership. While this duality is particularly marked in the relations between law and sociology, it is a much more general phenomenon, derived from the social role of the sociologist. The legal scholar has a similarly dual role in relation to his subjects. He observes and describes the judge and the legislator, but he also gives advice to them, and he is always in some sense bound by them.

Part One Law and Social Structure

The selections in this first part illustrate different approaches to the more general problems concerning the relationships between law and society. Durkheim and Maine wanted to use legal forms as a diagnostic tool in the classification of societies. Their classificatory schemes have as a background an evolutionary theory of society. Renner, as a Marxist theorist, also assumes a social development in terms of definable structural stages. His view on law differs from that of Durkheim and Maine in so far as he is concerned with the stability of legal forms under drastically changing economic and social conditions. Legal forms mask underlying power relationships and struggling interests. Although Renner is very clear in his view on law as an instrument in a power conflict, his emphasis upon the stable and somewhat sacrosanct forms of law connects him with the two more recent writers on the social function of law, Arnold and Bredemeier. In one form or another they emphasize the socially integrative function of legal institutions, as did Durkheim.

1 Emile Durkheim

Types of Law in Relation to Types of Social Solidarity

Excerpts from Emile Durkheim, *The Division of Labor in Society*, Free Press of Glencoe, 1964, pp. 68–132.

Since law reproduces the principal forms of social solidarity, we have only to classify the different types of law to find therefrom the different types of social solidarity which correspond to it. It is now probable that there is a type which symbolizes this special solidarity of which the division of labor is the cause. That found, it will suffice, in order to measure the part of the division of labor, to compare the number of juridical rules which express it with the total volume of law. [. . .]

To proceed scientifically, we must find some characteristic which, while being essential to juridical phenomena, varies as they vary. Every precept of law can be defined as a rule of sanctioned conduct. Moreover, it is evident that sanctions change with the gravity attributed to precepts, the place they hold in the public conscience, the role they play in society. It is right, then, to classifiy juridical rules according to the different sanctions which are attached to them.

They are of two kinds. Some consist essentially in suffering, or at least a loss, inflicted on the agent. They make demands on his fortune, or on his honor, or on his life, or on his liberty, and deprive him of something he enjoys. We call them repressive. They constitute penal law. It is true that those which are attached to rules which are purely moral have the same character, only they are distributed in a diffuse manner, by everybody indiscriminately, whereas those in penal law are applied through the intermediary of a definite organ; they are organized. As for the other type, it does not necessarily imply suffering for the agent, but consists only of *the return of things as they were*, in the re-establishment of troubled relations to their normal state, whether the incriminated act is restored by force to the type whence it deviated, or is annulled, that is, deprived of all social value. We must then separate juridical rules into two great classes, accordingly as they have organized repressive sanctions or only restitutive sanctions. The first comprise all penal law; the second, civil law, commercial law, procedural law, administrative and constitutional law, after abstraction of the penal rules which may be found there.

Let us now seek for the type of social solidarity to which each of these two types corresponds. [...]

The link of social solidarity to which repressive law corresponds is the one whose break constitutes a crime. By this name we call every act which, in any degree whatever, invokes against its author the characteristic reaction which we term punishment. To see the nature of this link is to inquire into the cause of punishment, or more precisely, to inquire what crime essentially consists of. [...]

The method of finding the permanent and pervasive element in crime is surely not by enumerating the acts that at all times and in every place have been termed crimes, observing, thus, the characters that they present. For if, as it may be, they are actions which have universally been regarded as criminal, they are the smallest minority, and, consequently, such a method would give us a very mistaken notion, since it would be applied only to exceptions. These variations of repressive law prove at the same time that the constant characteristic could not be found among the intrinsic properties of acts imposed or prohibited by penal rules, since they present such diversity, but rather in the relations that they sustain with some condition external to them. [...]

In effect, the only common characteristic of all crimes is that they consist in acts universally disapproved of by members of each society. We ask ourselves these days whether this reprobation is rational, whether it would not be wiser to see in crime only a malady or an error. But we need not enter upon these discussions; we seek to determine what is or has been, not what ought to be. Thus, the reality of the fact that we have just established is not contestable; that is, that crime shocks sentiments which, for a given social system, are found in all healthy consciences. [...]

Every written law has a double object: to prescribe certain obligations, and to define the sanctions which are attached to them. In civil law, and more generally in every type of law with restitutive sanctions, the legislator takes up and solves the two questions separately. He first determines the obligation with all possible precision, and it is only later that he stipulates the manner in which it should be sanctioned. For example, in the chapter of the French civil code which is devoted to the respective duties of married persons, the rights and obligations are announced in a positive manner; but no mention is made of what happens when these duties are violated by one or the other. We must go elsewhere to find this sanction. Sometimes it is totally lacking. Thus, article 214 of the civil code orders the wife to live with her husband; we deduce from that that the husband can force her to remain in the conjugal domicile, but this sanction is nowhere formally indicated. Penal law, on the contrary, sets forth only sanctions, but says nothing of the obligations to which they correspond. It does not command respect for the life of another, but kills the assassin. It does not say, first off, as does civil law: Here is the duty; but rather: Here is the punishment. No doubt, if the action is punished, it is because it is contrary to an obligatory rule, but this rule is not expressly formulated. There can be only one reason for this, which is that the rule is known and accepted by everybody. When a law of custom becomes written and is codified, it is because questions of litigation demand a more definite solution. If the custom continues to function silently, without raising any discussion of difficulties, there is no reason for transforming it. Since penal law is codified only to establish a graduated scale of punishments, it is thus the scale alone which can lend itself to doubt. Inversely, if rules whose violation is punished do not need a juridical expression, it is because they are the object of no contest, because everybody feels their authority (cf. Binding, 1872, p. 6 ff.). [. . .]

The functioning of repressive justice tends to remain more or less diffuse. In very different social systems, it does not function through the means of a special magistracy, but the whole society participates in a rather large measure. In primitive societies, where, as we shall see, law is wholly penal, it is the assembly of the people which renders justice. This was the case among the ancient Germans (Tacitus, *Germania*, Chapt. 12). In Rome, while civil affairs were given over to the *praetor*, criminal matters

19

were handled by the people, first by the *curile comites,* and then, beginning with the law of the Twelve Tables, by the *centurial comites.* Until the end of the republic, even though in fact it had delegated its powers to permanent commissions, the people remained, in principle, the supreme judge of this type of process. In Athens, under the legislation of Solon, criminal jurisdiction partly rested in the 'Ηλιαία', a vast assemblage which nominally comprised all the citizens over the age of thirty (cf. Gilbert, 1881, p. 138). Then, among Germano-Latin peoples, society, in the person of the jury, intervened in the exercise of these same functions. The diffused state in which this part of judicial power is thus found would be inexplicable, if the rules whose observation it assured, and, consequently, the sentiments to which these rules correspond, were not immanent in all consciences. It is true that, in other cases, the power is wielded by a privileged class or by particular magistrates. But these facts do not lessen the demonstrative value of the preceding, for simply because collective sentiments are enforced only through certain intermediaries, it does not follow that they have ceased to be collective while localizing themselves in a restricted number of consciences. This delegation may be due either to the very great multiplicity of affairs which necessitate the institution of special functionaries, or to the very great importance assumed by certain persons or certain classes and which makes them the authorized interpreters of collective sentiments. [. . .]

The totality of beliefs and sentiments common to average citizens of the same society forms a determinate system which has its own life; one may call it the collective or common conscience. No doubt, it has not a specific organ as a substratum; it is, by definition, diffuse in every reach of society. Nevertheless, it has specific characteristics which make it a distinct reality. It is, in effect, independent of the particular conditions in which individuals are placed; they pass on and it remains. It is the same in the North and in the South, in great cities and in small, in different professions. Moreover, it does not change with each generation, but, on the contrary, it connects successive generations with one another. It is, thus, an entirely different thing from particular consciences, although it can be realized only through them. It is the psychical type of society, a type which has its properties, its conditions of existence, its mode of development, just as individual types, although in a different way. Thus understood, it has the right to be denoted by a special word. [. . .]

We must not say that an action shocks the common conscience because it is criminal, but rather that it is criminal because it shocks the common conscience. We do not reprove it because it is a crime, but it is a crime because we reprove it. As for the intrinsic nature of these sentiments, it is impossible to specify them. They have the most diverse objects and cannot be encompassed in a single formula. We can say that they relate neither to vital interests of society nor to a minimum of justice. All these definitions are inadequate. By this alone can we recognize it: a sentiment, whatever its origin and end, is found in all consciences with a certain degree of force and precision, and every action which violates it is a crime. [. . .]

It is an error to believe that vengeance is but useless cruelty. It is very possible that, in itself, it consists of a mechanical and aimless reaction, in an emotional and irrational movement, in an unintelligent need to destroy; but, in fact, what it tends to destroy was a menace to us. It consists, then, in a veritable act of defense, although an instinctive and unreflective one. We avenge ourselves only upon what has done us evil, and what has done us evil is always dangerous. The instinct of vengeance is, in sum, only the instinct of conservation exacerbated by peril. Thus, vengeance is far from having had the negative and sterile role in the history of mankind which is attributed to it. It is a defensive weapon which has its worth, but it is a crude weapon. As it has no realization of the services which it automatically renders, it cannot, in consequence, regulate itself; but it responds somewhat haphazardly to blind causes which urge it on and without anything moderating its activities. Today, since we better understand the end to be attained, we better know how to utilize the means at our disposal; we protect ourselves with better means and, accordingly, more efficiently. But, in the beginning, this result was obtained in a rather imperfect manner. Between the punishment of today and yesterday there is no chasm, and consequently it was not necessary for the latter to become something other than itself to accommodate itself to the role that it plays in our civilized societies. The whole difference derives from the fact that it now produces its effects with a much greater understanding of what it does. But, although the individual or social conscience may not be without influence upon the reality that it clarifies, it has not the power to change its nature. The internal structure of phenomena remains the same, whether they be conscious of it or not. We thus reach the conclusion that the essential elements of punishment are the same as of old.

And in truth, punishment has remained, at least in part, a work of vengeance. It is said that we do not make the culpable suffer in order to make him suffer; it is none the less true that we find it just that he suffer. Perhaps we are wrong, but that is not the question. We seek, at the moment, to define punishment as it is or has been, not as it ought to be. It is certain that this expression of public vindication which finds its way again and again into the language of the courts is not a word taken in vain. In supposing that punishment can really serve to protect us in the future, we think that it ought to be above all an expiation of the past. The proof of this lies in the minute precautions we take to proportion punishment as exactly as possible to the severity of the crime; they would be inexplicable if we did not believe that the culpable ought to suffer because he has done evil and in the same degree. [. . .]

The nature of punishment has not been changed in essentials. All that we can say is that the need of vengeance is better directed today than heretofore. The spirit of foresight which has been aroused no longer leaves the field so free for the blind action of passion. It contains it within certain limits; it is opposed to absurd violence, to unreasonable ravaging. More clarified, it expends less on chance. One no longer sees it turn against the innocent to satisfy itself. But it nevertheless remains the soul of penality. We can thus say that punishment consists in a passionate reaction of graduated intensity. [. . .]

Every strong state of conscience is a source of life; it is an essential factor of our general vitality. Consequently, everything that tends to enfeeble it wastes and corrupts us. There results a troubled sense of illness analogous to that which we feel when an important function is suspended or lapses. It is then inevitable that we should react energetically against the cause that threatens us with such diminution, that we strain to do away with it in order to maintain the integrity of our conscience. [. . .]

Since, therefore, the sentiments which crime offends are, in any given society, the most universally collective that there are; since they are, indeed, particularly strong states of the common conscience, it is impossible for them to tolerate contradiction. Particularly if this contradiction is not purely theoretical, if it affirms itself not only by words, but by acts – when it is thus carried to its maximum, we cannot avoid rising against it passionately. A simple restitution of the troubled order would not suffice for us; we must have a more violent satisfaction. The force against which the crime comes is too intense to react with very much moderation. Moreover, it cannot do so without enfeebling itself, for it is thanks to the intensity of the reaction that it keeps alive and maintains itself with the same degree of energy. [...]

Thus, the nature of collective sentiments accounts for punishment, and, consequently, for crime. Moreover, we see anew that the power of reaction which is given over to governmental functionaries, once they have made their appearance, is only an emanation of that which has been diffuse in society since its birth. The one is only the reflex of the other. The extent of the first varies with that of the second. Let us add, moreover, that the institution of this power serves to maintain the common conscience itself. For it would be enfeebled if the organ which represents it did not partake of that which inspired it and the particular authority that it exercises. But it cannot participate in it unless all the acts which offend it are opposed and combatted as those which offend the collective conscience, even though the collective conscience is not directly affected. [...]

Although punishment proceeds from a quite mechanical reaction, from movements which are passionate and in great part non-reflective, it does play a useful role. Only this role is not where we ordinarily look for it. It does not serve, or else only serves quite secondarily, in correcting the culpable or in intimidating possible followers. From this point of view, its efficacy is justly doubtful and, in any case, mediocre. Its true function is to maintain social cohesion intact, while maintaining all its vitality in the common conscience. Denied so categorically, it would necessarily lose its energy, if an emotional reaction of the community did not come to compensate its loss, and it would result in a breakdown of social solidarity. It is necessary, then, that it be affirmed forcibly at the very moment when it is contradicted, and the only means of affirming it is to express the unanimous aversion which the crime continues to inspire, by an authentic act which can consist only in suffering inflicted upon the agent. Thus, while being the necessary product of the causes which engender it, this suffering is not a gratuitous cruelty. It is the sign which witnesses that collective sentiments are always collective, that the communion of spirits in the same faith rests on a solid foundation, and accordingly, that it is repairing the evil which the crime inflicted upon society. That is why we are right in saying that the criminal must suffer in proportion to his crime, why theories which refuse to punish any expiatory character appear as so many spirits subversive of the social order. It is because these doctrines could be practised only in a society where the whole common conscience would be nearly gone. Without this necessary satisfaction, what we call the moral conscience could not be conserved. We can thus say, without paradox, that punishment is above all designed to act upon upright people, for, since it serves to heal the wounds made upon collective sentiments, it can fill this role only where these sentiments exist, and commensurately with their vivacity. Of course, by warning already disturbed spirits of a new enfeeblement of the collective soul, it can even stop attacks from multiplying, but this result, however useful, is only a particular blow. In short, in order to form an exact idea of punishment, we must reconcile the two contradictory theories which deal with it: that which sees it as expiation, and that which makes it a weapon for social defense. It is certain that it functions for the protection of society, but that is because it is expiatory. Moreover, if it must be expiatory, that does not mean that by some mystical virtue pain compensates for the error, but rather that it can produce a socially useful effect only under this condition.

The result of the preceding is this: there exists a social solidarity which comes from a certain number of states of conscience which are common to all the members of the same society. This is what repressive law materially represents, at least in so far as it is essential. The part that it plays in the general integration of society evidently depends upon the greater or lesser extent of the social life which the common conscience embraces and regulates. The greater the diversity of relations wherein the latter makes its action felt, the more also it creates links which attach the individual to the group; the more, consequently, social cohesion derives completely from this source and bears its mark. But the number of these relations is itself proportional to that of the repressive rules. In determining what fraction of the juridical system penal law represents, we, at the same time, measure the relative importance of this solidarity. It is true that in such a procedure we do not take into account certain elements of the collective conscience which, because of their smaller power or their indeterminateness, remain foreign to repressive law while contributing to the assurance of social harmony. These are the ones protected by punishments which are merely diffuse. But the same is the case with other parts of law. There is not one of them which is not complemented by custom, and as there is no reason for supposing that the relation of law and custom is not the same in these different spheres, this elimination is not made at the risk of having to alter the results of our comparison. [. . .]

The very nature of the restitutive sanction suffices to show that the social solidarity to which this type of law corresponds is of a totally different kind. What distinguishes this sanction is that it is not expiatory, but consists of a simple return in state. Sufferance proportionate to the misdeed is not inflicted on the one who has violated the law or who disregards it: he is simply sentenced to comply with it. If certain things were done, the judge reinstates them as they would have been. He speaks of law; he says nothing of punishment. Damage-interests have no penal character; they are only a means of reviewing the past in order to reinstate it, as far as possible, to its normal form. [. . .]

The pleader who has lost in litigation is not disgraced, his honor is not put in question. We can even imagine these rules being other than they are without feeling any repugnance. The idea of tolerating murder arouses us, but we quite easily accept modification of the right of succession, and can even conceive of its possible abolition. It is at least a question which we do not refuse to discuss. Indeed, we admit with impunity that the law of servitudes or that of usufructs may be otherwise organized, that the obligations of vendor and purchaser may be determined in some other manner, that administrative functions may be distributed according to different principles. As these prescriptions do not correspond to any sentiment in us, and as we generally do not scientifically know the reasons for their existence, since this science is not definite, they have no roots in the majority of us. [...]

The relations governed by cooperative law with restitutive sanctions and the solidarity which they express, result from the division of social labor. We have explained, moreover, that, in general, cooperative relations do not convey other sanctions. In fact, it is in the nature of special tasks to escape the action of the collective conscience, for, in order for a thing to be the object of common sentiments, the first condition is that it be common, that is to say, that it be present in all consciences and that all can represent it in one and the same manner. To be sure, in so far as functions have a certain generality, everybody can have some idea of them. But the more specialized they are, the more circumscribed the number of those cognizant of each of them. Consequently, the more marginal they are to the common conscience. The rules which determine them cannot have the superior force, the transcendent authority which, when offended, demands expiation. It is also from opinion that their authority comes, as is the case with penal rules, but from an opinion localized in restricted regions of society. [...]

This law definitely plays a role in society analogous to that played by the nervous system in the organism. The latter has as its task, in effect, the regulation of the different functions of the body in such a way as to make them harmonize. It thus very naturally expresses the state of concentration at which the organism has arrived, in accordance with the division of physiological labor. Thus, on different levels of the animal scale, we can measure the degree of this concentration according to the development of the nervous system. Which is to say that we can equally measure the degree of concentration at which a society has arrived in accordance with the division of social labor according to the development of cooperative law with restitutive sanctions. We can foresee the great services that this criterion will render us. [...]

We shall recognize only two kinds of positive solidarity which are distinguishable by the following qualities:

1. The first binds the individual directly to society without any intermediary. In the second, he depends upon society because he depends upon the parts of which it is composed.

2. Society is not seen in the same aspect in the two cases. In the first, what we call society is a more or less organized totality of beliefs and sentiments common to all the members of the group: this is the collective type. On the other hand, the society in which we are solidary in the second instance is a system of different, special functions which definite relations unite. These two societies really make up only one. They are two aspects of one and the same reality, but none the less they must be distinguished.

3. From this second difference there arises another which helps us to characterize and name the two kinds of solidarity.

The first can be strong only if the ideas and tendencies common to all the members of the society are greater in number and intensity than those which pertain personally to each member. It is as much stronger as the excess is more considerable. But what makes our personality is how much of our own individual qualities we have, what distinguishes us from others. This solidarity can grow only in inverse ratio to personality. There are in each of us, as we have said, two consciences: one which is common to our group in its entirety, which, consequently, is not ourself, but society living and acting within us; the other, on the contrary, represents that in us which is personal and distinct, that which makes us an individual. Solidarity which comes from likenesses is at its maximum when the collective conscience completely envelops our whole conscience and coincides in all points with it. But, at that moment, our individuality is nil. It can be born only if the community takes smaller toll of us. There are, here, two contrary forces, one centripetal, the other centrifugal, which cannot flourish at the same time. We cannot, at one and the same time, develop ourselves in two opposite senses. If we have a lively desire to think and act for ourselves, we cannot be strongly inclined to think and act as others do. If our ideal is to present a singular and personal appearance, we do not want to resemble everybody else. Moreover, at the moment when this solidarity exercises its force, our personality vanishes, as our definition permits us to say, for we are no longer ourselves, but the collective life.

The social molecules which can be coherent in this way can act together only in the measure that they have no actions of their own, as the molecules of inorganic bodies. That is why we propose to call this type of solidarity mechanical. The term does not signify that it is produced by mechanical and artificial means. We call it that only by analogy to the cohesion which unites the elements of an inanimate body, as opposed to that which makes a unity out of the elements of a living body. What justifies this term is that the link which thus unites the individual to society is wholly analogous to that which attaches a thing to a person. The individual conscience, considered in this light, is a simple dependent upon the collective type and follows all of its movements, as the possessed object follows those of its owner. In societies where this type of solidarity is highly developed, the individual does not appear. Individuality is something which the society possesses. Thus, in these social types, personal rights are not yet distinguished from real rights.

It is quite otherwise with the solidarity which the division of labor produces. Whereas the previous type implies that individuals resemble each other, this type presumes their difference. The first is possible only in so far as the individual personality is absorbed into the collective personality; the second is possible only if each one has a sphere of action which is peculiar to him; that is, a personality. It is necessary, then, that the collective conscience leave open a part of the individual conscience in order that special functions may be established there, functions which it cannot regulate. The more this region is extended, the stronger is the cohesion which results from this solidarity. In effect, on the one hand, each one depends as much more strictly on society as labor is more divided; and, on the other, the activity of each is as much more personal as it is more specialized. Doubtless, as circumscribed as it is, it is never completely original. Even in the exercise of our occupation we conform to usages, to practices which are common to our whole professional brotherhood. But, even in this instance, the yoke that we submit to is much less heavy than when society completely controls us, and it leaves much more place open for the free play of our initiative. Here, then, the individuality of all grows at the same time as that of its parts. Society becomes more capable of collective movement, at the same time that each of its elements has more freedom of movement. This solidarity resembles that which we observe among the higher animals. Each organ, in effect, has its special physiognomy, its autonomy. And, moreover, the unity of the organism is as great as the individuation of the parts is more marked. Because of this analogy, we propose to call the solidarity which is due to the division of labor, organic.

At the same time, the preceding analyses furnish us with the means to calculate the part which remains to each of these two social links in the total common result which they concur in producing through their different media. We know under what external forms these two types of solidarity are symbolized, that is to say, what the body of juridical rules which corresponds to each of them is. Consequently, in order to recognize their respective importance in a given social type, it is enough to compare the respective extent of the two types of law which express them, since law always varies as the social relations which it governs.

References
BINDING, K. (1872), *Die Normen und Ihre Uebertretung*,
    vol. 1, Leipzig.
GILBERT, G. (1881), *Handbuch der Griechischen Staatsalterthümer*
    vol. 1, Leipzig.

2 Henry Maine

From Status to Contract

Excerpt from Sir Henry Maine, *Ancient Law*, Dent, 1917, pp. 99–100.

The movement of the progressive societies has been uniform in one respect. Through all its course it has been distinguished by the gradual dissolution of family dependency and the growth of individual obligation in its place. The Individual is steadily substituted for the Family, as the unit of which civil laws take account. The advance has been accomplished at varying rates of celerity, and there are societies not absolutely stationary in which the collapse of the ancient organization can only be perceived by careful study of the phenomena they present. But, whatever its pace, the change has not been subject to reaction or recoil, and apparent retardations will be found to have been occasioned through the absorption of archaic ideas and customs from some entirely foreign source. Nor is it difficult to see what is the tie between man and man which replaces by degrees those forms of reciprocity in rights and duties which have their origin in the Family. It is Contract. Starting, as from one terminus of history, from a condition of society in which all the relations of Persons are summed up in the relations of Family, we seem to have steadily moved towards a phase of social order in which all these relations arise from the free agreement of Individuals. In Western Europe the progress achieved in this direction has been considerable. Thus the status of the Slave has disappeared – it has been superseded by the contractual relation of the servant to his master. The status of the Female under Tutelage, if the tutelage be understood of persons other than her husband, has also ceased to exist; from her coming of age to her marriage all the relations she may form are relations of contract. So, too, the status of the Son under Power has no true place in law of modern European societies. If any civil obligation binds together the

Parent and the child of full age, it is one to which only contract gives its legal validity. The apparent exceptions are exceptions of that stamp which illustrate the rule. The child before years of discretion, the orphan under guardianship, the adjudged lunatic, have all their capacities and incapacities regulated by the Law of Persons. But why? The reason is differently expressed in the conventional language of different systems, but in substance it is stated to the same effect by all. The great majority of Jurists are constant to the principle that the classes of persons just mentioned are subject to extrinsic control on the single ground that they do not possess the faculty of forming a judgement on their own interests; in other words, that they are wanting in the first essential of an engagement by Contract.

The word Status may be usefully employed to construct a formula expressing the law of progress thus indicated, which, whatever be its value, seems to me to be sufficiently ascertained. All the forms of Status taken notice of in the Law of Persons were derived from, and to some extent are still coloured by, the powers and privileges anciently residing in the Family. If then we employ Status, agreeably with the usage of the best writers, to signify these personal conditions only, and avoid applying the term to such conditions as are the immediate or remote result of agreement, we may say that the movement of the progressive societies has hitherto been a movement *from Status to Contract*.

3 O. Kahn-Freund

Introduction to Karl Renner's *The Institutions of Private Law and their Social Functions*

Excerpt from Karl Renner, *The Institutions of Private Law and their Social Functions*, Routledge and Kegan Paul, 1949, pp. 1–2.

It is one of the tasks of a sociology of law to explore the social forces which bring about the creation of legal norms and institutions and changes in the positive law. Renner's work does not deal with this aspect of the interrelation between law and society. It does not investigate the problem how and why legal principles like that of the freedom of contract or of the owner's unfettered right of disposition come into being at a given stage of social development. He pre-supposes the stability and relative immutability of legal institutions such as property and contract, and he asks: How is it possible that, given unchanged norms, unchanged conceptions of ownership and sale, contract and debt, mortgage and inheritance, their social function can nevertheless undergo a profound transformation? How is it possible that – to take the most prominent example and the central theme of Renner's work – as a legal institution 'property' can mean the same thing, say, in 1750 and in 1900, and yet in the latter year produce economic and social effects almost diametrically opposed to those it had in the former? How can one account for the functional transformation of a norm which remains stable? What, in particular, is the technique used by a developing capitalist society in order to adapt pre-capitalist and early capitalist legal conceptions to the needs of high capitalism without changing those conceptions themselves? How does society use the institutions of the law, what does it make of them, how does it group and re-group them? How does it put them to new services without transforming their normative content? How, in particular, has property been able to become the legal framework of a capitalist economy?

4 Karl Renner

The Development of Capitalist Property and the Legal Institutions Complementary to the Property Norm

Excerpts from Karl Renner, *The Institutions of Private Law and their Social Functions*, Routledge and Kegan Paul, 1949, pp. 105–8, 114–22.

Journeymen and apprentices used to live in the master's household. Their relation was in the nature of a subjection determined by public law, on the lines of the Germanic *patria potestas*, which served the purposes of education, training, and mastery of the craft,[1] and whose function therefore was to ensure the continuity of the working population. This relationship was abolished by the mere force of facts; it was replaced by the private contracts of *do ut facias*. The old regulation of labour is dissolved, and for a while there is no new regulation.

But the property-object (*res*) as it develops into and assumes the functions of capital, itself inaugurates a process of education for the owner no less than for the dispossessed.

We saw, in a former chapter, that a certain minimum amount of capital was necessary, in order that the number of labourers simultaneously employed . . . might suffice to liberate the employer himself from manual labour, convert him from a small master into a capitalist, and thus formally to establish capitalist production. . . . We also saw that, at first, the subjection of labour to capital was only a formal result of the fact that the labourer, instead of working for himself, works for and consequently under the capitalist. By the cooperation[2] of numerous wage-labourers, the sway of capital develops into a requisite for carrying on the labour process itself, into a real requisite of production. That a capitalist should command on the field of production, is now as

1. For the Germanic *patria potestas* and its fate in this country, see Pollock and Maitland (1895, pp. 436 ff.). For general descriptions of the Germanic *patria potestas*, see Schröder and Künsberg (1922, pp. 71, 350) and Hübner (1915, p. 90).

2. Marx distinguishes three stages in the development of industrial production: co-operation, manufacture and machinofacture (the factory system) and we shall adhere to his division.

indispensable as that a general should command on the field of battle. ... The work of directing, superintending and adjusting, becomes one of the functions of capital, from the moment that labour, under the control of capital, becomes co-operative. Once a function of capital it acquires special characteristics (Karl Marx, *Capital*, vol. 1, pp. 320–21).

What is the essence of this power of command? It is based on contract. But so was the relation of the feudal lord to his vassal, yet this was essentially of a public nature. An element of domination is without doubt implied in this system of superordination and subordination, and in spite of the form of contract it remains essentially a system of power.

The question is whether this control is still in essence the Germanic medieval *mundium*, that reflection of paternal power. Is it established in favour of the ruled or of the ruling, is it a government of protection or of exploitation? What are its essential features?

The directing motive, the end and aim of capitalist production, is to extract the greatest possible amount of surplus-value, and consequently to exploit labour-power to the greatest possible extent. ... The control exercised by the capitalist is not only a special function, due to the nature of the social labour-process, and peculiar to that process, but it is, at the same time, a function of the exploitation of a social labour-process, and is consequently rooted in the unavoidable antagonism between the exploiter and the living and labouring raw material he exploits. ... Moreover, the co-operation of wage-labourers is entirely brought about by the capital that employs them. Their union into one single productive body and the establishment of a connexion between their individual functions, are matters foreign and external to them, are not their own act, but the act of the capital that brings and keeps them together. Hence the connexion existing between their various labours appears to them, ideally, in the shape of a pre-conceived plan of the capitalist, and practically in the shape of the authority of the same capitalist, in the shape of the powerful will of another, who subjects their activity to his aims (ibid., pp. 321–2).

In the eyes of the law, the property-subject is related to the object only, controlling matter alone. But what is control of property in law, becomes in fact man's control of human beings, of the wage-labourers, as soon as property has developed into capital. The individual called owner sets the tasks to others, he makes them subject to his commands and, at least in the initial stages of capitalist development, supervises the execution of his commands. The owner of a *res* imposes his will upon *personae*, autonomy is converted into heteronomy of will.

Capital extends its scale, it expands beyond the sphere of the capitalist's personal control. 'Just as at first the capitalist is relieved from actual labour, . . . so now, he hands over the work of direct and constant supervision, . . . to a special kind of wage labourer. . . . The work of supervision becomes their established and exclusive function' (ibid., p. 322).

We see that the right of ownership thus assumes a new social function. Without any change in the norm, below the threshold of collective consciousness, a *de facto* right is added to the personal absolute-domination over a corporeal thing. This right is not based upon a special legal provision. It is the power of control, the power to issue commands and to enforce them. The inherent urge of capital to beget constantly further capital provides the motive for this *imperium*.

This power of control is a social necessity, but at the same time it is profitable to the owners – it establishes a rule not for the purpose of protection but for the purpose of exploitation, of profit.

The subordination of the workers which at the same time effects their mutual co-ordination, is a corresponding phenomenon. Is this co-ordination also based on contract? The workers are not asked whether their neighbour appeals to them, yet they are forced into close proximity and in this way they become united into an association of workers. What is it that brings about this passive association of the workers? What is it that correlates their functions and shapes them into a unified productive body? There is no doubt that these workers who contribute partial operations form a compulsory association according to all rules of legal doctrine.

This association receives its individuality from the capital that collects the workers in one place and keeps them there. Just as the law is the norm for the citizens, so the plan, the plan of production, is the abstract and impersonal norm for this compulsory association, supported by the ultimate and most concrete authority of the capitalist, the power of an alien will. Supervision is delegated to special functionaries, and thus relations of superordination and subordination are made into an organic whole.

Thus the institution of property leads automatically to an organization similar to the state. Power over matter begets personal power.

It is not because he is a leader of industry that a man is a capitalist; on the contrary, he is a leader of industry because he is a capitalist. The leadership of industry is an attribute of capital, just as in feudal times the functions of general and judge were attributes of landed property (ibid., p. 323).

We see that even at the first stage of capitalism, that of cooperation, the old microcosm is replaced by a new one which derives its unity from capital, which here is the aggregate of the technical means of production, that is, objects of ownership. These new organizations bring about a gradual transformation of man and matter, without any norm imposed by the state. [. . .]

At this stage it is useful to realize the original implications of the institution of property: it is not a mere order of goods. It is just in respect of the deliberate planned social distribution of goods that it first abdicates. It merely protects him who has possession by virtue of an unassailable title, but it does not distribute goods according to a plan. Contrast with this the law of property of the feudal epoch. How richly diversified was its catalogue of *jura in rem*. The property law of bourgeois society leaves the order of the goods to the goods themselves. It is only thus that they become commodities and capital, only thus that they organize themselves and accumulate in accordance with the specific laws of capitalist circulation. At this stage we see already that this anonymous and anarchial regulation of 'goods' becomes control over men in their capacity as potential labour. We also see that in our time this factual regulation of 'goods' presumes to dictate the social regulation of power and labour. We see further that this regulation of power and labour remains concealed to the whole of bourgeois legal doctrine which is aware of nothing but its most formal, general and extraneous limitations, namely, its foundation on the contract of employment.

Wage labour is a relation of autocracy with all the legal characteristics of despotism. The factory is an establishment with its own code with all the characteristics of a legal code. It contains norms of every description, not excluding criminal law, and it establishes special organs and jurisdiction. Labour regulations and the conventions valid within economic enterprises deserve just as well to be treated as legal institutions as the manorial law of the feudal epoch. This, too, was based upon private rule, upon the will of a Lord, one manorial custom differing from another only in details. Even if this difference had been so fundamental as to exclude all understanding and exposition on a common basis – and this cannot even be imagined – these institutions would still remain an integral part of the legal system of that period. The same applies to factory law, the general regulations of labour in economic enterprises. No exposition of our legal order can be complete without it, it regulates the relations of a large part of the population. If material differences were to prevent a general exposition, there would still remain the fundamental problem of the intrinsic nature of this right.

Once we have raised this question, all the fictions of bourgeois legal doctrine disappear, above all the distinction between public and private law. The right of the capitalist is delegated public authority, conferred indiscriminately upon the person who will use it for his own benefit. The employment relationship is an indirect-power relationship, a public obligation to service, like the serfdom of feudal times. It differs from serfdom only in this respect, that it is based upon contract, not upon inheritance.[3] No society has yet existed without a regulation of labour peculiar to it, the regulation of labour being as essential for every society as the digestive tract for the animal organism. The period of simple commodity production when in fact the working *persona*, the instruments of labour and the labour product merged into one another, was the only period in which the process of production and reproduction, the very life process of society, was independent of social consciousness. As an individual process, it

3. In 1940 Lord Atkin, in *Nokes* v. *Doncaster Amalgamated Colleries Ltd* (1940) A.C. 1014, said that there was 'ingrained in the personal status of a citizen under our laws ... the right to choose for himself whom he would serve, and that this right of choice constituted the main difference between a servant and a serf'. From a legal point of view the 'right of choice' is the essence of the distinction between serfdom and service. The lawyer ignores the question: to what extent do economic conditions permit the servant to exercise this right.

remained private, not revealing any underlying correlations of power and labour. The co-operative labour-process, however, is social; in its very essence it cannot be private. The contents of the right have assumed a public nature, though legal doctrine still conceives of it in terms of private law.[4]

During Karl Marx's lifetime the capitalist is still in full control, legislative, executive and judiciary, of his enterprise. His power contains all the elements of state absolutism, mitigated only by the fact that it is founded upon a contract which can be dissolved by notice. Up to this period capital knows no 'separation of powers'. This purely legal limitation, however, becomes illusory, as soon as we conceive of capitalists and wage labourers confronting each other as classes. If we accept this, it becomes evident at once that the worker, though he can exchange one individual capitalist for another, cannot escape from the Capitalist. There is no doubt that in the sphere of production the bourgeoisie as a class has absolute control of the non-propertied classes as far as the law is concerned. Restrictions of their power in fact are imposed only by bourgeois self-interest and fear of the 'subjects of steam power'. Such is the position at the height of capitalist development.

Since no society can live without the eternal and natural necessity of labour, it is a naïve conception that any society could exist without a regulation of labour, an organized power of disposal over the whole of its available labour-power. It is exclusively the merit of Marx to have discovered this hidden regulation of labour within bourgeois society, to have explored its nature and to have analysed its functions. The 'natural laws' of society which normally achieve this regulation within capitalist society are sufficient only so long as labour-power remains actually chained to the *res*.

If a revolt of the workers loosens these chains, society throws off its mask of torpor. It suddenly becomes conscious of its mission to regulate labour. Then it applies direct and authoritative measures of coercion against labour in the form of laws. 'In the ordinary run of things, the labourer can be left to the "natural

4. Or, to use Maine's formula (Pollock, 1906, p. 174), what outwardly appears as 'contract' is in essence a matter of 'status'. The *legal* development from contract to status has often been discussed (e.g. by Dicey, 1962, lecture 8).

laws" of "production"' (ibid, p. 761). But whenever these laws fail, bourgeois legislation has recourse to direct force outside the economic field. So, above all, at the stage of primitive accumulation (ibid., chapter 26). It was only upon the completion of the capitalist order of economy that the wage-regulating laws were repealed. 'They were an absurd anomaly, since the capitalist regulated his factory by private legislation' (ibid. p. 764). 'The machine was Lycurgus, Draco and Solon at the same time, it converted labour into the actual appendage of capital, its psychological embodiment, just as a building is an appendage of an estate in the eyes of the law. Occasionally the capitalist, that psychological incarnation of capital, even unblushingly asserts the proprietary rights of capital over labour-power' (ibid. p. 587). 'I allow that the workers are not a property, not the property of Lancashire and the masters; but they are the strength of both; they are the mental and trained power which cannot be replaced for a generation; the mere machinery which they work might much of it beneficially be replaced, nay improved, in a twelve-month. Encourage or allow (!) the working power to emigrate, and what of the capitalist?' (Potter, quoted by Marx, ibid. p. 588). Capital demands no less than that public authority should maintain the labour which it has appropriated, even if, owing to lack of raw material, the machines stand idle. It demands that the state should store labour in the work-houses, capital's general public reserve dumps. If ever labour remembers its personal freedom in fields where it is manifest even to the most stupid brain that work is a function of the social body (e.g. in the railway industry or the provision trade), if labour makes use of this freedom by strike, then the bourgeoisie makes labour a military institution or replaces free labour by a labour organization on military lines, achieving a direct socialization of labour.

New functions thus accrue to the legal character 'person' who also has the economic character 'proprietor'. Now he regulates labour, ruling and exploiting. Property, from a mere title to dispose of material objects, becomes a title to power, and as it exercises power in the private interest, it becomes a title to domination.

At the same time the free person, the labourer with no property, becomes a subject *sui generis*, as history does not repeat itself.

Among all those who have the power and are destined to be his master, he may choose the master who most appeals to him, but as a class the subjects are chained to the class of the masters.

We see that property at the stage of simple commodity production endows the worker with the detention of his means of production, making man the master of matter. Now property changes its function without a corresponding change in the law. It gives the legal detention of the means of production to the individuals who do not perform any labour, making them thus the masters of labour. Property automatically takes over the function of regulating power and labour, and it becomes a private title to domination. The law endows this non-worker with the legal detention of the means of production, but in any society only the worker can actually hold them, as he must have them in his hands in order to work with them. Thus the law, by means of a complementary institution, the contract of service, takes actual detention away from the owner. The worker may mind the machine, but he must pay the price of submitting himself to exploitation. A permanent state of war between legal and actual detention is thus established.

A generation and a half have passed away since the death of Karl Marx, two generations since the first publication of *Das Kapital*. Yet his analysis of the transformation of property not only gives a complete picture of the phase which it had reached in his days, it extends much further. Nevertheless, contemporary development, which has by no means remained static, has overtaken Marx's analysis and again transformed the substratum of the norms. Above all, much has matured which at the time of Marx could only be seen in its initial stages. These two generations, however, have changed the world of norms much more than the world of the substratum. Although exposition and explanation of this transformation of norms is beyond the scope of this inquiry, we endeavour to outline it briefly in order to achieve a clearer understanding.

'The most surprising fact is the lack of social observation. Millions of people live among changing conditions, they daily feel their practical impacts, yet their theoretical implications do not become conscious to them. They think in concepts of a bygone generation' (Renner, 1918, p. 51).

In order to illustrate this transformation, as well as the contradictions implied in our social order, we consider the following two examples.

Upon its enclosed estate there stands the manor house of the old noble family, and the peasant's farm is surrounded by his own land. Property is distinctly fenced off, notice-boards announce that it is 'private' and that 'trespassers will be prosecuted'. In contrast, let us consider the most striking example of modern development, a privately owned railway. We enter the station hall, but though this is registered property like the manor and the farm, it does not even come into our minds that we have entered somebody else's property. No one inquires who is the owner, his identity has become a matter of indifference. We go to the booking office. There, the lawyers assure us, we conclude a contract for a *facere*, not for a *dare*. But nobody else thinks of it in this way. We get our ticket which the other party is obliged to give us, there is no trace of bargaining, of freedom of contract, of conditions and terms; published bye-laws fix everything in advance. We board the train and do not think for a split second that we have hired Mr X's private vehicle, though lawyers may still construe it in this way. We know that we have acquired the privilege, conferred upon us by public law, to make use of a public utility, against payment of the usual fee which is also fixed or confirmed by public law, and that we have thus submitted ourselves to the public regulations of the bye-laws. The owner, Mr X, has no significance whatever in any of these proceedings and, more than that, he remains outside the sphere of our consciousness.

In the first case the substratum and the norm coincide at least as regards the main aspect. One's own property is clearly distinguished from that of other persons, property appears as what it is: as private. In the second case, on the other hand, property has become everybody's own; the owner himself, if he books a ticket for a journey, is now like a stranger. As far as the economic and social function of the *res* is concerned, the legal owner has become completely irrelevant. Yet he continues to perform an invisible part.

In this instance it has become evident that private property has been transformed into a public utility, though it has not become public property. The old peasant farm and the old manor are nothing of the kind. This example leads us to suspect that rights of ownership have outgrown the limitations of private law. In this particular case this is so evident that even the law takes cognisance of it, by creating a number of norms public and private, which convert property into a public utility. The private character of property has been forced into the background by complementary institutions of public law.

But these new norms, which, as we have stressed repeatedly, belong to another branch of research, could not accomplish more than to give a precise legal form to what had existed in the world of facts long before they intervened. The specific features of a public utility were established in the substratum before the norm got hold of them. In innumerable other cases, this change within the substratum has not been recognised or admitted, though property indeed advertises its new character of a public utility. The cobbler's shop advertises itself as a 'shoe-repairing service', thus declaring that the whole public acquires the right to its services against payment of the scheduled fee. This kind of shop sign is more than a joke, thousands of similar signs express a new public opinion *vis-à-vis* a gradual creation of new law. It is the profession of lawyers to disregard and deny this; for this very purpose they have been led for years through the labyrinth of Roman Law. But let us leave the cobbler. We give our soiled linen to a laundering establishment and get their receipt in exchange. The two contracting parties, as a rule, do not even know each other's name, they never see each other. It is a mere fiction that a private 'contract' is here agreed on, though it might be so 'construed'. A peasant farm adjoining that mentioned in our example above may have become a dairy and thus an establishment that owes to the public certain services against payment of specified and advertised fees. The transformation of private property into public utility is completed in form as well, as soon as the licensing authorities make it obligatory to serve everybody and to exhibit a tariff of charges. But even without this, public opinion regards every owner of such an establishment as under a legal obligation. Private property has now become accessible to everyone, it is put at everybody's disposal. I think that this change is remarkable enough. During the war this already existing trend of development has suddenly become strikingly apparent. The sovereign owner of private property has suddenly, by one stroke of the pen, been converted into a subject who has public duties. The landowner must cultivate his land or some other person seizes it for cultivation, he must sell, he must charge the controlled price instead of the market price, he must dispatch his corn to the railway or mill, and so forth.

All of a sudden it becomes apparent to us that property has developed into public utility.

This is an indication of the trend of the future development of legislation. It will not only shamefacedly hint at this new character of property by complementary institutions, the norm itself will openly reveal it, and all property-units which today already have become the substratum of public utility, will accordingly become establishments of public law. This is the first unavoidable step towards nationalization of private property. Even more striking is the development which has taken place at the other pole of society, that of labour. It was not in vain that the workers, thrown together by the capitalists into compulsory associations, were in revolt for fifty years. According to Marx, and in fact during his lifetime, the capitalist hired the individual worker on the labour market for a wage that was individually agreed and took him into the workshop. The labour relation in its entirety was based upon individual regulation. But today the position is different, thanks to a century of struggle.

The prospective employee registers with a labour exchange, which is either a private establishment or run by the state, a municipality or a trade union. He is assigned to a job by rote. This state of affairs is unintelligible in an economy based upon freedom of contract, which can explain it no more than pure science can explain the working of a typewriter, which is a technical product. If the worker is accepted, at terms which are fixed beforehand and scarcely mentioned, he goes on the job. Formerly based upon contract, the labour relationship has now developed into a 'position', just as property has developed into public utility. If a person occupies a 'position', this means that his rights and duties are closely circumscribed, the 'position' has become a legal institution in character much like the fee of feudal times. The 'position' comprises the claim to adequate remuneration (settled by collective agreement or works rule), the obligation to pay certain contributions (for trade unions and insurance), the right to special benefits (sickness, accident, old age, death) and finally certain safeguards against loss of the position or in case of its loss.

What is the meaning of this development from the contract of employment to the position of work and service? The private contract, by means of the complementary institutions of collective agreement, labour exchanges, social insurance and the like, has become an institution of public law. It is still largely determined by the private will of the individuals concerned, yet this influence is continually decreasing, and the state element is almost of greater importance than the private element, the collective element more important than the individual element. It predominates today, when the job is becoming the 'established position'. The development of the law gradually works out what is socially reasonable. Labour, in fact, never is and never was a merely private affair, it has always been public service. Only an economic science unrelated to the state has transformed and disfigured the social necessity of labour into the private pleasure of individual capitalists and workers whose relations are established by acts of exchange.

Yet it is true that this development to 'establishment' and 'position' has affected only a part of property and labour and even this only partially. The fundamental character of society is undergoing a process of change. The ultimate direction of this change is clearly determined and its results are unequivocal, but they have neither undergone theoretical analysis, nor have they entered common consciousness. Human society, unconscious or only half conscious of its own needs, drags itself forward, driven on by obscure urges.

References
DICEY, A. V. (1962), *Law and Public Opinion in England*, Macmillan.
HÜBNER, R. (1915), *Deutsches Privatrecht*, 2nd edn, Leipzig.
MARX, KARL, *Capital*, vol. 1, translated by Moore-Aveling, London, 1920.
POLLOCK, F. (1906), *Introduction and notes to Sir Henry Maine's 'Ancient Law'*, Murray.
POLLOCK, F. and MAITLAND, F. W. (1895), *The History of English Law*, vol. 2, Cambridge University Press.

RENNER, K. (1918), *Marxismus, Krieg und Internationale*, 2nd edn, Stuttgart.

SCHRÖDER, R., and V. KÜNSBERG. E. F. (1922), *Lehrbuch der deutschen Rechtsgeschichte*, 6th edn, vol. 1, de Gruyter.

5 Thurman W. Arnold

Law as Symbolism

Excerpts from Thurman W. Arnold, *The Symbols of Government*, Harcourt, Brace and World, 1962, pp. 33–70.

The thing which we reverently call 'Law' when we are talking about government generally, and not predicting the results of particular lawsuits, can only be properly described as an attitude or a way of thinking about government. It is a way of writing about human institutions in terms of ideals, rather than observed facts. It meets a deep-seated popular demand that government institutions symbolize a beautiful dream within the confines of which principles operate, independently of individuals.

The fact that today as a necessary gesture towards a new habit of thought the 'Law' is dressed up to look like a 'science' does not change it as a way of thought. It means only that the earliest conception that the law came from God and the later conception that it rose from logic and reason have both been worn thin. However, the new word 'science' has not given the law a different point of view. It has merely set up a new line of defense against the attacks of those detached observers who insist upon recording what they see.

Of course, there are countless rules, institutional habits, and various kinds of social compulsions in every society. These are often called law. It is not with these that we are dealing when we study 'Law' in Western civilization. The fundamental principles of law do not represent what we do, but what we ought to do. The science of the law is not the method which judges actual use, but the method which they ought to use. It is a sort of Heaven which man has created for himself on earth. It is a characteristic of all paradises that they should be different from what we actually experience in everyday affairs. Otherwise there would be no object in creating them. Therefore no one should be surprised because there is so little similarity between the ideals of the law and what the courts actually do. It is part of the function of 'Law' to give recognition to ideals representing the exact opposite of established conduct. Most of its complications arise from the necessity of pretending to do one thing, while actually doing another. It develops the structure of an elaborate dream-world where logic creates justice. It permits us to look at the drab cruelties of business practises through rose-colored spectacles.

The principles of law are supposed to control society, because such an assumption is necessary to the logic of the dream. Yet the observer should constantly keep in mind that the function of law is not so much to guide society, as to comfort it. Belief in fundamental principles of law does not necessarily lead to an orderly society. Such a belief is as often at the back of revolt or disorder. Respect for fundamental principles of law performs the same function in stiffening the morale of those who are in revolt against established institutions as it does in holding in line those who defend these institutions. Everyone should respect and obey the law in this country even if he does not like it. But no one should be hindered or prevented from relying on his constitutional rights, and if this involves disobeying mere statutes, the act of disobedience intended for this purpose is most praiseworthy. Thus the law at the same time contains both the contradictory philosophies of obedience and revolt.

'Law' is primarily a great reservoir of emotionally important social symbols. It develops, as language develops, in spite of, and not because of, the grammarians. Though the notion of a 'rule of Law' may be the moral background of revolt, it ordinarily operates to induce acceptance of things as they are. It does this by creating a realm somewhere within the mystical haze beyond the courts, where all our dreams of justice in an unjust world come true. Thus in the realm of the law the least favored members of society are comforted by the fact that the poor are equal to the rich and the strong have no advantage over the weak. The more fortunately situated are reassured by the fact that the wise are treated better than the foolish, that careless people are punished for their mistakes. The trader takes heart by learning that the law ignores the more profitable forms of dishonesty in deference to the principle of individual freedom from governmental restraint. The preacher, however, is glad to learn that all forms of dishonesty which can be curbed without interfering with freedom or with economic law are being curbed. The dissatisfied minority is cheered by the fact that the law is elastic and growing. The conservative is convinced that it is becoming more and more certain. The industrial serf is told that no man, not even his great employer, is above the law. His employer, however, feels secure in the fact that his property is put above ordinary legislative law by the Constitution, which is the highest form of law there is. It protects us on the one hand from arbitrary power exercised without regulations. It saves us from the mob, and also from the dictator. It prevents capitalism from turning into communism, democracy from becoming the rule of an unthinking people. It gives all people an equal chance for success, and at the same time protects those who have been born in more favored positions of privilege and power.

From a practical point of view it is the greatest instrument of social stability because it recognizes every one of the yearnings of the underprivileged, and gives them a forum in which those yearnings can achieve official approval without involving any particular action which might joggle the existing pyramid of power. It permits the use of an argumentative technique by which powerful institutions can be defended on the ground that taking away privileges from them would take away freedom from the poor. [. . .]

Obviously, 'Law' can never be defined With equal obviousness, however, it should be said that the adherents of the legal institution must never give up the struggle to define law, because it is an essential part of the ideal that it is rational and capable of definition, rather than a psychological adjustment to conflicting emotional needs. Hence the verbal expenditure necessary to the upkeep of the ideal of 'Law' is colossal and never ending. The legal scientist is compelled by the climate of opinion in which he finds himself to prove that an essentially irrational world is constantly approaching rationality; that a cruel world is constantly approaching kindliness, and that a changing world is really stable and enduring. [. . .]

'Law' represents the belief that there must be something behind and above government without which it cannot have permanence or respect. Even a dictator cannot escape this psychology of his time. He does not quite believe in his own government unless he is able to make gestures toward this prevailing ideal. It is child's play for the realist to show that law is not what it pretends to be and that its theories are sonorous, rather than sound; that its definitions run in circles; that applied by skilful attorneys in the forum of courts it can only be an argumentative technique; that it constantly seeks escape from reality through alternate reliance on ceremony and verbal confusion. Yet the legal realist falls into grave error when he believes this to be a defect in the law. From any objective point of view the escape of the law from reality constitutes not its weakness but its greatest strength. Legal institutions must constantly reconcile ideological conflicts, just as individuals reconcile them by shoving inconsistencies back into a sort of institutional subconscious mind. If judicial institutions become too 'sincere', too self-analytical, they suffer the fate of ineffectiveness which is the lot of all self-analytical people. They lose themselves in words, and fail in action. They lack that sincere fanaticism out of which great governmental forces are welded.

The abstract ideals of the law require for their public acceptance symbolic conduct of a very definite pattern by a definite institution which can be heard and seen. In this way only, can they achieve the dramatic presentation necessary to make them moving forces in society. Any abstract ideal which is not tied up with a definite institution or memorialized by particular ceremonies, becomes relegated to the limbo of metaphysics and has little social consequence. The institutions which throw about the law that atmosphere of reality and concreteness so necessary for its acceptance are the court and the law school. The one produces the ceremonial ritualistic trial; the other produces a theoretical literature which defends the ideal from attack by absorbing and weaving into its mystical pattern all the ideas of all of the critics. In other words, trials today are the product of courts; books the product of law schools. [. . .]

As we have shown, the law consists of a large number of mutually contradictory symbols and ideals. Such contradictions are apparent to any man in the street who becomes involved in the judicial process. He must therefore believe, if he is to keep his faith that government is symmetrical and rational, that there exists somewhere, available to him if he only could get time to study it, a unified philosophy of science of law.

Therefore he believes that there exists a science of jurisprudence, and gives a place in the social scheme to a priesthood whose duty it is to expound that science, unmoved by the irrelevancies of practical day-to-day governmental action.

An official admission by a judicial institution that it was moving in all directions at once in order to satisfy the conflicting emotional values of the people which it served would be unthinkable. It would have the same effect as if an actor interrupted the most moving scene of a play in order to explain to the audience that his real name was John Jones. The success of the play requires that an idea be made real to the audience. The success of the law as a unifying force depends on making emotionally significant the idea of a government of law which is rational and scientific.

The unifying principles which are behind all of the various activities of admittedly legal institutions are the concern of jurisprudence. Its task is to prove that such principles exist, and to define them in general terms sufficiently broad so that all the little contradictory ideals appearing in the unending procession of particular cases will appear to be part of one great set of ideals. Functionally the primary purpose of the science of the law is to be a sounding board of both the prevalent hopes and the prevalent worries of those who believe in a government of law and not of men; to reconcile these hopes and worries somewhere in the mists of scholarship and learning; and never to admit that this is what it is doing. [. . .]

We may describe jurisprudence or the science of the law in our present day as the effort to construct a logical heaven behind the courts, wherein contradictory ideals are made to seem consistent. Naturally the contradictions are reconciled in the only way logical contradictions can ever be reconciled, by giving each a separate sphere to work in, and pushing the inconsistencies back into the obscurity of great piles of books which are taken on faith and seldom read. [. . .]

We may finally define jurisprudence as the shining but unfulfilled dream of a world governed by reason. For some it lies buried in a system, the details of which they do not know. For some, familiar with the details of the system, it lies in the depth of an unread literature. For others, familiar with this literature, it lies in the hope of a future enlightenment. For all, it is just around the corner. [...]

In the science of jurisprudence all of the various ideals which are significant to the man on the street must be given a place. It must prove that the law is certain and at the same time elastic; that it is just, yet benevolent; economically sound, yet morally logical. It must show that the law can be dignified and solemn, and at the same time efficient, universal and fundamental, and a set of particular directions. Jurisprudence must give a place to all of the economic, and also the ethical, notions of important competing groups within our society, no matter how far apart these notions may be. In its method it must make gestures of recognition to the techniques of each separate branch of learning which claims to have any relation with the conduct of individuals, no matter how different these techniques may be.

Such a task can only be accomplished by ceremony, and hence the writings of jurisprudence should be considered as ceremonial observances rather than as scientific observations. This is shown by the fact that the literature of jurisprudence performs its social task most effectively for those who encourage it, praise it, but do not read it. For those who study it today it is nothing but a troubling mass of conflicting ideas. However, it is not generally read, so that its troubles are known only to the few people who read it for the purpose of writing more of it. For most of those who reverence the law the knowledge that there is a constant search going on for logical principles is sufficient.

6 Harry C. Bredemeier

Law as an Integrative Mechanism

Harry C. Bredemeier, 'Law as an integrative mechanism', in William M. Evan (ed.), *Law and Sociology*, Free Press of Glencoe, 1962, pp. 73-88.

It is important to distinguish between two kinds of enterprises relating sociology and law: one is denoted by the phrase 'sociology *of* the law', the other by 'sociology *in* the law'. The first makes 'the law' a focus of sociological investigation in the same way that 'small groups' and 'voting' are foci. The goal here is either to describe the significance of the law for the larger society or to describe its internal processes or both. The second aims to facilitate the law's performance of its functions by adding sociological knowledge to its stock of tools. Clearly, the second aim depends on the first; there can be no sociological knowledge that is useful to the law until there is sociological knowledge about the functions of the law and mechanisms of performing those functions. For that reason, in the first part of this paper I set out an analysis of the functions of the law and their relationships to other functional subsystems of the society. I then discuss some of the salient lines of research in sociology of the law suggested by that analysis, and the place of sociology *in* the law.

The framework I employ is that developed by Talcott Parsons and his colleagues, particularly as stated in *Economy and Society* (Parsons and Smelser, 1956). This framework posits four major functional processes to be observed in a social system: adaptation, goal pursuance, pattern maintenance, and integration. Parsons and Smelser have identified adaptation with economic processes, and goal pursuance with political processes. Pattern-maintenance processes may very roughly, but adequately for present purposes, be identified with what we ordinarily refer to as socialization. Integrative processes are not so neatly identified with familiar patterns; but I propose to identify them in part with 'the law', that is, with legal processes.

The function of the law is the orderly resolution of conflicts. As this implies, 'the law' (the clearest model of which I shall take to be the court system) is brought into operation after there has been a conflict. Someone claims that his interests have been violated by someone else.[1] The court's task is to render a decision that will prevent the conflict – and all potential conflicts like it – from disrupting productive cooperation. In order to do this, the court needs three things – or, in the language of Parsons and his colleagues, the court is dependent upon three kinds of 'inputs'.

In the first place, the court needs an analysis of cause-and-effect relationships. It needs a way of ascertaining both the *past* relationship between the alleged act of the defendant and the alleged injury of the plaintiff, and the probable *future* relationship between the decision and the activities of defendant and plaintiff (and all persons similarly situated). I suggest that this input comes from the adaptive system, in return for an immediate output of 'organic' as distinguished from 'mechanical' solidarity.

In the second place, as is implied by the phrase 'productive cooperation', the court needs a conception of what the division of labor is *for*; what the goals of the system are, what state of affairs is to be created or maintained by the exercise of power. In other words, it needs standards by which to *evaluate* the conflicting claims and the anticipated effects of a decision on the role structure. I suggest that this is the primary input from the goal-pursuance or political system, in exchange for which the court's primary output is 'interpretation' of the meaning in a particular case of the abstract language of legislation, or the even more abstract language of the society's 'ideals'.

Finally, in order to perform its function the court needs a willingness on the part of potential litigants to *use* the court as a conflict-resolving mechanism. This motivation to accept the court and abide by its decisions is an input from the pattern-maintenance or socialization system, and the court's immediate return output is what is termed 'justice'.

1. Whether it is a district attorney claiming that the 'public interest' he 'represents' has been violated by an alleged 'criminal', or a citizen claiming (for example) that his interest in esteem has been violated by a libel or slander, the court's procedure is essentially the same.

The Law and Adaptive Processes

Adaptation refers essentially to the production of instrumental facilities for coping with obstacles to the achievement of system goals. As mentioned earlier, Parsons and Smelser associate this function on a societal level with the economic system. I prefer a somewhat different association, broader in some respects, narrower in others. I want to conceive of adaptive structures, at least for modern Western societies, as those of science and technology. (So far as I can see, this does not modify the analysis of *Economy and Society* except to give it greater scope.)

When the courts receive a signal, in the shape of a lawsuit, that there has been a clash of interests, the first requirement is 'to understand it'. This means two things. First, it means discovering the factual connexion between the alleged harm and the event alleged to have caused it. Second, it means discovering the functional context of the action of plaintiff and defendant – that is to say, (a) the roles they are performing, (b) the functional significance for the system of those roles, and (c) the necessity (for efficient performance) of playing the roles in the manner in which the litigants had in fact been playing them.

These 'discoveries' are made on the basis of certain cognitive generalizations, beliefs, and theories concerning cause-and-effect relationships; and they are made with the aid of techniques for ascertaining 'truth'. The elaborate equipment and techniques of crime-detection laboratories; the statistics contained in a 'Brandeis-type' brief; the mortality tables used in calculating potential earning power in order to assess the 'damages' of a death; psychiatric examinations; public opinion polls showing the amount of confusion existing between trade-marks or brand-names – all those are examples of inputs to the legal system from the adaptive system of the society.

Not only technique and factual knowledge are involved in this input, but also cognitive theories regarding the necessity of certain kinds of behavior if certain functions are to be efficiently performed. An important example of such an input is the use by the courts of classical economic theory.

The very fact that Justice Holmes found it necessary to admonish his colleagues on the Supreme Court that the Fourteenth

Amendment 'does not enact Mr Herbert Spencer's social statics'[2] is evidence that in fact the Fourteenth Amendment had, for all practical purposes, done precisely that. In interpreting concepts such as 'property' and 'due process' the Court for a very long time based its reasoning about economic conflicts of interest on a specific theory of what was necessary to achieve productive co-ordination of economic activities.

Not only in constitutional law, but in all areas of decision-making, the courts (more or less systematically) use as a decision-making criterion the expected impact of a decision on productive efficiency. In tort law, for example, such perennial issues as the distinction among trespassers, licensees, and invitees, or the problem of the immunity of governmental agencies or charitable institutions from liability for their negligence, are nearly always debated in the context of the question, 'What will be the impact on people's ability to carry out their responsibility?'

The court utilizes these inputs of knowledge (together with the other inputs that will be discussed below) to make a decision. The decision, which will of course be binding on all persons in the same class or category as the particular litigants at bar, is an output to the adaptive system of the society. It is an output of *organization* or structure.

The decision asserts a set of rights, duties, liabilities, exposures, immunities, and privileges that either alter or reinforce the organization of roles in the division of labor. For example, the extension of the protection of the Fourteenth Amendment to corporations, regarded as 'legal persons', vividly affected the adaptive machinery of the society. Other examples are the holding of minimum wage laws to be unconstitutional and the later reversal of that holding, and the holding that a state may not keep for itself certain natural resources that would benefit interstate commerce.

In Durkheim's terminology, the court's integrative contribution to the adaptive system may be regarded as an output of organic solidarity. That is, the court's contribution to adaptation is an imposition of rights and obligations *in the interests of efficient organization*. It is dependent for this, however, on knowledge of what efficient organization *is*, and what can contribute

2. *Lochner* v. *New York*, 198 U.S. 45, at 75 (1905).

to it. For example, employers now have what is called a 'qualified privilege' to defame employees, which means that they are not liable for defamatory remarks, even if proved false. The ground of this privilege is that employers are thought to need freedom to express their opinions to other employers without having to worry about possible legal penalties.

How important is this freedom today for labor recruitment? What effect does it have on labor mobility? What pressures does it put on employees to see particularistic relations with employers as a safeguard against defamation? And are there different answers to these questions for different categories of employees, so that the law errs (merely on pragmatic grounds) in dealing only with the gross category 'employees'?

As part of the adaptive system, sociology potentially has much to contribute to the legal system, by way of answering such questions, by way of facilitating the predictions of how people will behave when exposed to new liabilities, by way of delineating the obstacles to efficient performance of functions, and by way of understanding what kinds of actions are and are not required for meeting various responsibilities.

But even supposing that sociologists are in a position to contribute such knowledge, a further problem is raised concerning the channels of communication by which it is transmitted to the legal system, and the return channels by which a secondary output of the legal system is communicated to the adaptive system – namely, *queries*, or expression of need for certain kinds of knowlege.

The most conspicuous mechanism relied upon at present for effecting this transmission is the adversary system, which is based, at least in part, on the assumption that if each of two adversaries is motivated to get in the record all the evidence most favorable to his *own* case, the chances are maximized of getting *all* relevant considerations before the court, and of forcing on the attention of 'scientists' the need for certain kinds of knowledge.

How well this system works or the degree to which it in fact obstructs and obscures the collection of pertinent evidence, is something on which there is more folklore than scientific knowledge. Similarly, we know very little about the utility of legal education for acquainting the practising lawyer with the possible sources of reliable knowledge, or about the nature of the obstacles he encounters in obtaining it from 'experts', even if he knows the sources.

Furthermore, on the other side of the transaction, there is a difficulty in making scientists, especially social scientists, sensitive to the needs of the legal system – that is, aware of them in the first place, and responsive to them in the second. The difficulty is illustrated in the conspicuous lack of communication between lawmen and social scientists even on the same university campus. The results are that some useful raw materials for sociological analysis remain locked in the law schools and law journals; an important market for sociological knowledge remains untapped; and the quality of 'organizational efficiency' put out by the legal system may fall below possibly realizable standards.

The Law and the Polity

In modern democratic societies the prototype of the sovereign may be taken to be the legislature. Legislative determination of policy – the actual uses to which power is put – is one of the primary sources of the law's conception of goals, or standards for evaluating the 'efficiency' of a given or anticipated role structure.

The legislature's primary input into the legal system is, in other words, a description of the ideal state of affairs for which social resources are to be mobilized through the exercise of power. The immediate corresponding output of the legal system is the *application* of general policy statements to the specific conflict at hand. This, of course, means that the courts can by no means be passive or mechanical 'implementers' of the legislative policy; the statute must be interpreted, and its interpretation is a creative act, giving real effect to the abstract language of the legislature. It is an indispensable adjunct to the legislative exercise of power. In return for the output of interpretation, the legal system receives from the polity a secondary input, the sanction of *enforcement*. Judicial decisions become binding on the litigants through the power of the state; and – also to be included in the concept of enforcement – it is by the legislature that the courts are *empowered* to resolve disputes and are given the facilities for doing so: courthouses, judgeships, salaries, and so on.

These interchanges, of course, do not occur in any automatic or inevitable way. The transactions between the legal system and the polity may break down. Courts may 'interpret' the life out of legislative policies; or they may even ignore a statute. In turn, the polity may refuse to enforce legal decisions, and may fail to give any clear indication of public policy as a guide to judicial action. These interchanges are often precariously balanced, just as are the interchanges between the output of consumers' goods by business firms and the spending of money by households. The point is that when the exchanges are not completed smoothly, some re-adjustment is likely to occur, in the first place; and in the second place there will be repercussions in other subsystems of the society.

The exchange of policy directives for interpretation of such policies is especially susceptible to disruption because the legislature, subject to the influence of whimsical shifts in public opinion and to the private demands of various interest groups, often enacts contradictory policies. The court in such cases must choose between different policies of the state.

American courts, for example, are often required to choose between a policy involving the use of the police power to secure collective goals, on the one hand, and the policy of maximum individual liberty, on the other. For a long period, the courts steadily rejected the use of police power in economic affairs in favor of a policy of freedom of contract. Today, they seem willing to accept almost any legislative policy concerning economic matters, regardless of its interference with individual liberty. This is true to such an extent that Maine's famous generalization concerning a transition from status to contract may be in the process of reversal, at least as regards economic relations (cf. Friedmann, 1953, pp. 144–5). At the same time, the courts more frequently reject policies that attempt to place national security – or 'mechanical solidarity' – above individual liberty. The decision in the *Jencks* case,[3] for example, was a rejection of the policy of protecting FBI efficiency in favor of allowing defendants maximum opportunity to defeat prosecution.

3. *Jencks* v. *U.S.*, 350 U.S. 980 (1956).

That the courts must choose between conflicting policies means they have a secondary kind of output to make the polity in exchange for the secondary input of enforcement. In a sense, the court becomes a legitimator of legislative decisions; and this adds to the polity's dependence on a successful completion of the exchange.

This adds significance to the sociological problem of locating extralegislative sources of the court's own goal conceptions. The social origins of judges and law professors probably point to one such source; another is the socialization received by lawmen in the traditions of the law, both formally in the law schools and informally in interaction with peers and clients. Further, the mechanisms by which lawmen maintain some degree of insulation from the fluctuating pressures to which legislators are exposed, and the process of reinforcement of an independent legal self-image, are problems to which sociologists could profitably direct their attention.

The transaction between the political and the legal systems may also break down on the other side. There is no automatic guarantee that judicial decisions will be enforced. From the time when the State of Georgia sent Cherokee Indians on something close to a death march in response to the Supreme Court's declaration that Georgia could not expropriate Cherokee lands, until recently when Congress refused to empower the Attorney General to file contempt proceedings against officials who defy the Court's desegregation order, it has been clear that the input of enforcement may be withheld. The withholding of enforcement under certain conditions tends to move the system in the direction of totalitarian forms of state-court relationships, and is hence not only a theoretically strategic but also a value-strategic focus of sociological study.

One of the most important conditions affecting the supply of enforcement is the need of the polity for the legitimation by the courts. This need seems to be a function of the esteem in which the courts are held; and that in turn seems to be a function of the relationships prevailing between the pattern-maintenance and the legal systems.

The Law and Pattern Maintenance

Presupposed by all that I have said so far, a third condition is necessary if the legal system is to contribute to integration through the resolution of conflicts. This is the obvious fact that conflicts must be brought to the courts' attention. People must be motivated to turn to the law for protection of their interests, and this implies that they must feel that the law will in fact give them justice. It is thus in the offer of 'justice' that the legal system makes its major output, in exchange for the input of motivations to accept the court as a problem-solving structure.

To do the proverbial rushing in, I want to define 'justice' for present purposes simply as the subjective feeling that one has got what's coming to him, that one has received his 'due'. This amounts to saying that internalized expectations have been met.

It is perhaps in connexion with these interchanges between the legal system and the pattern-maintenance system that there are the most familiar breakdowns. On the side of the pattern-maintenance system, one reason for the breakdown, it is sometimes suggested, is that no one really wants what the courts offer. As political boss Martin Lomassey put it to Lincoln Steffens, in a remark revitalized in Merton's discussion of the political machine, what people often want is simply *help* – 'Help, you understand; none of your law and justice, but help' (Merton, 1949, p. 74).

This dislike of justice may be put in other terms. It is a feeling that the court's conceptions of legitimate expectations are very different from one's own. And this is likely to be true, partly because of differences between the reference groups of judges and clients, and partly because of the nature of one important mechanism relied upon by the court to insure conformity to institutionalized expectations.

The mechanism I refer to is the doctrine of *stare decisis*, the doctrine that the courts are bound by their own precedents, and that lower courts are bound by the old decisions of higher courts. The justification for the doctrine is usually that it provides the best insurance that 'justice' will be served by respecting the expectations that have been built up on the basis of previous decisions.

The 'certainty and predictability' of the law, so important to acceptance of the law as an integrative mechanism, is sought, then, by the law's own moral commitment to precedent. This commitment, though, interferes with another condition necessary for public acceptance of the legal process: a flexibility sufficient to adapt to changed circumstances, new interests, and different dangers and liabilities attendant upon social change.

The traditional devices relied upon by the common law to balance *stare decisis* on the one hand and the need for flexibility on the other were the familiar ones of 'legal fictions', 'equity', and concepts of 'natural law' (cf. Friedmann, 1953, pp. 320–29). These still operate to some extent to preserve the law from rigor mortis; but a more important device in modern societies is legislation, which, as was pointed out above, constitutes an input into the legal system of policy determination from an agency more responsive than the courts to rapidly changing needs.

So important has this device become, indeed, that courts may be found rendering decisions that are labelled by the court itself as unjust and inefficient but which, the court insists, it is bound to render nonetheless, until the legislature rescues it from the consequence of a prior decision. Justice Brandeis once declared that 'It is usually more important that a rule of law be settled than that it be settled right. Even where the error in declaring the rule is a matter of serious concern, it is ordinarily better to seek correction by legislation. Often this is true although the question is a constitutional one' (Frankfurter, 1956, p. 64).

The rationale for this position is that the legislative procedure can give clear notice to everyone that after a certain date, rights and obligations will be changed in a certain way, whereas the courts can reverse a precedent only in the context of an actual case, which would involve injustice to the litigant who had been relying upon the validity of the court's previous judgement. The courts do, of course, still reverse decisions, on the alleged basis of new facts, as in the desegregation cases, or even on the alleged finding of simple error in previous decisions. They are, however, reluctant to do this; and such actions are not predictable enough to be relied on. Changed community sentiments regarding the meaning of 'justice', therefore, tend not so readily to be reflected in judicial decisions.

Furthermore, a related aspect of *stare decisis* also contributes to the law's lack of receptivity to new claims. This is the persistence, to some extent, of the doctrine that only those *interests* will be recognized that were previously recognized. That is to say, new needs for which court protection is sought may be dismissed by the court with the deadly sentence, 'Plaintiff has failed to state a cause of action', which means that he has failed to demonstrate that any court in the past has even been willing to listen to evidence on such a violation of an expectation.

The central condition responsible for such dismissal seems to be that the court's *manifest* function is to apply an already-existing law; the latent function of resolving disputes *efficiently* is seldom recognized.

Two additional mechanisms by which the court's output of justice may be kept in fairly close balance with community sentiments should, however, be noted. One is the jury system. Although nominally only a 'trier of facts' when facts are in dispute, the jury probably tries a good many things besides facts behind its closed doors. Without overt changes in the legal doctrines, then, justice – according to the community's views – may nonetheless be served, although, to be sure, in a mysterious and somewhat 'chancy' way.

A second such mechanism is the system of communication internal to the legal system itself. I include in this both law schools and the extensive commentaries and criticism of judicial opinions in law journals. It is commonly supposed, for example, that it was an academic article by Brandeis and Warren in the *Harvard Law Review* that was responsible for judicial recognition of a new tort, invasion of privacy (Brandeis and Warren, 1890). To the unknown degree to which the journals are considered by the bench and bar, the legal system may be kept in fairly close touch with prevailing community sentiments – depending also, of course, on the degree to which academic jurists are themselves in touch with them.

The fact remains, however, that 'the law' is for many people something to be avoided if at all possible. There is not a very good market for the law's output of justice; and – the other side of the same coin – the law is not widely regarded as the place to take one's conflicts, except as a last resort.

A deeper reason for this than any I have so far considered

may be related to the fact that, almost by definition, 50 per cent of the people involved in litigation must have their expectations violated. Someone has to lose.

While the adversary system may work tolerably well as a transmission belt for inputs of facts and policy considerations, it can hardly work very well in persuading a litigant that his cause is being considered on its merits and with respect, except possibly by his own lawyer, who by definition is not in control of the situation.

Furthermore, there are two related characteristics of the law that contribute to making its output of 'justice' unpalatable. One is the fact that the legal system tends to have written into it the assumption that in any dispute one side is right and the other side is wrong. The adversary system is built on this assumption and helps to reinforce it; and the court is ordinarily empowered only to decide a winner and a loser – not to find a way to help the loser adjust to his loss, or to avoid in the future the action that led to the loss, or to alter the conditions that led to the loser's behaving as he did.

The second difficulty is related to this. An assumption implicit in the operation of the law is that once rights and obligations have been authoritatively stated, individuals have only one mode of adaptation available to them: acceptance. The assumption, in other words, is that *learning* is the only response to a deprivation.

In fact, of course, there is good reason to believe that learning – that is, a reorganization of the individual's personality system so as smoothly to adapt to the new reality – is not even a very likely response, except under special conditions, such as those summarized by Leonard Cottrell (1947) or those suggested by Parsons (1951, chapt. 7).

The legal system does not include the machinery for insuring the amount of permissiveness, support, denial of reciprocity, and conditional reward required to make the court experience a learning experience. To the contrary, the obscure and complicated legal procedures remain a baffling barrier to the litigant's understanding of what happened to him, except to the degree to which his attorney informally plays the role of therapist. In consequence, the major impact may be frustration, with little to prevent the frustration from leaving a permanent residue of hostility.

63

It is interesting in this connexion, moreover, that a device that under certain conditions *could* help the losing litigant to adjust to his loss – and even, conceivably, to change his expectations and behavior – does not in fact function toward that end, and so far as I can discern is not even intended to do so. I refer to the written opinion delivered by appellate courts, setting forth the reason for the decision. An explanation of the decision addressed to the litigants might contribute to consensus in the long run; but the legal tradition seems to be rather to address the explanation to other lawyers – who, again, may or may not attempt to translate it for their clients in a way that might gain their acceptance of it.

To the degree that there is a reluctance to accept the courts as problem-solving agencies, the question must be raised as to what in fact is substituted for them. I shall here only propose certain tentative suggestions, approaching the problem by calling attention to a fact that at first glance seems to contradict what I have just said concerning a lack of demand for the court's output.

This is the fact that, in a sense, the demand for the court's services exceeds the supply. At least this might be a reasonable way of expressing the widely publicized figures of the backlog of cases on the judicial dockets in many jurisdictions, which results in delays of up to three or four or even six years between the filing of a suit and its final settlement. Why is the supply not increased?

One reason may be found in the consideration reviewed above. Widespread skepticism about the quality of justice put out by the legal system is an obstacle to any general support for legislation to increase the number of courts. Justice costs money, and people who purchase it either have a lot of money or have a desperate need for it. Those in immediate need may not be so numerous at any given time as to be able to affect legislative behavior; and those not in immediate need may not be sufficiently impressed by the quality of the stuff to be interested in increasing its supply.

Another factor tending to prevent an expansion of facilities is the obvious fact that those with an immediate demand do not have direct access to the courts; their immediate purchase is a purchase of lawyers' services. The supply of lawyers, therefore, might be expected to be more responsive to demand for legal adjudication than the supply of courts.

In so far as this occurs, the *de facto* system of conflict resolution tends to become, not the court system, but a system of direct bargaining and negotiation between lawyers. Conflicts may then be settled not on the basis of the considerations discussed above, but on the basis of straight bargaining power and ability to wait. Furthermore, there may be two classes of persons for whom the inadequate supply of judicial facilities is functional rather than dysfunctional. These are lawyers who can use the very existence of delays to persuade clients to settle out of court, and thus increase the turnover of cases, and defendants.

For example, a litigant who has experienced, say, $20,000 worth of damages and who, let us say, has a very strong case, is put in the position of having to choose between having $20,000 six years from now or considerably less today. If he is awarded $20,000 six years later, he has lost and the defendant has gained the interest on that amount, which at 5 per cent would be $1000 a year.

What other differential consequences for integration flow from this kind of substitution of direct bargaining and power relations for judicial review can only be a matter of conjecture, until considerably more research is done. One conjecture is that of Herbert Croly, quoted by Merton, that 'The lawyer having been permitted to subordinate democracy to the Law, the Boss had to be called in to extricate the victim, which he did after a fashion and for a consideration' (Merton, 1949, pp. 72–73).

At any rate, a widespread attitude toward the law seems to be that conveyed by the slogan, 'First thing we do, let's hang all the lawyers'. The incidence of this negative view, and its sources and implications for conflict resolution, offer another fertile field for sociological research.

Summary

The suggestion of this paper is that the legal system be viewed as an integrative mechanism, contributing 'co-ordination' to the society. This contribution takes the form of certain 'outputs' to other sectors of the society, in exchange for certain 'inputs'.

1. From the political system, goals and enforcement, in exchange for interpretation and legitimation.

2. From the adaptive system, knowledge and 'acceptance of queries' as research directives in exchange for organization and 'demand' for knowledge.

3. From the pattern-maintenance system, conflicts and esteem in exchange for resolution and 'justice'.

The legal system's effectiveness in contributing to integration is a function of the stability of these interchanges. Some factors making for instability have been tentatively suggested:

1. The possible development inside the law of goal-conceptions inconsistent with the polity's.

2. The responsiveness of legislatures to short-run fluctuations in private interests.

3. The lack of communication of accurate knowledge to courts.

4. The lack of facilities for turning litigation into a 'learning experience'.

5. The development in the pattern-maintenance system of values resistant to 'justice'.

6. The lack of channels by which demand for court facilities might lead to an increase in supply.

Finally, certain strategic areas for sociological research have been suggested:

1. Possible sources of extra legislative conceptions of collective goals, such as the social origins of lawmen and their legal socialization experiences.

2. The mechanism of reinforcement of and support for legal 'ideals' within the legal profession.

3. The channels of communication to lawmen of scientific knowledge.

4. Public perceptions of the legal system and the bases of those perceptions.

5. The reactions of individuals to the legal imposition of new liabilities.

6. The devices used as alternatives to the legal system for resolving conflicts.

It is the central suggestion of this paper that a frame of reference such as that essayed here might not only help to overcome the barriers of sociolegal stereotypes, but also point the way to areas of sociolegal cooperation that would enrich both sociology and the administration of justice.

References
BRANDEIS, L. D., and WARREN, S. D. (1890), 'The right to privacy' *Harvard Law Review*, vol. 4, pp. 193–220.
COTTRELL, L. S. (1947), 'The adjustment of the individual to his age and sex roles', in T. M. Newcomb and E. L. Hartly (eds.), *Readings in Social Psychology*, Henry Holt, pp. 370–73.
FRANKFURTER, F. (1956), 'The social views of Mr Justice Brandeis', in E. H. Pollack (ed.), *The Brandeis Reader*, Oceana Publications.
FRIEDMANN, W. G. (1953), *Legal Theory*, Stevens and Sons Ltd.
MERTON, R. K. (1949), *Social Theory and Social Structure*, The Free Press.
PARSONS, T. (1951), *The Social System*, The Free Press.
PARSONS, T., and SMELSER, N. J. (1956), *Economy and Society*, The Free Press.

Part Two Legislation, Law Enforcement and the Public

There exist two contrasting views on the relationship between legal precepts and public attitudes and behaviour. According to the one, law is determined by the sense of justice and the moral sentiments of the population, and legislation can only achieve results by staying relatively close to prevailing social norms. According to the other view law, and especially legislation, is a vehicle through which a programmed social evolution can be brought about. The selections in this part illustrate both views. Several of the extracts try, in a limited way, to confront the two views and determine the conditions under which the law may change social relationships (Aubert, Dror, Gorecki). Podgorecki is primarily concerned with the possible innovative functions of law and of the machinery of enforcement. Dicey, however, was more concerned to demonstrate the dependence of law upon public opinion. And Banton, who studied the actual encounter between the law and the public in the role of the policeman, emphasizes strongly the primacy of other social norms.

7 A. V. Dicey

Law and Public Opinion in England

Excerpts from A. V. Dicey, *Lectures on the Relation between Law and Public Opinion in England during the Nineteenth Century*, Macmillan, 1905, pp. 1-42.

The existence and the alteration of human institutions must, in a sense, always and everywhere depend upon the beliefs or feelings, or, in other words, upon the opinion of the society in which such institutions flourish.

As force [writes Hume] is always on the side of the governed, the governors have nothing to support them but opinion. It is, therefore, on opinion only that government is founded; and this maxim extends to the most despotic and most military governments, as well as to the most free and most popular. The Soldan of Egypt, or the Emperor of Rome, might drive his harmless subjects, like brute beasts, against their sentiments and inclination; but he must, at least, have led his mamelukes, or praetorian bands, like men, by their opinion (Hume, *Essays*, vol. 1, Essay 4).

And so true is this observation that the authority even of a Southern planter over his slaves rested at bottom upon the opinion of the negroes whom he at his pleasure flogged or killed. Their combined physical force exceeded the planter's own personal strength, and the strength of the few whites who might be expected to stand by him. The blacks obeyed the slave-owner from the opinion, whether well or ill founded, that in the long run they would in a contest with their masters have the worst of the fight; and even more from that habit of submission which, though enforced by the occasional punishment of rebels, was grounded upon a number of complicated sentiments, such, for example, as admiration for superior ability and courage, or gratitude for kindness, which cannot by any fair analysis be reduced to a mere form of fear, but constitute a kind of prevalent moral atmosphere. The whites, in short, ruled in virtue of the opinion, entertained by their slaves no less than by themselves, that the slave-owners possessed qualities which gave them the might, and even the right, to be masters. With the rightness or wrongness of this conviction we are not here in any way concerned. Its existence is adduced only as a proof that, even in the most extreme case conceivable, Hume's doctrine holds good, and the opinion of the governed is the real foundation of all government.

But, though obedience to law must of necessity be enforced by opinion of some sort, and Hume's paradox thus turns out to be a truism, this statement does not involve the admission that the law of every country is itself the result of what we mean by 'public opinion'. This term, when used in reference to legislation, is merely a short way of describing the belief or conviction prevalent in a given society that particular laws are beneficial, and therefore ought to be maintained, or that they are harmful, and therefore ought to be modified or repealed. And the assertion that public opinion governs legislation in a particular country, means that laws are there maintained or repealed in accordance with the opinion or wishes of its inhabitants. Now this assertion, though it is, if properly understood, true with regard to England at the present day, is clearly not true of all countries, at all times and indeed has not always been true even of England. [...]

There are three different reasons why we cannot assert of all countries, or of any country at all times, that laws are there the result of public opinion. No 'opinion', in the proper sense of that word, with regard to the change of the law may exist; the opinion which does direct the development of the law may not be 'public opinion'; and lastly, there may be lacking any legislative organ adapted for carrying out the changes of the law demanded by public opinion.

In England, however, the beliefs or sentiments which, during the nineteenth century, have governed the development of the law have in strictness been public opinion, for they have been the wishes and ideas as to legislation held by the people of England, or, to speak with more precision, by the majority of those citizens who have at a given moment taken an effective part in public life.

And here the obvious conclusion suggests itself that the public opinion which governs a country is the opinion of the sovereign, whether the sovereign be a monarch, an aristocracy, or the mass of the people.

This conclusion, however, though roughly true, cannot be accepted without considerable reservation. The sovereign power may hold that a certain kind of legislation is in itself expedient, but may at the same time be unwilling, or even unable, to carry this conviction into effect, and this from the dread of offending the feelings of subjects who, though they in general take no active share in public affairs, may raise an insuperable opposition to laws which disturb their habits or shock their moral sentiment; it is well indeed to note that the public opinion which finds expression in legislation is a very complex phenomenon, and often takes the form of a compromise resulting from a conflict between the ideas of the government and the feelings or habits of the governed. This holds good in all countries, whatever be their form of government, but is more manifest than elsewhere in a country such as England, where the legislation enacted by Parliament constantly bears traces of the compromise arrived at between enlightenment and prejudice. [. . .]

The principle that the development of law depends upon opinion is, however, open to one objection.

Men legislate, it may be urged, not in accordance with their opinion as to what is a good law, but in accordance with their interest, and this, it may be added, is emphatically true of classes as contrasted with individuals, and therefore of a country like England, where classes exert a far more potent control over the making of laws than can any single person.

Now it must at once be granted that in matters of legislation men are guided in the main by their real or apparent interest. So true is this, that from the inspection of the laws of a country it is often possible to conjecture, and this without much hesitation, what is the class which holds, or has held, predominant power at a given time. [. . .]

The answer to the objection under consideration is, however, easy to find. 'Though men', to use the words of Hume, 'be much governed by interest, yet even interest itself, and all human affairs, are entirely governed by *opinion*' (Hume, *Essays*, vol. 1, Essay 7). Even, therefore, were we to assume that the persons who have power to make law are solely and wholly influenced by the desire to promote their own personal and selfish interests, yet their view of their interest and therefore their legislation must be determined by their opinion; and hence, where the public has influence, the development of the law must of necessity be governed by public opinion. [. . .]

Individuals, indeed, and still more frequently classes, do constantly support laws or institutions which they deem beneficial to themselves, but which certainly are in fact injurious to the rest of the world. But the explanation of this conduct will be found, in nine cases out of ten, to be that men come easily to believe that arrangements agreeable to themselves are beneficial to others. A man's interest gives a bias to his judgement far oftener than it corrupts his heart. [. . .]

Public legislative opinion, as it has existed in England during the nineteenth century, presents several noteworthy aspects or characteristics. They may conveniently be considered under five heads – the existence at any given period of a predominant public opinion; the origin of such opinion; the development and continuity thereof; the checks imposed on such opinion by the existence of counter-currents and cross-currents of opinion; the action of laws themselves as the creators of legislative opinion.

First, there exists at any given time a body of beliefs, convictions, sentiments, accepted principles, of firmly-rooted prejudices, which, taken together, make up the public opinion of a particular era, or what we may call the reigning or predominant current of opinion, and, as regards at any rate the last three or four centuries, and especially the nineteenth century, the influence of this dominant current of opinion has, in England, if we look at the matter broadly, determined, directly or indirectly, the course of legislation.

It may be added that the whole body of beliefs existing in any given age may generally be traced to certain fundamental assumptions which at the time, whether they be actually true or false, are believed by the mass of the world to be true with such confidence that they hardly appear to bear the character of assumptions. [. . .]

The large currents, again, of public opinion which in the main determine legislation, acquire their force and volume only by degrees, and are in their turn liable to be checked or superseded by other and adverse currents, which themselves gain strength only after a considerable lapse of time. For example, the whole way in which, during the sixteenth and the seventeenth centuries, men looked at the regulation of labour or the fixing of prices by the State, a view which finds expression in Tudor legislation and has the closest connexion with the Elizabethan poor law, is the result of a body of beliefs favouring State intervention in matters of trade, no less than in matters of religion, and had been growing up during many generations. This confidence in the authority of the State was in the seventeenth and eighteenth centuries superseded by a different body of beliefs which pointed at any rate towards the conclusion that the chief, though not the sole, duty of the State is to protect men's persons and property,[1] so as to secure the maximum of freedom for each man compatible with the existence of the like freedom on the part of others. All that need here be noted is that any fundamental change of convictions which inevitably affects legislation in all directions has, in England at least, always gone on slowly and gradually, and has been in this respect like the gradual rising of the tide. Nor does the likeness end here, for an alteration in the condition of opinion more often than not, begins just at the very time when the predominant beliefs of a particular age seem to exert their utmost power. The height of the tide immediately precedes its ebb.

Secondly, the opinion which affects the development of the law has, in modern England at least, often originated with some single thinker or school of thinkers.

No doubt it is at times allowable to talk of a prevalent belief or opinion as 'being in the air', by which expression is meant that a particular way of looking at things has become the common possession of all the world. But though a belief, when it prevails, may at last be adopted by the whole of a generation, it rarely happens that a widespread conviction has grown up spontaneously among the multitude. 'The initiation', it has been said, 'of all wise or noble things comes, and must come, from individuals; generally at first from some one individual' (Mill, *On Liberty*); to which it ought surely be added that the origination of a new folly or of a new form of baseness comes, and must in general come, at first from individuals or from some one individual. The peculiarity of individuals, as contrasted with

1. Compare Macaulay's essay on 'Gladstone on Church and State'.

the crowd, lies neither in virtue nor in wickedness, but in original-ity. [. . .]

The course of events in England may often at least be thus described: A new and, let us assume, a true idea presents itself to some one man of originality or genius; the discoverer of the new conception, or some follower who has embraced it with enthusiasm, preaches it to his friends or disciples, they in their turn become impressed with its importance and its truth, and gradually a whole school accept the new creed. These apostles of a new faith are either persons endowed with special ability or, what is quite as likely, they are persons who, owing to their peculiar position, are freed from a bias, whether moral or intel-lectual, in favour of prevalent errors. At last the preachers of truth make an impression, either directly upon the general public or upon some person of eminence, say a leading statesman, who stands in a position to impress ordinary people and thus to win the support of the nation. Success, however, in converting man-kind to a new faith, whether religious, or economical, or political, depends but slightly on the strength of the reasoning by which the faith can be defended, or even on the enthusiasm of its adherents. A change of belief arises, in the main, from the occurrence of circumstances which incline the majority of the world to hear with favour theories which, at one time, men of common sense derided as absurdities, or distrusted as paradoxes. [. . .]

Thirdly, the development of public opinion generally, and therefore of legislative opinion, has been in England at once gradual, or slow, and continuous. [. . .]

Owing to the habitual conservatism to be found even among ardent reformers when leaders of Englishmen, and to the customs of our parliamentary government, the development of legislative opinion is rendered still slower by our inveterate preference for fragmentary and gradual legislation. Only in exceptional cases and under the pressure of some crisis can English legislators be induced to carry out a broad principle at one stroke, to its logical and necessary consequences. [. . .]

The slowness with which legislative opinion acts is not quite the same thing as its continuity, though the bit-by-bit or gradual system of law-making dear to Parliament, does in truth afford strong evidence that the course of opinion in England has certainly during the nineteenth century, and probably ever since parliamentary government became to any degree a reality, been continuous, i.e. has been rarely marked by sudden breaks. In any case it is certain that during the nineteenth century the legislative opinion of the nation has never veered round with sudden violence. [. . .]

This continuity is closely connected with some subordinate characteristics of English legislative opinion.

The opinion which changes the law is in one sense the opinion of the time when the law is actually altered; in another sense it has often been in England the opinion prevalent some twenty or thirty years before that time; it has been as often as not in reality the opinion not of today but of yesterday.

Legislative opinion must be the opinion of the day, because, when laws are altered, the alteration is of necessity carried into effect by legislators who act under the belief that the change is an amendment; but this law-making opinion is also the opinion of yesterday because the beliefs which have at last gained such hold on the legislature, as to produce an alteration in the law, have generally been created by thinkers or writers who exerted their influence long before the change in the law took place. Thus it may well happen that an innovation is carried through at a time when the teachers who supplied the arguments in its favour are in their graves, or even – and this is well worth noting – when in the world of speculation a movement has already set in against ideas which are exerting their full effect in the world of action and of legislation. [. . .]

Nor is there anything mysterious about the way in which the thought or sentiment of yesterday governs the legislation or the politics of today. Law-making in England is the work of men well advanced in life; the politicians who guide the House of Commons, to say nothing of the peers who lead the House of Lords, are few of them below thirty, and most of them are above forty years of age. They have formed or picked up their convictions, and, what is of more consequence, their prepossessions, in early manhood, which is the one period of life when men are easily impressed with new ideas. Hence English legislators retain the prejudices or modes of thinking which they acquired in their youth; and when, late in life, they take a share in actual legislation, they legislate in accordance with the doctrines which were current, either generally or in the society to which the law-givers belonged, in the days of their early manhood. [. . . .]

Fourthly, the reigning legislative opinion of the day has never, at any rate during the nineteenth century, exerted absolute or despotic authority. Its power has always been diminished by the existence of counter-currents or cross-currents of opinion which were not in harmony with the prevalent opinion of the time.

A counter-current here means a body of opinion, belief, or sentiment more or less directly opposed to the dominant opinion of a particular era.

Counter-currents of this kind have generally been supplied by the survival of ideas or convictions which are gradually losing their hold upon a given generation, and particularly the youthful part thereof.

Counter-currents, again, may be supplied by new ideals which are beginning to influence the young. The hopes or dreams of the generation just coming into the field of public life undermine the energy of a dominant creed.

Counter-currents of opinion, whatever their source, have one certain and one possible effect.

The certain effect is that a check is imposed upon the action of the dominant faith. Thus, from 1830 to 1850 the Benthamite liberalism of the day, which then exerted its highest authority, was held in check by the restraining power of the older and declining toryism. Hence the progress of parliamentary reform, that is, the advance towards democracy, was checked. [. . .]

The possible, but far less certain, result of a strong counter-current may be to delay a reform or innovation for so long a time that ultimately it cannot be effected at all, or else, when nominally carried out, becomes a measure of an essentially different character from the proposal put forward by its original advocates. [. . .]

A cross-current of opinion may be described as any body of belief or sentiment which, while strong enough ultimately to affect legislation, is yet in a measure independent of, though perhaps not directly opposed to, the dominant legislative creed of a particular era. These cross-currents arise often, if not always, from the peculiar position or prepossessions of particular classes, such as the clergy, the army, or the artisans, who look upon the world from their own special point of view. Such a cross-current differs from a counter-current in that it does not so much directly oppose the predominant opinion of a given time as deflect and modify its action. [. . .]

Fifthly, laws foster or create law-making opinion. This assertion may sound, to one who has learned that laws are the outcome of public opinion, like a paradox; when properly understood it is nothing but an undeniable though sometimes neglected truth.

Every law or rule of conduct must, whether its author perceives the fact or not, lay down or rest upon some general principle, and must therefore, if it succeeds in attaining its end, commend this principle to public attention or imitation, and thus affect legislative opinion. Nor is the success of a law necessary for the production of this effect. A principle derives prestige from its mere recognition by Parliament, and if a law fails in attaining its object the argument lies ready to hand that the failure was due to the law not going far enough, i.e. to its not carrying out the principle on which it is founded to its full logical consequences. The true importance, indeed, of laws lies far less in their direct result than in their effect upon the sentiment or convictions of the public.

The Reform Act of 1832 disfranchised certain corrupt boroughs, and bestowed on a limited number of citizens belonging mainly to the middle class the right to vote for members of Parliament. But the transcendent importance of the Act lay in its effect upon public opinion. Reform thus regarded was revolution. It altered the way in which people thought of the constitution, and taught Englishmen, once and for all, that venerable institutions which custom had made unchangeable could easily, and without the use of violence, be changed. It gave authority to the democratic creed, and fostered the conviction or delusion that the will of the nation could be expressed only through elected representatives.

8 O. Kahn-Freund

Labour Law and Public Opinion

Excerpt from O. Kahn-Freund, 'Labour law', in M. Ginsberg (ed.), *Law and Opinion in England in the Twentieth Century*, Stevens and Sons, 1959, pp. 215–27.

At the risk of seeming to indulge in a paradox, I must begin my discussion of the relation between public opinion and labour law by stating that few branches of the law have been less changed in their fundamentals since Dicey's day. When in 1914 Dicey published the second edition of his book, most of the great legislative and judicial battles in this field had been fought, and the foundations of social and industrial legislation had been well and truly laid. In some respects the principal patterns of labour legislation had been established in the nineteenth century, such as the codes intended to reduce the risk of industrial accidents in factories and mines, to regulate the hours of work of women and young persons, and to determine the method of wage payments, and the major rules governing the status of trade unions. In many ways, however, the era of the Liberal Governments of Campbell-Bannerman and of Asquith was the formative period of British labour law: between the South African War and the First World War minimum wage legislation was inaugurated, and the cornerstone was laid of the edifice of modern social security law, the nineteenth-century legislation designed to safeguard the individual's freedom of organization and freedom of strike was completed by the Trade Disputes Act, 1906, and, one year before Dicey published his second edition, the burning question of the trade unions' political activities was answered by a compromise. Although the Ministry of Labour and its Industrial Relations Department had not yet seen the light of day, the principle functions of that Department in settling disputes were already exercised by the Board of Trade under a statute passed in 1896, two years before Dicey delivered his lectures at the Harvard Law School.

This is a somewhat haphazard and incomplete enumeration of

legislative measures, but it will suffice to show that what has been achieved in this field since the outbreak of the First World War was a very considerable widening of the scope of existing principles rather than the formulation of new ones. With a good deal of exaggeration I may say that all the tendencies of legal development I am about to discuss had already become visible when Dicey sent the manuscript of the famous Introduction to his second edition to the printers.

You will probably say that this is surprising. After all, you may say, is it not true that middle-class opinion towards trade unions underwent a remarkable change in this half-century? Have collective bargaining methods not been thoroughly transformed, and has the volume of industrial stoppages not been reduced to a fraction of what it used to be? Are we not talking about a period which included two world wars, a general strike, and a depression and unemployment of unheard-of dimensions? Can it really be suggested that the general pattern of British labour law emerged unscathed from this multiple ordeal by fire?

The plain fact is that it did. Still, no miracle has occurred, unless you call it a miracle that the social structure of this island is exceptionally stable and its population exceptionally homogeneous. Even so it is noteworthy that almost all the major legislative measures in relation to labour which were taken under the impact of the two world wars and of the general strike have again disappeared. Compulsory arbitration, so important a feature of the First World War, was abolished even before the Peace Treaties had been signed, and though it persisted after the Second World War – in a sense it is still with us – it was at least deprived of its 'teeth' as soon as in peacetime it attempted a modest 'bite'. Wartime controls of the labour market, from the Munitions of War Acts of the First World War to the direction of labour and Essential Work Orders of the Second, vanished in the sun of peace like snow in the spring, and 'freedom of contract' emerged triumphant. The anti-trade union Trade Disputes and Trade Unions Act of 1927, a measure passed by a Conservative Government after the general strike, was repealed by a Labour Government in 1946. We have not heard of any plan to reintroduce it. Nor did the Labour Government replace it by another measure: in the decisive question of the trade unions' political fund it simply restored the law as it had been before 1926, that is, as it had been enacted a year before Dicey published his second edition. Characteristically enough, two measures during both wars on which organized labour insisted were aimed at the 'restoration of pre-war trade practices'. I do not, of course, mean to suggest that the period since 1914 has been an era of what Dicey called 'legislative quiescence'. Very far from it. But in the field of labour it was not a period of legislative inventiveness. In the development of industrial relations, war has been the father of many things, but in the creation of new legal principles it contributed, in this country, very little of permanent importance. This is not a matter of course, as the contrast to Continental countries plainly shows.

You can easily see that my task is very different from that of Professor Gower who, a few weeks ago, spoke in this series on Business and the Law. Remember how very different the relation between government and business was in 1914 from what it is today, and remember also the great and fundamental changes in the law of controls which have occurred during this period. The triangular relationship between organized labour, organized management and government, which is the framework of all labour law in this country, obtained firm foundations after 1914, but it was already there before that year. If, in 1914, individualism and *laissez faire* in the traditional sense were still a living legal ideology in the world of business, they were certainly rapidly ceasing to be so in the world of industrial relations. The free play of competition, of the laws of supply and demand, was, in the commodity markets, acceptable to a large segment of public opinion, but the social conscience of the nation had long ago been powerfully aroused against a corresponding policy for labour. State intervention and the impact of collective forces on individual relationships might still, at least nominally, be rejected in business, but they had to be accepted in the relations between labour and management. This, I submit, is the background to the Introduction of Dicey's second edition, the theme of which is the victory of what Dicey called 'collectivism' or 'socialism'. Dicey lived until 1922, but this Introduction was his political testament. It was the political testament of a dying generation, a lament for *laissez faire*.

The catalogue of legislation which Dicey stigmatized as 'collectivist' or 'socialist' is not by chance, to a large extent, taken from labour law. Let us have a look at his list of gravamina to see what precisely he meant by 'socialism' or 'collectivism'. The list includes the Old Age Pensions Act of 1908, by which non-contributory old age pensions were first introduced – contributory pensions did not come until after Dicey's death – and, as you may have expected, Lloyd George's National Insurance Act of 1911, that is to say, the first beginnings of health and – viewed with special misgivings by Dicey – of unemployment insurance. But the list also covers the fixing of a maximum shift for coal miners underground by the Coal Mines Regulation Act of 1908, and Winston Churchill's Trade Boards Act of 1909, the root of our minimum wage law. Much more surprising, in the same context Dicey also mentions the Trade Disputes Act of 1906 and the Trade Union Act of 1913, although both these statutes do not increase but greatly reduce the possibilities of State intervention. How can we explain the uniform classification by as acute a thinker and lawyer as Dicey of all these variegated items under the heading of 'socialist' or 'collectivist'? Was the explanation simply that Dicey was – as no doubt he was – politically out of sympathy with the Liberal Governments of the day, and that, to give the dog a bad name, he called their doings 'socialist' however much they may have been treading in the legislative footsteps of Bismarck, much as twenty years later in a similar situation American conservatives sometimes called Roosevelt's New Deal 'socialism'?

Such an explanation would be far too simple. The true explanation lies, I think, in Dicey's analysis of public opinion in relation to labour legislation and in what to our eyes must appear as the naïveté of this analysis. 'Collectivism' (and that word was for Dicey synonymous with 'socialism') denoted not only State intervention, but also what he called 'Preference for Collective Action'. All legislation designed to strengthen trade unions was 'collectivist' in this sense, and, even if consisting in the withdrawal of State intervention, contrary to his conception of 'individualism'. 'Individualism' and 'collectivism' were clear opposites. State intervention by legislation such as Factory Acts or Minimum Wage Acts, Public Health Acts or statutes promoting school meals for children were 'collectivist', but so was the removal of trade union liability in tort. The greater the power of the unions, the greater, under a democratic franchise, the pressure for State intervention. In the light of nineteenth-century experience, Dicey was persuaded that legislation strengthening the unions and legislation regulating the employment relationship were politically prompted by kindred motives and likely to lead to similar political and social results.

We cannot ignore the factual basis, the richness of the evidence on which this judgement was founded. The evidence can be seen in the description by Sidney and Beatrice Webb (*Industrial Democracy*, 1926 edn, Part 2, esp. Chapts. 2 and 4) of the methods used for the establishment of standards by the trade unions in the nineteenth century, the familiar and classical methods of mutual insurance, of collective bargaining, and of legal enactment. The Webbs showed the eclecticism, or empiricism, of the unions in the choice of these methods. In the chapter of *Industrial Democracy* (Part 2, chapt. 4) which bears the heading 'The Method of Legal Enactment' we find a demonstration how, in the nineteenth century, the inclination or disinclination of the unions to seek the aid of legislation varied with their power as what today we should call political pressure groups. Thus, the 'enfranchisement of the town artisan in 1867 and that of the county operative and the miner in 1885' (ibid., pp. 250 ff.) led almost immediately to a greatly increased demand on the part of the unions for legislation, and anyone familiar with the course of British labour legislation in the nineteenth century knows the significant results of this aspect of trade union policy in the seventies and eighties. We can understand why to Dicey growth of union power and growth of State intervention must have seemed almost identical.

Nevertheless, whilst as a diagnosis of nineteenth-century legislation Dicey's analysis may have had a good deal of validity, as a prognosis of twentieth-century developments it was wrong. During our century, and especially in the course of and after the First World War and even more so during and since the Second World War, the political pressure power of the unions grew beyond anything to be found in the descriptive analysis of the Webbs. Yet, if one studies the legislative developments of our time, one does not come to the conclusion that the nineteenth-century tendencies observed by the Webbs were continued after the First World War. On the contrary: the more trade union power grew, the clearer did it become that – to use the Webbs' terminology – the method of collective bargaining outweighed the reliance on legal enactment. Permit me here to give one simple example: No sooner was the Representation of the People Act, 1867, on the Statute-book than the unions renewed their demand for the regulation by law of the working hours of adult male workers. We may surmise that, if at any time when the political constellation was favourable to them, the trade unions had resuscitated this demand in our century, they would have been much more likely to be successful than they were ninety years ago. Nevertheless, this country has never even ratified the I L O Washington Convention of 1919 on the 48-hour week. To this day the working hours of adult men are regulated by law only in a number of exceptional cases. Perhaps the most important of these is the regulation of the shift hours of coal miners underground by the amended Coal Mines Regulation Act, 1908, which (to use Dicey's words, p. li) 'interfered ... with the right of a workman of full age to labour for any number of hours agreed upon between him and his employer'. It might have surprised Dicey that, with all the growth of union power after the First and the Second World Wars, the only major example of legislation of this kind to have been enacted since 1914 is road traffic legislation which has restricted the working hours of certain categories of drivers in order to protect the public against the obvious dangers resulting from long hours worked by those in charge of buses, lorries, etc. Generally speaking, the unions were content to rely on collective bargaining. From the point of view of social justice it is not always an unmixed blessing that the trade unions rely so much more on their industrial than on their political strength for the purpose of creating and enforcing standards of social protection. Sometimes it may mean that in sectors of the economy where trade union organization is weak social standards lag behind those enforced in other countries in which more emphasis lies on legislation and less on collective bargaining. Does not perhaps the fate of the recommendations in the Gowers Report on the health, safety and welfare of office workers provide a lesson? The Report was published in 1949, and had been preceded by no less than eleven Office Regulation Bills, introduced by private members between 1923 and 1936, but so far these recommendations have not been implemented. Can one doubt that, if the unions relied on legislation, that is on political pressure power in our time as, according to the Webbs, they did in the nineteenth century and as, according to Dicey, they could be expected to do in the twentieth, the Gowers Recommendations would, shortly after 1949, have become law? And, if I may for a moment indulge in political speculation, is it not true that the potential beneficiaries of such legislation belong to the 'new middle class,' the black-coated or white-collared workers, who are said to supply a not inconsiderable proportion of the 'floating vote'? Would you not, on the basis of Dicey's analysis of the impact of public opinion on labour law, have expected politicians to strain every nerve to enact such politically important legislation? And does not the fact that it was not passed provide further proof that the relation between law and opinion in these matters is quite different from what Dicey thought it would be? That the pressure of opinion on law-making is exercised through organized pressure groups, and that the unions as pressure groups are far less interested in legislation than they were even half a century ago?

What Dicey did not see, then, and what he could have hardly seen in his day, was that the continued and growing success of British trade unionism would not involve a commensurate increase in the intervention of legislative action in labour relations. On the contrary: the spectacular rise of the trade unions since the First World War ensured in many areas the defeat of the principle of State intervention. Dicey's antithesis of *laissez faire* and collectivism was too simple. He took too little account of the regulatory function of collective forces in society, and in a sense he ignored the rapidly developing pluralistic character of the British Constitution. This, I think, explains his failure to see that in labour relations and possibly elsewhere *laissez faire* may have two very different meanings. It may, of course, mean the free play of the laws of a market between individuals assumed to be equal, and the use of the law to prevent the interference of collective entities such as trade unions with the operation of supply and demand. But it may also mean allowing free play to the collective forces of society, and to limit the intervention of the law to those marginal areas in which the disparity of these forces, that is, in our case, the forces of organized labour and of organized management, is so great as to prevent the successful operation of what is so very characteristically called 'negotiating machinery'. It so happens that in this country (but not by any means in other capitalist countries as well) this principle of, if you like, 'collective *laissez faire*', came to be a preponderant characteristic of labour law in the course of the first half of our century. The British labour movement, and especially the trade union movement, has, to an extent certainly not contemplated by Dicey, been heir not only to a Socialist tradition, but decisively also to the Liberalism of the nineteenth century. Seen from the lawyer's point of view, its main characteristic today is its aversion to legislative intervention, its disinclination to rely on legal sanctions, its almost passionate belief in the autonomy of industrial forces. What is more, this principle of 'collective *laissez faire*' has come to dominate not only the attitude of the unions but also that of the employers and their associations and of the civil service, and, in our own time that of the courts. The increase in the influence of legislation on labour since 1914 bore no relation to that of the political influence of those collective forces which, far more than the law and the State, came to be the fundamental factors in organizing the labour-management relationship.

In the telescope of academic analysis one can discern and distinguish – again using Dicey's term – three 'currents of legislative opinion', the interaction of which accounts for much in the development of labour law in our century. First, there is this policy of 'collective *laissez faire*' I have mentioned, the retreat of the law from industrial relations and of industrial relations from the law. Secondly, there is the tendency to use legislation for the expansion of patterns of protection established in the nineteenth century and during the Edwardian period, and, especially, the increasing use made of legislation as a substitute for collective bargaining, as a stop-gap where dis-equilibrium of social forces makes its intervention inevitable. In so far, and in so far only, the tendency described by Dicey as 'collectivist' continues during our period. Thirdly, there is, to an extent perhaps not anticipated by Dicey, the continued and permanent influence of individualism:

the insistence on the contract of employment – however formal – as the legal basis of the labour management relation and in peacetime the firm rejection of anything that even remotely resembles compulsory labour. Indeed, we may say of our century that its conception of the need for protecting the individual is more enlightened and more differentiating than that of our grandfathers. Even among lawyers there is a belated recognition that, to paraphrase Lassalle, not only the Houses of Parliament and the Ministry of Labour, but also the General Council of the Trades Union Congress, the British Employers' Confederation, Imperial Chemical Industries, Ltd., the Prudential Assurance Company and the Transport and General Workers Union are a part of the British Constitution, and that it is necessary to protect the individual's freedom of action not only against the so-called 'State' but also against other social forces, whether of business or trade unionism, whose direct impact on the reality of law was not fully within Dicey's range of vision.

I should like to make three further observations on general tendencies in legal development which seem to me to be of special importance for my subject. The first is about what you might call the 'centri-petal' tendency of public opinion, or, to put it differently, the simple fact that a great number of things such as the existence and recognition of trade unions, and the principle of social insurance, which were still highly controversial fifty years ago, have, generally speaking, become parts of the accepted pattern of life. The reduction of the area of the 'disputed' and the constant enlargement of the area of the 'accepted' principles of social organization seem to me to be characteristic for the development of public opinion in this country.

The second general observation I was anxious to make also transcends my subject but is of particular significance for labour relations: it is the growth of 'pluralism': that is, of the participation in legislation, in administration, even in the judicial process, above all in policy making, of representatives of the interests concerned. The line between 'State' and 'society' has been blurred very deliberately, or to put it differently, the 'pressure' of the pressure groups has been so organized as to work inside the legislative, administrative, judicial and policy making processes. This is of special importance in considering the relation between collective bargaining and legislative action.

My third general observation is even more general, and it may sound very platitudinous to anybody who has had no opportunity of looking at the British scene from outside: It is the remarkable respect, not indeed for the lawyers, but for the law among the British people, and in particular among the working classes. The determination, even in a desperate situation, to remain within the law was cogently demonstrated at the time of the General Strike of 1926 when the verdict of a well-known lawyer (who was also a politician), in and out of Parliament, and that of a Chancery judge that the strike was illegal, appear to have had a considerable effect on public opinion, although not perhaps on the strikers themselves. How many countries are there in the world in which, in a national crisis of this kind, public opinion could be influenced by the utterances of a lawyer-politician and of a judge? Is it not perhaps partly the fact that people take the law so seriously which makes them anxious to keep it at arm's length and to shrink from calling for its intervention? Where the law is less respected, where in this regard public opinion is a little more cynical, the intervention of the law in human affairs in general and in industrial relations in particular is perhaps viewed with greater equanimity and therefore accepted more willingly.

9 Yehezkel Dror

Law and Social Change

Excerpt from Yehezkel Dror, 'Law and social change', *Tulane Law Review*, vol. 33 (1959), pp. 749–801.

There is nearly always a certain difference between actual social behavior and the behavior demanded by the legal norm; the existence of a certain 'tension' between actual behavior and legally desired behavior (and between legally required behavior and morally demanded behavior) belongs to the characteristics of law in all societies (Kelsen, 1945, 436–7) and does not by itself signify the existence of a lag between law and social change. A lag appears only when there is more than a certain tension, when the law does not in fact answer the needs arising from major social changes or when social behavior and the sense of obligation generally felt towards legal norms significantly differs from the behavior required by law. In other words, while a certain difference between actual behavior and legally required behavior can be found in all societies, the concept of lag applies to law and social change in dynamic situations, after either social change or changes in the law occur and no parallel changes and adjustment processes take place in law or society respectively.

Some illustrations will clarify the concept of lag relative to law and social change. After the invention of the automobile, the totally unsuitable laws developed for horse-drawn carriages were applied.[1] After the industrial revolution the various laws against conspiracy were applied to workers' organizations in a way which constituted a clear lag behind the new social situation, which included both new techniques and ways of economic organization and new public sentiments and ideologies. It took the law in England and other countries a long time to catch up with these social developments and provide answers to the problems raised

1. On the necessity of developing special law-making procedures to deal with this problem in France, see Sieghart (1950, pp. 267–8).

by them (Dicey, 1919).[2] A contemporary illustration concerns the development of atomic energy and of public international law; public international law lags behind modern developments in nuclear techniques and has not yet adjusted itself to the new situations created by them. When space flight becomes technically feasible, even more urgent and difficult problems of adjustment to technological and social change will be posed before law.

All these illustrations deal with lag of the law behind social change. Though the very high rate of social change in contemporary societies confronts the agencies in charge of changing the law with difficult problems, the relative ease of legislation and the new modes of changing the law provide rather simple ways of adjusting the law to social change. In some jurisdictions, especially the international society and to some extent countries with rigid constitutions and judicial review powers over the constitutionality of legislation, the use of legislation to adjust the law to social change is somewhat limited; in all countries difficulties are faced concerning the problem of the best way of effecting this adjustment. In general, the use of conscious legislation in modern societies makes the process of adjustment of the law to social change rather easy. At a time when legislative action was not accepted as readily and legislatures were composed of conservative elites generally opposed to social change and averse to corresponding changes in the law, the lag of the law behind social change was very formidable indeed, and the primary responsibility for changing the law was imposed on the courts (themselves often composed of judges opposed to social change). But today the general orientation of nearly all strata and elites is in favor of change, and popular elections in democratic countries, as well as support requirements in many a dictatorship, assure the necessary sensitivity of the legislative organs and their willingness in general to change the law and adjust it to social change. More and more the issue here becomes one of preserving legal security, which is endangered by the rapid changes in the law, rather than one of preventing lag of law behind social needs and developments.

More novel, both from the theoretical and the practical point

2. For a critique of Dicey's method and analysis see Stone (1950, p. 473).

of view, is the problem of the lag of society after changes in the law. How far, if at all, can changes in the law be used to bring about social change? The first question is whether it is feasible and possible to change society through changing the law. Classical Marxian theory would answer in the negative. Regarding law as a superstructure on technology and the economy, that theory admitted the possibility of a lag of law behind social change and fully conceived that it might take some time for changes in technology and economy to be reflected in the law; but it would be inconceivable, from a Marxian point of view, for law to bring about changes in the basic technology and economy of society. Today, Soviet jurists recognize the possibility of using law to bring about social change and influence its direction (Kechekyan, 1956, p. 42),[3] and in fact Soviet Russia uses law extensively to bring about and regulate social change.[4]

A different argument against the possibility and desirability of using law to bring about social change was made by the historical school of jurisprudence and its founder, Savigny. Savigny, applying to law parts of Hegel's philosophy, regarded law as an organic growth indigenous to every society (see Savigny, 1814). Therefore, he opposed legislation, and especially legislation adopting foreign institutions and laws.[5]

These arguments have been clearly overruled by the facts of reality. The growing use of law as a device of organized social action directed toward achieving social change seems to be one of the characteristics of modern society which is in need of intensive study. The relative novelty of the conscious, systematic and large-scale use of law as a device of social action and the apparent contradiction and real tension between the ideology of the rule of law – which regards law as the stable foundation of social order – and the instrumental orientation towards law associated with the utilization of law as a means of social action, may provide a partial explanation for the lack of attention paid to these crucial

3. Kechekyan, a professor at the Moscow Law Institute, recognizes the use of law as an instrument in directing social change.

4. See Hazard (1953) and Berman (1950), where the use of 'parental law' as an instrument for changing society through education by law is discussed.

5. It is interesting to note the influence of Savigny and his students on one of the founders of the social study of law, namely Eugen Ehrlich (1913).

evolutions in the role of law and law-making in modern society.

Closer analysis of the role of law *vis-à-vis* social change leads us to distinguish between the direct and the indirect aspects of the role of law.

Law plays an important indirect role in regard to social change by shaping various social institutions, which in turn have a direct impact on society. Thus, a law setting up a compulsory educational system has a very important indirect role in regard to social change, by enabling the operation of educational institutions which play a direct role in social change. On the other hand, law interacts in many cases directly with basic social institutions in a manner constituting a direct relationship between law and social change. Thus, a law designed to prohibit polygamy has a great direct influence on social change, having as its main purpose the bringing about of changes in important patterns of behavior. This distinction is not free from difficulties, caused mainly by the multiple character of most parts of law, which are both in a direct and in an indirect relationship with social changes. The distinction is not an absolute but a relative one: in some cases the emphasis is more on the direct and less on the indirect impact of social change, while in other cases the opposite is true.

The indirect influence of law on social change is closely interwoven with the functions of the various social institutions of which, as already mentioned, parts of law are an important element. Full examination of the indirect aspect of the role of law in relation to social change requires, therefore, analysis of social institutions outside the scope of this article. We will therefore limit ourselves to citing illustrations designed to clarify this aspect of the relation between law and social change.

To a considerable extent, law exerts an indirect influence on general social change by influencing the possibilities of change in the various social institutions. For example, the existence of a patent law protecting the rights of inventors encourages inventions and furthers change in the technological institutions, which in turn may bring about basic general social change.[6] The absence of freedom to associate and disseminate ideas can prevent, or at least delay, the spread of new social ideas, and thus exert a very

6. The importance of the role of patent law in this respect has been recognized also in the U.S.S.R. (Hazard, 1953, chapter 8).

important basic influence on the processes of social change in society (Rose, 1956, p. 59). The extent to which contact with other societies is limited or encouraged by law regulates one of the basic factors bringing about social change, and so on. Here, law as part of the various institutions (technology, political and social control, external relations) influences the chances of changes in these social institutions and through them the processes of social change in general.

A somewhat different indirect relationship between law and social change concerns the indirect use of law in directed social change. The legal basis of organized social action in all modern societies – associated as they are with the internal functional needs of large-scale bureaucratic societies (Heller, 1934, p. 216) – calls for the reliance on legal means as indirect aids for nearly all conscious attempts to bring about directed social change. Thus, if the state desires to set up a public body the functions of which include bringing about certain social changes, it is necessary to use law to set up the body and define its powers; here, law indirectly serves social change by setting up organs which directly try to further various social developments. The act setting up the Tennessee Valley Authority in the United States[7] and the acts dealing with new towns in England[8] illustrate this functioning of law as an indirect factor in social change.

A slightly different illustration of the indirect use of law in organized social action involving social change, is the creation of legal duties which in turn enable direct action to bring about social change. One of the most important instruments of directed social change relied upon in many countries is education. But in order for the educational network to operate effectively it is necessary to create a duty to study in them. Hence, as already mentioned, compulsory education laws indirectly serve the operation of the educational institutions, which in turn function as a direct factor in social change.

A very interesting additional way in which law indirectly serves social change is the role of law in preserving and assuring the operation of a free market economy, which is one of the more

7. 48 Stat. 58 (1933), 18 U.S.C. para. 831 (1952).

8. New Towns Act, 1946, 9 & 10 Geo. 6, c. 68; cf. Town and Country Planning Act, 1947, 10 & 11 Geo. 6, c. 51.

important mechanisms of social change in many countries, especially the United States.

Further ways in which changes in the law indirectly serve or reflect social change could be enumerated, but the important fact is the distinction between direct and indirect aspects of the relationships between law and social change. While there are many marginal cases and the difference is often one of degree, this distinction is of primary importance in obtaining a comprehensive and inclusive view of the relationships between law and social change.

Every collection of statutes and delegated legislation is full of illustrations of the direct use of law as a device for directed social change. This is true for all modern societies. But the more interesting and extreme examples of the use of changing the law as a device to bring about social change from which we can hope to study its processes and problems are provided by those cases where a revolutionary or intellectual minority obtains legislative power and uses it in its efforts to bring about extensive changes in social structure and culture. This was the case in Japan and Turkey, where whole parts of Western law were received with the intention thus to further the Westernization of these countries, and this was also the case in Soviet Russia. To some extent the efforts of various colonial powers, especially France, to introduce their law into various territories under their rule was also motivated by the desire to shape the social realities of those places.

Illustrations of the use of law to bring about substantial social change can also be found in modern Western countries. An interesting case illustrating an ambitious effort to shape social behavior through the use of law was the enactment of prohibition in the United States.[9] It was also one of the most conspicuous failures, showing that there are strict limits to the effective uses of law to bring about social change.

Consideration of the conditions for effective use of law as a device for directed social change and the limits of such use, is of the utmost practical and theoretical importance, as such a study provides a key to the development of a policy-study of legislation

9. For an interesting though outdated description of various efforts to control the consumption of alcohol through various legal devices see Catlin (1931).

and to an understanding of some of the basic social processes associated with law and social behavior.

This question can be approached in two principal ways. One possible method would require examination of the psychological and socio-psychological processes through which law operates, and definition of the conditions under which individuals and groups adjust their behavior to new laws and, conversely, definition of the conditions under which new laws do not significantly influence behavior. It is not certain whether the study of psychology and social psychology has developed far enough to permit the use of this method. The role of law within the motivational system of the individual and the psychological processes by which law commands obedience under certain conditions are not understood, and are not likely to be thus understood, until a great deal of progress is made in the study of more elementary socio-psychological phenomena, about which too little is known. Therefore this avenue to the investigation of the effectiveness of law is closed at present.

Fortunately, there is another way in which this question can be dealt with at least partially, i.e. through a comparative empiric investigation of the effects of attempts to use law to induce social change in various societies. While little research has been done in this direction, published material together with a case-study from Israel, permit suggestion of a preliminary hypothesis concerning some of the independent variables determining the effectiveness of the use of law to induce social change.

Recently published material on the impact of the reception of Western law on society in Turkey[10] clearly brings out two facts: the reception did have a significant influence on some aspects of social life, while certain other aspects were but little influenced by the new laws meant to regulate them. It seems that the aspects of social action of a mainly instrumental character, such as commercial activities, were significantly influenced by new law, while those aspects of social action involving expressive activities and basic beliefs and institutions, such as family life and marriage

10. *International Social Science Bulletin*, vol. 60 (1956), includes a series of articles on the reception of foreign law in Turkey, based on a symposium on this subject held by the International Committee of Comparative Law in 1955 at Istanbul.

habits, were very little changed despite explicit laws trying to shape them.

This conclusion from the Turkish experience is reinforced by the failure up to the present time to change family habits of certain immigrant groups in Israel through legal norms. While Israel itself has not received a foreign legal system (Akzin, 1956), the legal pattern of Israel constitutes a new legal environment for the immigrants who came from various oriental and Arab countries; moreover, some laws have been enacted especially in order to bring about social change among them and among the Arab population of Israel. The Marriage Age Law, 1950,[11] serves as an interesting illustration.

This act sets the minimum age of seventeen for marriage, admitting pregnancy as the only exception, and imposes a criminal sanction on anyone who marries a girl below the age of seventeen without a permit from the district court or who assists in the marriage ceremony. By fixing the minimum age at seventeen, the law tried to impose a rule of behaviour strictly opposed to the customs and habits of some of the sections of the Jewish population of Israel which came from Arab and oriental countries, where marriage was generally contracted at a lower age.[12] In relation to this part of the population, as well as in relation to parts of the Moslem and Druze population of Israel, the law constituted a determined effort to bring about social change through law.

In fact, while no systematic field-investigation has been conducted in this matter, it seems that this act has had only limited effect on social action. Those communities which formerly permitted marriage of females at an early age continue to do so.[13] The main impact of the law on social action was to create a situation where many marriages are contracted without formal registration, while the real purpose of the act is not being achieved. At present, the failure of the act to bring the desired social change is generally recognized, and it seems that the law will be amended so as to fix the minimum age of marriage at sixteen and grant

11. 4 *Laws of Israel* 158.

12. On Jewish marriage laws and customs in various countries and periods see Freeman (1945).

13. This information is based on conversations with officials of the Ministry of Religious Affairs and the Ministry of Social Welfare, who are responsible for some aspects of the execution of the law.

free discretion to the courts to permit marriage after the age of fifteen.

It seems that here the Israeli experience supports the conclusion that can be drawn from the Turkish experience and supports our hypothesis that changes in law have more impact on emotionally neutral and instrumental areas of activity than on expressive and evaluative areas of activity. Basic institutions rooted in traditions and values, such as the family, seem to be extremely resistant to changes imposed by law.

Further comparative study is urgently needed to throw more light on the subject and to enable re-examination and elaboration of this basic hypothesis. The difficulties encountered in all countries when trying to use law as an instrument to control economic activities, evidenced by the everpresent phenomenon of the black market in periods of shortage and rationing, requires additional study which may well modify our hypotheses in important respects. Additional comparative study of the experience of various countries, including, *inter alia*, the experiences of Japan, Communist China and some of the so-called underdeveloped countries, could provide important relevant material, thus furthering the study of the direct relationship between law and social change and allowing us to grasp more fully the possibilities and limitations of the use of law as a means to induce social change.[14]

14. For an important recent study posing some basic problems of the relationship between law and social change and dealing with them through a close analysis of historical material see Hurst (1956).

References
AKZIN, B. (1956), 'Codification in a new state: a case study of Israel' *Am. J. Comp. L.*, vol. 60, pp. 44–7.
BERMAN, H. J. (1950), *Justice in Russia*, Cambridge, Mass.
CATLIN, G. E. G. (1931), *Liquor Control*, Holt.
DICEY, A. V. (1919), *Lectures on the Relations between Law and Public Opinion in England during the Nineteenth Century*, 2nd edn, Macmillan.
EHRLICH, E. (1913), *Grundlegung der Soziologie des Rechts*, München.
FREEMAN, (1945), *Kidushin and Marriage Customs and Law*.
HAZARD, J. N. (1953), *Law and Social Change in the U.S.S.R.*, London.
HELLER, H. (1934), *Staatslehre*, Leiden.
HURST, J. W. (1956), *Law and the Conditions of Freedom* University of, Wisconsin Press.
KECHEKYAN, (1956), 'Social progress and law', in *Transactions of the Third World Congress of Sociology*, vol. 6.

KELSEN, H. (1945), *General Theory of the Law and the State*, Cambridge, Mass.

ROSE, A. M. (1956), 'The use of law to induce social change', in *Transactions of the Third World Congress of Sociology*, vol. 6.

SAVIGNY, F. K. V. (1814), *Von dem Beruf unserer Zeit zur Gesetzgebung und zur Rechtswissenschaft*, Heidelberg.

SIEGHART. (1950), *Government by Decree*.

STONE, H. (1950), *The Province and Function of Law*, Harvard University Press.

10 Jan Górecki

Divorce in Poland – A Socio-Legal Study

Jan Górecki, 'Divorce in Poland – a socio-legal study', *Acta Sociologica* vol. 10 (1966), pp. 68–80.

Some General Remarks

1. The present paper gives an account of some of the main ideas contained in a broader study on divorce (Górecki, 1965). The method applied in the study differs from that commonly in use in the legal sciences: it has been based on empirical investigations. My intention was not to analyse the meaning of the legal rules, but to find out how they work, that is, to bring to light whether, and how their purposes are being achieved. The explanation of these purposes and the empirical investigation of their fulfilment constitute the main contents of the study.

The legal rules which I examined as a working institution are the Polish divorce rules. I chose them for two reasons. *First*, only rules in frequent use may be the topic of this type of socio-legal study: the divorce rate is rather high in Poland, in 1962 the courts pronounced 18,068, in 1963 – 19,455 divorce decrees all over the country, which means respectively 6·0 and 6·3 divorces per 10,000 of the total population. *Secondly*, the effects of these rules are highly controversial, and therefore there was no danger that the bringing of these effects to light would be a discovery of commonplace facts.

The effects of the divorce rules seem to be controversial in all countries which recognize divorce. This is particularly true in the East European countries, among them Poland: all these countries accept the breakdown of marriage as an all-embracing ground for divorce. In Poland there are two main limitations to this rule. The first (irrelevant to this study) concerns children: the court cannot decree a divorce if it is contrary to their welfare. The second is the recrimination rule: the guilty spouse cannot, in principle, claim divorce, unless his (or her) innocent partner agrees to divorce.[1] With these two exceptions, the complete and permanent breakdown of marriage is sufficient and, simultaneously, the only ground for divorce. However, it is always the duty of the divorce court to act against divorce: to try to reconcile the parties, not only at a special conciliatory session at the beginning of each trial, but also later.

What is the intended purpose of these rules? Apparently the four main purposes are easily deduced from the very contents of these rules, when the latter are explained against their social and historic background, and, to a certain degree, from the published motives of the legislative bodies or their members, and decrees of the Supreme Court. The first purpose is to ensure liberal access to divorce: whenever a marriage is completely broken down, the spouses should be free to dissolve their union. The second purpose is the limitation of the first: the union must be dissolved only when the breakdown of the marriage is indeed complete and permanent. The third purpose is to bring about a reconciliation whenever possible. Finally, there are some moral, and, one may say, pedagogical purposes of the rule of recrimination. To investigate whether, and to what extent these four purposes are being realized, is the main aim of this study.

2. For research, it was necessary to collect a great deal of factual data throwing light on the whole course of divorce trial, on some antecedences and behind-the-scenes happenings of the trial, and on some aspects of the situation which emerge after divorce. For instance, to answer the question whether divorces are decreed only in cases of the complete and permanent breakdown of marriage, I had to learn how the court investigates the degree and durability of the breakdown: an observation of trials and interviewing of judges, barristers, and divorced persons appeared necessary. All these means, as well as interviewing a sample of reconciled persons, have been used to learn the practical value of reconciliation by the court. In all, the following investigations

1. The word 'recrimination' is used here in a meaning which differs from that in use in English legal language. In England and in the United States, where matrimonial offences of either spouse constitute the main grounds for divorce, and the general principle of breakdown of marriage is unknown, the doctrine of recrimination requires that the plaintiff in a divorce suit be innocent of the matrimonial offence justifying the petition.

were carried out. First, I observed a random sample of 153 trials attended, in principle, from the very beginning (except the conciliatory session) till decree. I also observed an additional sample of a further thirty-four trials. Secondly, a random sample of eighty-four conciliatory sessions was observed. Both these observations were preceded by a pilot study, and, the pilot study included, they continued from spring 1961 till summer 1963. They were carried on in the divorce court in Cracow which at that time served over two million inhabitants. To extend these observations in time and space I interviewed forty-one judges (who had been altogether charged by approximately 26,750 divorce cases), and sixty barristers (with 4280 cases); these were all the divorce judges, and small samples of barristers of Cracow, Warsaw, Lublin and Katowice. I was unable to arrange these interviews in all the forty-four divorce courts in Poland. I chose the courts mentioned because they to some extent differ from each other as regards type of population and legal training, that is those two factors which greatly influence the course of the divorce trial. If considerable divergencies existed in the practice of various Polish courts, they would probably come to light in the interviews from these four courts. On the contrary, if similarities appeared among these four courts, they would probably be characteristic of the majority, if not of all of the divorce courts in Poland. To learn some antecedents and behind-the-scenes elements of divorce trials, as well as some of the sequences, 152 divorced and reconciled persons were interviewed: this was a sample drawn mainly from the suits filed in the first 103 days of 1959 in Cracow. The interviewing of judges and barristers mentioned above was also used to extend, in time and in space, the data revealed by divorced and reconciled spouses. These data, and the data collected in the course of the observation of trials, were supplemented by information drawn from the court's records. There also appeared, mainly in order to be able to evaluate the recrimination rule, the necessity of some public opinion research. In this I was helped by the Public Opinion Research Centre in Warsaw which, in 1962, interviewed a sample of 2355 respondents, representative of the whole country. However, these last interviews were not sufficient. To complete them, I put some questions to a sample of 323 students of law at the University of

Cracow. Lastly, I used published as well as unpublished statistical data, collected by the Ministry of Justice and by the Central Statistical Office.

Breakdown of Marriage

1. The first of the four mentioned purposes of the legislator is: *always* let the spouses divorce if their marriage is completely and permanently broken (provided there are no other reasons, especially the child's welfare, to hinder divorce). Several considerations indicate the advisability of accepting this aim, among them the frustration and hardship which follow the necessity of remaining in an unhappy union, and the absuses – such as migratory divorce, resort to groundless annulment of marriages or production of bogus grounds for divorce – which appear under those legal systems that make divorce of broken marriages difficult. The introduction of the rule that the breakdown of marriage is a sufficient ground for divorce is, however, not enough to realize this aim. Its achievement is dependent upon two further conditions. First, free access to the divorce court must be secured. Secondly, the practice of the divorce court should be worked out in such a manner that, whenever any interested person wishes to take advantage of this access, the court will always decree divorce if the marriage is completely and permanently broken.

In contemporary Poland free access to the divorce court is limited by two factors. The first is the expense connected with a divorce trial; however, information drawn from the interviews with divorced persons, judges, barristers, and from the court's records seem to suggest that these expenses do not bar access to the divorce court to any great extent. The second factor is various social pressures, strongest in the country and mainly of a customary, religious, and, above all, economic nature: the rural family, being not only a consumptive, but also a productive economic unit, is joined by economic ties which make it difficult or even impossible to divorce in the case of maladjusted marriage. This seems to be the main reason for which the divorce rate among the farmers, who constitute approximately 50 per cent of the whole Polish population, is about eight times lower than in the urban areas. This situation is to be deplored: in the light of the social premises of Polish law it is shocking that reasons of economic dependency should compel spouses to live in a broken union. This pressure is, however, an effect of the socio-economic structure of the Polish country, and it can only decrease under the influence of a change in this structure, in particular as a result of urbanization and industrialization of the country. To decrease this pressure is therefore not in the power of those who codify the divorce rules, and, consequently, cannot be their reasonably intended legislative aim.

On the other hand, the legislator undoubtedly intends the court always to pronounce divorce, when divorce proceedings are under way and a complete and permanent breakdown of the marriage is apparent. This aim is not being fully realized. Some divorce suits lead to dismissals: dismissals constitute approximately 10 per cent of all the final decrees in divorce cases all over Poland. Some of these dismissals are, as far as I can see, groundless. The mistake may be caused by the fact that the court erroneously finds the complete and permanent failure of a given marriage to be insignificant or only temporary; it may be that in reality, contrary to the opinion of the court, the child's welfare is not a reason against divorce; that, contrary to the court's opinion, the plaintiff is not entirely guilty. It is clear that in all these cases the purpose of the legislator, which I am considering, is not achieved.

In order to find out the proportion of dismissals decreed apparently without ground, an analysis of trials observed and of the data drawn from interviews with barristers were carried out. It appeared that the figure for groundless dismissals, somewhat higher in the first instance, decreases owing to the corrective function of the appeal-court. One hundred and twenty-eight of the 153 trials observed resulted in final decrees pronouncing divorce, eleven of the trials in final dismissals. In two of the eleven dismissals there appeared some likelihood – but not certainty – of groundlessness: this makes 18 per cent of dismissals and 1 per cent of all the final decrees pronounced in my sample of trials. This figure suggests that the practice of the Cracow Court is in accordance, at least in 99 per cent, with the purpose of the legislation which I am considering. This conclusion was confirmed by information from Cracow barristers; similar information was given by barristers from the other three courts mentioned above. The small figure of groundless dismissals deserves approval, for the collected data suggest that groundlessly dismissed cases usually return to the court, and eventually, after a long period of time, result in divorce after a new trial. As a result of two divorce trials, an extension of the period of suspense and waiting, and, owing to the delay, a decreasing chance of a new arrangement of each spouse's own family affairs, the parties in question suffer considerable inconvenience.

2. The second of the legislator's four purposes is: let the spouses divorce *only* if the breakdown of their marriage is complete and permanent. To what extent is this purpose realized? This question is the subject of controversial hypotheses suggested by a number of legal writers. To answer the question, one has to divide all the divorce trials into contested and uncontested cases. By 'contested cases' I mean those where the parties contest divorce, guilt, or the custody of the child, that is the three important points which may be the topic of a struggle between them. In my sample of 128 trials attended in which divorce was decreed, there were fifty-eight contested and seventy uncontested cases.

In the majority of the contested cases the main factors contributing to the breakdown of marriage and the symptoms of breakdown came out in the courtroom. The symptoms and the factors known to the parties came out, because in contested cases the quarreling parties bring to light all the facts they hope will be of any assistance in achieving their end; they present all possible documents (such as letters, photographs, medical certificates, various court decisions), and frequently call many witnesses. However, in the majority of the contested cases, the strained and hostile atmosphere of the trial was an important effect and additional evidence of the degree of breakdown. It is true that in some contested cases it was impossible to find out what the real factors and symptoms were: the parties and their witnesses contradicted each other from beginning to end so consistently that their statements seemed to be either equally true or equally false; however, even in these cases, the court's attention at least was called to all the relevant facts, and, moreover, the atmosphere of the trial indicated the degree of marital failure. On the whole, in all of the fifty-eight contested cases of my sample, the complete and permanent breakdown of marriage was proved in court: in forty-five of them with probability amounting to certainty, in twelve of them with a very high, and in one with a considerable degree of probability; several examples of cases – omitted here – explain the meaning of these degrees.

There were, however, seventy uncontested cases in my sample. In this type of case the danger of collusion, and of divorce decreed without a breakdown of the marriage, grows. What is the real extent of this danger under the Polish system? It is clear that an uncontested case does not necessarily mean a collusive one. There seem to be several groups of uncontested cases. The first, where not only the breakdown of marriage exists, but, moreover, the parties, in spite of the uncontroversial character of the trial, reveal all the known factors and symptoms of marital failure. The second group, where the breakdown exists, but some of its factors and symptoms, or even all of them, are hidden from the court by the parties. And, lastly, the third type, where no real breakdown has occurred, but where the parties falsely claim that it has. There are various reasons for which this kind of collusion sometimes occurs: it may be simple recklessness or a temporary whim on the part of immature parties; it may be a means of procuring a better flat, a way of escaping the liability for the other spouse's debts or of obtaining an immigration visa to a foreign country. I have tried to find out the number of these cases.

Obviously, I could only find an approximate, not an exact figure. I used various means to this end. The first of them was an observation of the above mentioned seventy uncontested cases which eventually resulted in divorce. Here, too, various elements witnessed to the degree of the breakdown and its permanency. One of these elements was, however, rather unexpected. In a considerable number of the uncontested cases not only the breakdown, but also its main known factors and symptoms, or at least some of them, came out in court: the parties were open, they revealed a lot of data. Their behaviour, highly emotional – recorded by me in each case – warranted a high degree of sincerity. There appeared in these cases hatred, mutual fault-finding, a tendency to clear oneself of charges or to seek revenge by telling the court about the adversary's guilt, sometimes a tragic situation for which none could be blamed. It may seem strange that such an atmosphere occurred in uncontested cases where one might have expected everything to proceed in a quiet way, and where, from the point of view of procedural tactics, any struggle between the parties was unnecessary. However, it appeared that the tendency toward emotional release and the emotional pressure of prolonged frustration were stronger than reasonable tactical calculation. This is more easily understood when one takes into account that, in a good many of these cases, the agreement concerning divorce and guilt did not appear between the parties until the initial part of trial, usually the conciliatory session; and at this session the agreement was rather the outcome of the barrister's or judge's advice, or even pressure,[2] than a spontaneous issue. Of a total of fifty-six uncontested cases complete and permanent breakdown of marriage was proved in court: in twenty-nine cases with probability amounting to certainty, in eighteen with a very high, in nine with a considerable degree of probability. In the remaining fourteen uncontested cases the court decreed divorce in spite of the fact that the evidence of breakdown was not really cogent: the parties disclosed neither emotion nor many reliable facts.

The following table affords a comparison of these figures with those mentioned above, concerning contested cases.

2. The judge's advice or pressure appeared frequently in the course of observation of trials, and was reported by divorced persons, barristers, and by about a half of all the judges interviewed; it appeared, in particular, in seventeen from among eighty-four conciliatory sessions observed. The judges interviewed indicated several reasons which inclined them toward those activities, the legality of which may be considered dubious. They pointed out that an uncontested trial takes much less time which is not only in the interest of themselves, but also, very frequently, in the interests of the parties. Moreover, in an uncontested trial the chance of a more civilized attitude of the parties grows, as well as the chance of a proper arrangement of the situation to emerge after divorce, in particular of the future relationships between either spouse and the common children; the last point was emphasized mainly by those judges who were inclined rather to help the parties in a common finding of their new paths than to make arbitrary decisions.

Table 1

Type of Trial and Degree of Probability of Completeness and Permanency of Breakdown

Type of Trial	Probability amounting to certainty	Very high degree of probability	Considerable degree of probability	No clear probability	Totals
Contested	45 (78%)	12 (20%)	1 (2%)	0 (0%)	58 (100%)
Uncontested	29 (41%)	18 (26%)	9 (13%)	14 (20%)	70 (100%)

It appears from the table that the cases where divorce was decreed on the grounds of the highest probability of complete and permanent breakdown of marriage constituted 78 per cent of contested, and 41 per cent of uncontested trials. The cases where the degree of probability was only considerable amounted to 2 per cent of contested, as opposed to 13 per cent of uncontested ones. Moreover, there were no contested cases in which the probability of complete and permanent breakdowns did not appear, and, on the other hand, it did not appear in 20 per cent of the uncontested. These figures throw some light on the difference between cognizance of breakdown by the court in the two types of divorce trials. It is a significant difference: $x^2 = 24 \cdot 13$ (P $< 0 \cdot 05$, df = 3).

The figure I am looking for – the number of divorces without breakdown, seems to be contained in the fourteen cases in which no clear probability appeared. To obtain a more accurate figure one of the parties in each of these cases was interviewed. In six of them the interviewers did not succeed; there were refusals and other difficulties. Eight interviews were given. In six of them the complete and permanent breakdown of marriage became quite evident in the course of long, sincere talks with the persons interviewed. In the seventh case the answers of the person interviewed were ambiguous. In the eighth one the lack of real breakdown clearly appeared: the person interviewed had claimed divorce because of an unimportant quarrel, she had hoped to be reconciled at court, and deplored that divorce had been decreed. These data suggest that divorce without breakdown occurred in one case, and its possibility in further seven cases; in other words: the figure for divorces without breakdown was, in my sample, somewhere between one and eight, that is between 1 and 6 per cent, and it seems to be a safe guess that it was rather near the lower limit. This guess became even more probable from the answers of the interviewed barristers. Their experience, as I have said above, was based upon approximately 4280 divorce trials from various courts. I asked all of them to estimate the number of divorces without breakdown: the mean value was 2 per cent for the Cracow barristers, and 2 per cent for the barristers of the three other courts; the median – 0·7 per cent and 1·5 per cent respectively. All these data seem to throw at least some light on the extent to which the purpose of the legislator mentioned above, is being realized under Polish law.

Reconciliation

The tendency to save marriages which are maladjusted but do not totally exclude any hope of their effective treatment, is closely connected with the idea of limiting divorce to the cases of complete and permanent marital failure. The outcome of this tendency is a conciliatory session at the very beginning of each divorce trial, as well as further efforts to be undertaken by the court during the whole course of the trial, to reconcile the spouses, whenever possible. It is true that a divorce trial is not the best time to use therapy: it should be applied by the marriage counselling centres at an earlier stage of marital conflict. However, these centres are only just starting their activities in Poland. The lack of properly developed marriage counselling is a real dilemma: the data gathered in the course of these investigations in the courtroom as well as in interviews with divorced and reconciled persons show the need for competent and friendly advice; they also throw some light on the harmful effects which appear if this need is not met. For want of properly arranged marriage counselling, the divorce court becomes the only agency whose duty it is to attempt reconciliation.

The real value of the court's conciliatory proceedings has become a matter of sceptical conjecture: several legal writers simply deny its effectiveness. On the other hand, according to the statistical data drawn from the Ministry of Justice, discontinuations of proceedings caused by reconciliation oscillated, in the years 1959–63, from 3·4 to 3·9 per cent of all the finally concluded divorce trials in Poland; these figures seem to suggest a comparatively high degree of effectiveness of reconciliation by the court.

In order to collect data concerning its real value, different means have been used, in particular observation of conciliatory sessions and the further course of divorce trials, interviews with divorced and reconciled persons, judges and barristers. It appeared that the conciliatory session, the main instrument of the conciliatory proceedings, is far from being a perfect tool, and that some of its deficiencies diminished the chance of reconciliation in cases where this chance existed. Among these deficiencies the formal atmosphere of the session should be mentioned, as well as the number of participants; both spouses always take part in the session, a judge and a registrar, usually barristers, sometimes laymen as well. The judges, neither selected nor trained for the purpose of marriage counselling, are not really competent. Shortage of time is another deficiency: the conciliatory sessions observed lasted from four to twenty-five minutes, with the mean value of twelve, the median of eleven minutes. It is most difficult to diagnose the marital disharmony in such a short period of time; the more so since some of this time is used by the judge to collect the personal data of both parties and to arrange for the further course of the trial.

The effort at conciliation made during the conciliatory session varies: it ranges from lack of any serious effort to a great one. A difference in attitudes is the reason for this. Some of the judges represent a sceptical attitude: they do not believe it possible to have any real influence on the behaviour of the parties. This opinion is a result of their own experience: they become aware of a lack of success in their conciliatory activities, and they explain this state of matters by the strength of the marital conflict between those who start a divorce trial, by the briefness of the conciliatory session, the impossibility of making a proper diagnosis, and shortcomings in their own skill. The opposite of this attitude is the optimistic approach: the belief that the conciliatory session gives a real chance of reconciliation. It seems that this belief is usually a result of the personal traits of some, not many, judges who contact the parties easily, who have intuition, capacity for arguing, experience, and moreover are, to a greater degree than the others, inclined to help the spouses. The difference between the behaviour of the judges representing these two different attitudes was confirmed by the effects of their activities, as well as by information given by divorced and reconciled persons; the statistical significance of the difference made known by the divorced and reconciled persons interviewed was tested by the Chi-square test. It seems that this difference grows smaller in the further course of the divorce proceedings: some judges, sceptical at the beginning of the trial, later make genuine efforts at conciliation, because, after having gathered some evidence, they are more easily able to diagnose the conflict, and, consequently, to choose the proper conciliatory arguments.

I examined the effect of conciliatory proceedings on the material furnished by suits filed at the Cracow Court in the first 103 days of 1959; those which resulted in reconciliation were concluded early enough to investigate the outcome of reconciliation. Two hundred and eighty-eight suits were investigated. Among them there were sixteen withdrawals and suspensions of proceedings which, in the light of the court's records, could have been the effect of reconciliation. In thirteen of these sixteen cases I succeeded in getting interviews from one of the spouses or both of them. It appeared that three couples interviewed had, in fact, not been reconciled at all, five further couples had been reconciled, but not as a result of any influence on the part of the court, and five had been reconciled under the influence of the court. However, in only three of the last five did there appear an improvement of a permanent character: the respondents were living with their spouses at the time of the interview, and believed they would never come to the divorce court again. These data were, in some measure, extended by the information drawn from interviews with barristers. Within these limitations they seem to contribute to knowledge of the conciliatory activity of the divorce court. They suggest that this activity is far from being so effective as one might have expected from studying the statistical data of the Ministry of Justice; it is, however, much more effective than is believed by the legal writers mentioned above who simply deny that this activity is of any value at all.

111

Recrimination

The last result of these investigations concerns recrimination: a rule that is a consequence of a broader and long-established principle that a man should not be allowed to profit from his own wrong-doing. The main purpose of this rule is to adjust the law to the moral views of the community: as the Supreme Court of Poland has frequently pointed out, it would contradict the moral principles generally accepted by the community if the guilty spouse could claim divorce against his (or her) innocent adversary's will. Another purpose, which has been also pointed out by the Supreme Court, is to influence people's behaviour: recrimination should deter people from the committing of matrimonial offences. Similar reasons are put forward by those, in various countries, who advocate recrimination.

As I mentioned above, 2355 people from all over the country were interviewed by the Public Opinion Research Centre. They were asked to choose one of the following points: 'Should the law prevent the guilty spouse from claiming divorce without the adversary's consent?', or: 'Should the guilty spouse be allowed to claim divorce regardless of his (her) fault?' Fourteen hundred and eighty-nine persons interviewed answered the question, the rest did not know what to answer, or in general opposed divorce. Seven hundred and eighty-seven subjects were for, 702 against recrimination: these figures are almost equal with a slight majority in favour of followers of recrimination. The respondents could not be asked to give reasons for their opinion, because questions concerning motives appeared, in the pilot study, to be too difficult for the average respondent. I therefore interviewed the above mentioned additional sample of 323 evening students of law at the University of Cracow. One hundred and fifty of them were for, 141 against recrimination: a similar result, in spite of the fact that the student sample was not representative of the whole population of the country. All these students were asked to give reasons for their opinion. Those for recrimination mainly gave moral reasons, those against represented the liberal tendency to enable the dissolution of all broken marriages, and moreover, argued that it is difficult to speak of any unilateral guilt in divorce at all. Possibly the reasons of people interviewed by the Public Opinion

Research Centre were the same, but were not felt clearly enough by all of them. In the light of these data it seems that, despite the Supreme's Court's opinion, the idea of recrimination is far from being a generally accepted moral principle in Poland; which, of course, does not necessarily mean that it is not a good moral principle.

There was no way of testing the impact of recrimination on human behaviour. It was impossible to divide the population of Poland into two comparable groups and to subject one of them to a legal system containing the rule of recrimination, and the other one to an identical system but without that rule, in order to compare the impact of the difference on the divorce rate. The experience of Finland, where the setting aside of recrimination in 1948 neither resulted in any significant rise of divorce rate, nor in major displacements among the figures of petitions for divorce filed on the ground of breakdown of marriage and of petitions filed on the other grounds (Snaevärr, 1957, 1959) is, because of differences in the social and historic background between the two countries, only of limited value in this study. The means I could use was to ask people whether the rule of recrimination stops them, as well as those with whom they are in touch, from acting contrary to the duties of husband or wife. The question was too complicated to set the sample interviewed by the Public Opinion Research Centre. I therefore asked the evening student sample: eighty of them believed, 228 (i.e. 71 per cent) did not believe in the preventive impact of recrimination. I also asked all the judges and barristers interviewed whether, in the light of their experience, the rule of recrimination had any preventive influence. Their answer was, in 85 per cent, negative: they argued that those who are inclined to violate marital duties act spontaneously, and do not consider their procedural position in an eventual divorce trial. However, their opinion may have been biased: they were used to meeting people in the process of divorce, not people (if there were any) whose marriages had been prevented from breakdown owing to recrimination.

Nevertheless, even if it is agreed that the rule of recrimination is a good moral principle, and has some preventive influence, its practical value is diminished because of some of its unexpected effects. I mentioned above that, under Polish law, this rule is limited to those cases only in which the innocent defendant does not consent to divorce. But for this limitation, this rule would possibly be too hard: limited in this way it gives rise to disadvantageous effects. The first of them consists in the law supporting base motives: the innocent spouse frequently refuses to consent from motives of malice and revenge, and the refusal, in spite of these motives, is an effective bar to divorce. This clearly appeared in trials attended, sometimes also in interviews with divorcees, in judges' and barristers' opinions. Of the barristers interviewed, 58·1 per cent found the innocent defendant's malice and revengefulness the most frequent cause for refusing consent. Another unfavourable consequence is the way in which the defendant's consent is obtained: the guilty plaintiffs use threats and bribery. Threats were reported in several trials attended and in interviews of divorcees: there were threats of physical force, of reporting the defendant's criminal offence to the authorities, of discontinuing payment of alimony, etc. Of barristers interviewed, 24·1 per cent met with threats in their practice. Payments to obtain a defendant's consent were even more frequent: they were made known in interviews of divorcees eleven times and 72 per cent of barristers met with them in their practice. There were various forms of payments: higher alimony, leaving of the common flat, unequal division of the matrimonial property, the giving of a sum of money, which in barrister's reports, varied from 2000 to 200,000 zlotys.[3] The evaluation of these payments is a complex problem. The former Polish law empowered the court to impose upon the guilty spouse damages for wrong suffered by his counterpart in effect of marital failure and divorce. This rule was set aside in 1950: an outcome of a more general tendency of socialist law to limit the damages for anguish. The data drawn from the courtroom and from interviews with divorcees brought to light how injurious its setting aside had been, and how strongly the damaged, in particular older women, deserted after many years of common life, felt their being set aside as an injustice on the part of the law; it is not surprising that for some of them payment for consent to divorce simply plays the role of damages. Moreover, it appeared in the course of my investigations that there are

3. The average monthly remuneration of working people in Poland being about 2000 zlotys.

judges who themselves at times, in the event of an exceedingly great wrong done to the innocent defendant, initiate payments for consent to divorce: an unexpected effect of the discrepancy between the law and the broadly accepted feeling of justice. However, it should be noted that not all the payments for consent play the role of a substitute of damages: the consent is frequently sold by defendants and a business is made of recrimination.

Threats by the plaintiffs and payments extend the figure of consents given, and consequently, limit the effectiveness of recrimination. Nevertheless, in spite of this limitation, the rule of recrimination seems to be the most frequent cause of dismissals, and dismissals, as I said above, constitute approximately 10 per cent of decrees of all the divorce courts in Poland.

Conclusion

The data presented and the considerations here put forward are of a monographic character: they are based mainly on an examination of a part of the practice of the Cracow Court and of some fragments of the practice of the other three divorce courts. They therefore justify qualitative rather than quantitative generalizations. Only with this provision may they be regarded, by a comparative lawyer or sociologist, as a report on the law in action in a country which has accepted the breakdown of marriage as an all embracing ground for divorce. It is, however, possible that the present divorce investigations will be continued in Poland. If this is the case, and if the samples drawn are broader, a transition to quantitative generalizations will become possible. It would not only mean an achievement of a higher level of knowledge, but it might also make a better contribution to the comparative science of living law, and moreover, supply, in the long run, a firmer basis for future legislations.

References
GÓRECKI, J. (1965), *Rozwód-Studium Socjologiczno-Prawne* (Divorce – A Socio-Legal Study), Panstoew Wydawnictwo Naukowe (Polish Scientific Publishers), Warszawa.
SNAEVÄRR, A. (1957, 1959), 'Verhandlungen des 21 nordischen Juristentages', *Helsingfors*, supp. 1, p. 32.

11 Vilhelm Aubert

Some Social Functions of Legislation

Abridged from Vilhelm Aubert, 'Some social functions of legislation', *Acta Sociologica*, vol. 10 (1966), pp. 99–110.

The purpose of the Norwegian Housemaid Law of 1948 is to protect the interests of domestic help. Work is limited to ten hours a day, including time for meals. Overtime is clearly defined, and a minimum pay for overtime service is stipulated. Overtime beyond a certain number of hours per week is prohibited. The housemaid can request a written contract and payment every other week. She is entitled to one free afternoon a week and every other Sunday free. Notice terminating employment must be given two weeks in advance. Wage levels remain unregulated, and the right to vacation follows from the general Law on Vacations. There are some other clauses in the Law on Housemaids which need not concern us here. The law limits the freedom to agree contractually to set the law aside.

The first aim of the empirical study of the impact of the Law on Housemaids,[1] was simply to establish the extent to which behaviour conformed to the rules laid down in the Law. A probability sample of 218 housewives and 221 housemaids in Oslo, drawn in pairs, were interviewed on their conduct, information, attitudes and motives in so far as these had a bearing upon the content of the Law on Housemaids. The results with respect to behaviour are easily summarized: Not more than one tenth of the sampled relationships showed complete conformity to the rules of the law. Many deviations are of minor importance, however. But the main requirement of the law, the ten-hour working day, was set aside in approximately half of the 233 households. In a consid-

1. The study which forms the basis of this article has been carried out in co-operation with Torstein Eckhoff, Knut Sveri and Per Norseng. Cf., the joint publication, *En lov i søkelyset* (A Law in the Searchlight), Oslo, 1952. The follow-up study was conducted by Eckhoff and Sveri and is published in *Instilling til lov om arbeidsvilkår for Hushjelp m. fl.*, 1960.

erable number of cases the violation was of great magnitude. Most other rules of the law were likewise frequently violated, although considerable variations occur between the different clauses.

Deviations tend to cluster in a certain number of households. Occurrence of one type of violation increases the likelihood of other offences as well. The more frequent the infringements of the law, and the greater the magnitude of these, the lower the pay; although in some households strenuous and illegal working conditions are compensated by high wages. In a large number of cases it is clear that the working conditions belong to precisely that category which the legislators aimed to abolish, and which some believed to have disappeared long ago.

Sumner claimed in his pioneer study of social norms that legislation had little or no independent influence upon behaviour. But he did not deny that laws were abided by. If they were, it was because they corresponded to, possibly originated in, and were at least supported by the already existing norms. Sumner ascribed little reformatory influence to laws, however. 'Vain attempts have been made to control the new order by legislation. The only result is the proof that legislation cannot make mores' (Sumner, 1906, p. 77). At first glance this seems to be a very adequate summary of the above data, irrespective of the general validity of Sumner's theory. Extensive deviance from the rules of a law is, however, no proof that the law has been without influence. Neither is conformity to rules certain evidence that it has been effective.

In order to understand the influence of a law it is necessary to study the variables which intervene between the promulgation of the law and the behaviour of the public. One of the most important of these is the level of information among the recipients of the legal communication. Thus, various measures of the level of information among housewives and housemaids were collected in the survey. Some of these refer to the amount of acquaintance with the law itself, while others refer to perceptions of norms, irrespective of their source.

A question which directed the attention of the respondents to possible recent changes in the working conditions of housemaids, and asked for the causes of such change, gave the result that only three housewives and three housemaids mentioned the law. But as soon as the Housemaid Law was mentioned by the interviewer, 80 per cent of the housemaids and 81 per cent of the housewives claimed to have at least heard about the law. Although less than one fifth of the respondents were completely unfamiliar with the law, 36 per cent of the housemaids and 26 per cent of the housewives were unable to mention a single clause in the law. Most of the others mentioned only one area regulated by the law. The ten-hour working day seems to have been the most publicized and most widely known part of the new law.

Table 1 shows how perceptions of norms are distributed among the areas regulated by the Housemaid Law. In these measures of the level of information, no attention has been paid to the sources of information, that is to say, whether it is derived from the law itself, from customs or from personal attitudes and experiences.

There are wide variations in the degree to which the norms of the law have become common knowledge. The norms fall into two relatively distinct classes. A fair amount of information exists with respect to the norms regulating termination of hire, days off and vacations. But the norms on the length of working hours, and especially on overtime and periods of wage payment, seem to be 'law in books' rather than 'law in action'. The gap between the two sets of rules must be interpreted in the light of Sumner's hypothesis. The rules which are fairly well known, happen to be those where the law (on Housemaids or on Vacations) corresponds to existing customs. The other, less known rules, are those where the Law on Housemaids has a reformatory function and lacks sanction in custom.

Table 1

The Percentage of Housemaids and Housewives who Possess Some Knowledge about the Different Clauses of the Law

Clause	Housemaids	Housewives
Termination of hire	83	76
Days off	76	73
Vacation	76	70
Length of working hours	34	33
Periods of wage payment	23	21
Pay for overtime work	16	25
Extension of overtime work	7	8

How can we further test the hypothesis that perceptions of norms derive more from customs than from laws? Obviously by correlating perception of norms and acquaintance with the law. Table 2 shows that correct perception of norms is closely dependent upon the respondent's degree of contact with the law. Those who have read the law are more frequently aware of the norms in question than those who have only heard about the law, while those who have not even heard about it, are even less aware of the legal norms.

These relationships between contact with the law and perception of norms, are not equally strong with respect to all rules. Most of those who have not even heard of the Housemaid Law, perceive quite correctly the norms regulating termination of hire, days off and vacations. These are precisely the norms which have a strong foundation in custom. However, with regard to the norms on hours of work, overtime and periodic payment of wages, the amount of contact with the law makes a very great difference. Some contact with the text of the law seems almost to be a prerequisite of correct perception of norms. This can be explained by the assumption that the clauses attempt to reform the state of affairs and lack support in old customs.

Table 2 goes contrary to Sumner's hypothesis, however, in another respect. Although the respondents were relatively unaware of the norms of the new law in so far as it had a reformative function, the few who did know the norms were people who had some contact with the law. The evidence is not conclusive, however, that the law is the source of their perception of the norms. The relationship may to some extent be explained by common dependence upon a third factor. It may be that those who have read the law, or have at least heard about it, belong to groups which for reasons unrelated to the law, practise norms similar to those stipulated by the Housemaid Law.

Of the several factors which seem to influence conduct as well as acquaintance with norms and the law, age is the most important. With respect to actual behaviour the difference between the age groups is significant among housemaids, but insignificant among housewives. The tendency is consistently in favour of the younger housemaids, with the exception of the very youngest who may not yet have realized their scarcity value, and who are used

Table 2
The Percentage of Housemaids and Housewives who Possess
Some Knowledge about the Contents of the Rules, Distributed
According to Whether they have Read the Law, Heard about
the Law, or not even Heard about it

| Clause | Housewives | | | Housemaids | | |
	Read law	Heard about law	Not heard about law	Read law	Heard about law	Not heard about law
Termination of hire	82	86	76	83	82	57
Days off	87	79	61	91	74	54
Vacation	80	85	70	88	74	46
Length of working hours	67	35	5	56	31	14
Periods of wage payment	36	25	12	46	17	8
Pay for overtime work	26	17	5	39	23	11
Extension of overtime work	28	3	0	26	4	0

to the diffuse and unprofessional work situation in a rural household. The housewives become more prone to violate the law as
they move up on the age scale; but the change is very moderate.

A strong and consistent relationship exists, however, between
the age of the housewife and her level of legal information. Young
housewives are better informed on legal norms than are the older
ones, and the decline in knowledge with age is gradual. Among
the housemaids too, a pattern is discernible, which links level of
legal information to age. The very young, below twenty, are
relatively ignorant compared to those between twenty and thirty
who again know more than the older ones. The differences are,
however, smaller and less significant than in the case of the housewives.

The housewives are usually better informed than the housemaids. It is not surprising that women of the urban middle or
upper middle classes should have easier access to legal material
than housemaids with little formal education and most often with
little training in handling problems of this kind. Only 2 per cent of
them were organized in the Housemaid's Union, which is generally known to enjoy very limited support. Thus, the housemaids

have been without that source of support and information which workers can count on in most other areas of labour legislation.

The evidence is ambiguous with respect to the crucial question: has the law influenced behaviour to any appreciable degree? We have seen that custom may have been a more important factor in determining conduct and perceived norms than the law itself. But we have also seen that contact with the law relates significantly to perceived norms. Both these factors are closely related to age, as is also behaviour, although less clearly so. The influence of age is, in part, influenced by differences between the generations in their evaluation of proper working conditions, derived from general economic and social trends. How, then, do actual working conditions correlate with the level of information among housewives and housemaids respectively?

There exists a nearly significant relationship among housewives between information and the index of violations, in the expected direction. Among the housemaids, however, there is rather more than less information in the high-violation households than in the low-violation ones, but the relationship is inconsistent and lacks statistical significance. The analysis of relationships between specific violations and corresponding information yields inconclusive results. It seems that information on the part of the housemaids has little or no bearing upon their actual working conditions. In general they enjoy the most favourable working conditions and are also best informed, if they belong to the twenty–thirty age group. But this must depend upon a third and independent factor. At that age the housemaid is in her prime as domestic help, she has some experience and some notion of her scarcity value. More often than not she will be employed by a relatively young housewife, familiar with the law or at least accustomed to modern views on labour relationships. Given this constellation of housewife and housemaid, one may find the optimum arrangements from the point of view of the law.

It has to be concluded that the law was, at least for some years, ineffective in the sense that actual conditions of work remained at variance with the norms laid down, and also in the sense that even conformity to the legal norms was rarely due to influence from the law. Why was it not effective, and why did the Parliament tend to overestimate the effects of the law as well as the current status of the housemaids when the law was issued?

Some specific circumstances concerning this statute might be expected to obstruct compliance without therefore necessarily throwing doubt upon the influence of other statutes. The law addresses groups which traditionally have had little connexion with laws and with public authorities. The recipients of the legal message consist of women who are not organized, and thus lack an intermediary link with the government. The law concerns an area traditionally protected against public inspection and control, the home. The place of work is isolated and the nature of the work relationship is intrinsically difficult to regulate. It is an area on the border-line between 'work' and 'private life', where it is sometimes hard to distinguish between the worker and the (slightly inferior) member of the family (cf. Aubert, 1961). Paternalistic, or maternalistic, relations are traditionally very strong, and are supported by the pronounced age differential between employer and employee (the average age of housewives was fifty-one, of housemaids thirty-six). Many housemaids are very young, inexperienced and unfamiliar with urban living conditions. They look upon their job as temporary. The turn-over is very high, continuously sapping the occupation of its most experienced members, those who might otherwise have fought to improve upon their common lot.

We shall leave these impediments aside, however, and concentrate on two other factors which may have counteracted an effective, or effectively enforced, Law on Housemaids. These two factors are of more general relevance, and they seem linked to latent functions which this law shares with other legislation. The first factor has to do with the language employed in the law, and the second has to do with the relationship between substantive and procedural clauses in the law.

Most of the respondents had no intimate acquaintance with the new piece of legislation, and even among those who had, compliance with the requirements of the law was far from complete. Both phenomena might in part be due to the technical aspects of the statute as a means of communication and to its terminology. In order to test the degree of comprehensibility of the language employed in the Housemaid Law, an experiment in legal interpretation was conducted in the course of the interview with the housewives and housemaids. A fairly large number of respondents gave contradictory or don't know answers, while the meaningful answers were rather evenly distributed among correct and false alternatives, although with a preponderance of correct answers. The conclusion is inescapable, however, that the law is far from being a reliable source of guidance for this particular type of audience. Pure guess-work or the tossing of a coin would not have yielded results drastically different from those found in the experiment.

Although it may be claimed that some of the relationships regulated by the Law on Housemaids are intrinsically complex and difficult to disentangle, there can be little doubt that the legislators did not achieve a maximum of clarity and simplicity in the text under scrutiny. Why not? Is the incomprehensibility of the Housemaid Law simply to be written off as a more or less unsystematic result of a legislative mistake, lack of care, ability and foresight? I do not believe so. The Housemaid Law has, above all, become hard to grasp for an audience of housewives and housemaids, because it is written in a language shaped by an entirely different function. It is written in the same kind of language as most statutes, a language which has been sharpened and made precise as a means of communication within the legal profession. It has developed as a means to the goal of resolving legal conflicts through the intervention of lawyers and judges.

It was not fully taken into consideration that this might be an area where lawyers are unlikely to become much involved and where the courts would rarely, if ever, be asked to settle disputes. At the time of the study no legal suit originating in the law on housemaids had been brought to the attention of the courts or of other legal authorities. Thus, the function of this law is almost wholly a question of its influence upon a lay audience, and of its ability to communicate a message to housewives and housemaids without legally trained intermediaries. In this respect it had, to a large extent, failed without achieving the subsidiary aim of easing conflict resolution before the courts or in negotiations between legal representatives of contending parties.

There are several reasons why conflict resolution by means of a court procedure is absent in this area. No official machinery, comparable to the Labour Inspectorate in industrial relations, exists to supervise the working conditions in households and instigate criminal procedure if violations are found. The initiative is left to the housemaid. For the same reasons that housemaids are unlikely to organize and become acquainted with a new law, they are also disinclined to litigate. Their best means of sanction, if they are at all aware of being exploited, is to leave their job at short notice and seek new employment, which will not be hard to find. Thus, a legal solution must have appeared to the thoughtful housemaid to be a costly, cumbersome, unpleasant and ineffective way of achieving good working conditions, when realistically compared to available alternatives.

Although conflict-resolution in legal form should foreseeably have presented itself as a remote possibility to the legislators, the Housemaid Law set out to influence working conditions in the home through an instrument developed in areas where conflict resolution is frequent and legal intervention the order of the day.

Because they are shaped by the traditional function of facilitating precise communication within the legal profession, many clauses of the Housemaid Law are unable to fulfill the more pressing function of communicating to housewives and housemaids. A social mechanism which has achieved its form when fulfilling one function, remains unaltered when faced with an entirely different function, and fails correspondingly.

The inaccessibility of the terminology is an impediment to the effective functioning of the law. So is the weak development of an enforcement machinery and the vagueness of the sanctions which can be invoked against violations.

The penal clause in the Housemaid Law is rather unique in making *repeated* violation, *in spite of protest* from the victim, a condition for sanctions. But in this area it is quite clear that a housemaid who is dissatisfied with her working conditions, and aware of this deviance from the law, will leave her job and seek more satisfactory employment. She will not vainly protest and then instigate cumbersome legal procedures, which would in the end make a continued work relationship intolerable anyway. It is hard to believe that the legislators can have been completely unaware of this state of affairs. Nor can they have overlooked that without a public agency charged with supervision, such a penal clause must become ineffective. Why did they, nevertheless, formulate such a hybrid system of enforcement and sanction?

The answer must be sought in the analysis of a function of legislation which is unrelated to the process of communicating norms and achieving compliance. This function relates to the need for compromise in the legislative assembly, turning legislative form into a means for resolving or ameliorating group-conflicts. In many cases this corresponds closely to a function which Thurman Arnold formulated thus: 'It is part of the function of Law to give recognition to ideals representing the exact opposite of established conduct. Most of its complications arise from the necessity of pretending to do one thing, while actually doing another' (Arnold, 1935, p. 34). What is pretended in the penal clause of the Housemaid Law is that effective enforcement of the law is envisaged. And what the legislature is actually doing is to see to it that the privacy of the home and the interests of housewives are not ignored.

The ambivalence and the conflicting views of the legislators, as they can be gleaned from the penal clause, appear more clearly in the legislative debate. A curious dualism runs through the debates. It was claimed, on the one hand, that the law is essentially a codification of custom and established practice, rendering effective enforcement inessential. On the other hand, there was a tendency to claim that the Housemaid Law is an important new piece of labour legislation with a clearly reformatory purpose, attempting to change an unacceptable *status quo*.

One and the same speaker in Parliament might use both kinds of argument on occasion. But there was also a tendency for the Conservatives to lean towards the claim that the Housemaid Law is nothing but a codification of established practice, while the Left would more frequently claim a reformatory function for the Law. Each type of argument may convince a different type of clientèle. The crucial point here is the remarkable ease with which such apparently contradictory claims were suffused in one and the same legislative action, which in the end received unanimous support from all political groups. It is also remarkable how references to facts or probable facts could go contrary to available evidence. It suggests that the legislator on occasion moves within a social reality very narrowly circumscribed by his political duties to party ideology and electorate, not to scientific truth.

References

ARNOLD, T. W. (1935), *The Symbols of Government*, New Haven.

AUBERT, V. (1961), 'The housemaid: an occupational role in crisis', in S. M. Lipset and N. J. Smelser (eds.), *Sociology, The Progress of a Decade*, Englewood Cliffs, pp. 414–20.

SUMNER, W. G. (1906), *Folkways*, Boston.

12 Michael Banton

Law Enforcement and Social Control

Excerpts from Michael Banton, *The Policeman in the Community*, Tavistock Publications, 1964, pp. 1–8, 166–81.

A cardinal principle for the understanding of police organization and activity is that the police are only one among many agencies of social control.

Though the police are concerned to a very important extent with law enforcement it is not a product of, nor is it to be attributed to the police. Indeed the police are relatively unimportant in the enforcement of law.

Consider, for example, some of the variations in criminality. In the average United States city of 500,000 people there were, in 1962, thirty-six cases of murder and non-negligent manslaughter, and sixty of forcible rape; where in Edinburgh in the same year there were two of murder, two of culpable homicide, and eight of rape. The Edinburgh figures are lower not because the police are more efficient, but because the community is more orderly. Social control – as Homans demonstrated so well in *The Human Group* (1950) – is a property of states of social relations, not something imposed from outside. The level of control, be it high or low, is determined by the kinds of social relationship that exist among the individuals who make up the society, and their effectiveness in getting people to follow prescribed patterns of behaviour. The number of people who obey the law and follow such patterns without ever a thought for police efficiency is striking testimony to the power of social norms and humanity's methods of training children to observe them: most people grow up so well conditioned that they cannot feel happy if they infringe the more important norms. Thus control is maintained by the rewards and punishments which are built into every relationship, and which are evident in the conferring and withholding of esteem, the sanctions of gossip, and the institutional, economic, and moral pressures that underlie behavioural patterns. Law and law-enforcement agencies, important though they are, appear puny compared with the extensiveness and intricacy of these other modes of regulating behaviour.

The communities with the highest level of social control are small, homogeneous, and stable – like small tribal societies in out-of-the-way regions, or the more remote villages in industrial nations. In such communities social order is maintained to a very large extent by informal controls of public opinion, and there is little resort to formal controls such as legislation or the full-time appointment of people to law-enforcement duties. Most tribal societies have no police forces, prisons, or mental hospitals: they are small enough to be able to look after their own deviants. The small society with a simple technology can afford to have its 'village idiot'; the large and complex one cannot, for many people would not recognize him and he might easily injure himself or create havoc in the affairs of others. Village societies are usually tightly knit communities because everyone is so dependent upon everyone else. If there is only one shop, everyone has to go there at some time or other, and the shopkeeper has to keep on reasonably friendly terms with all the local inhabitants. If there are two grocers, people may feel obliged to patronize the one who attends the same church as they do. Residents cannot disregard the opinion of their neighbours because there may come a situation in which they will need their co-operation. In these circumstances the job of the policeman is to oil the machinery of society, not to provide the motive power of law enforcement.

The orderliness of the small homogeneous society is not simply a matter of economics and social organization; as in any other kind of society it has moral qualities. In the village society, the rich are under greater obligation than their city counterparts to recognize responsibilities to the unfortunate; village people are involved in one another's affairs at work and in leisure whereas, in urban districts, social contacts and the sense of mutual commitment are more restricted. In homogeneous societies girls and boys grow up attuned to the social order, accepting their place in it and believing the distribution of rewards to be reasonably just. People who live together like this are agreed in what they consider right and wrong, so it can be said that the highly integrated society is characterized by a high level of consensus, or agreement on fundamental values. These moral judgements pervade social life and do not stop short when business relations are in question. The policeman obtains public co-operation, and enjoys public esteem, because he enforces standards accepted by the community. This gives his role considerable moral authority and sets him apart from the crowd socially, much as does the role of minister of religion.

Life in a small highly integrated society has many attractions, but most people find the rewards of economic progress even more attractive, and the two sets of values do not go well together. In the traditional kind of society the various social institutions are so interrelated that an alteration in one affects all the others and it is difficult to introduce changes. In an economically developing society, however, people and resources have to be moved around. Individuals have to pursue their private benefit and to fight the community controls that put a brake on change. Some people receive great rewards, greater than their moral deserts; others, who are scarcely less worthy, are much less fortunate. In a developing economy rewards are distributed according to economic criteria: the successful businessman is honoured because he has been successful – money comes itself to have a moral value. At many points economic values clash with community values and frequently break them. For instance, a man may have had an exemplary career for the first forty-five or fifty years of his life and hold an honoured if not particularly distinguished position in the community; then suddenly technological discoveries affect the industry in which he works. His skills become obsolete, the plant is reorganized, and he has to begin again. He may have to take a lower-paid job or to work under people who were previously his juniors, and this inevitably undermines his position in the community. In numerous sectors of industrial society, people appear to take many of their criteria for community ranking from the economic order and the occupational hierarchy. In one way and another industry is continually imposing on the community its own criteria of economic rewards.

Another example which makes the same point in a different way can be drawn from the effect of the introduction of the automobile upon the social structure of the Southern States of America. These were communities in which Negroes were expected to defer to Whites and to allow them precedence. When Negroes acquired automobiles the question arose whether precedence should be determined by the rule-of-the-road or by local custom. For a time the answer depended on the speed of the vehicle: below 25 m.p.h. the white driver, especially if it was a woman, expected the Negro driver to give way; above that speed no one took risks (Myrdal, 1944, p. 1368). Nowadays there is hardly any of this. Driving rules cannot be based upon particularistic criteria of skin colour: they must be the same for every driver, otherwise the confusion would be interminable. Thus new technical developments impose their own logic and upset community values of deference to older persons, to women, and, in some situations, to persons of superior social class or race.

No social changes are without their costs, and one of the principal costs of making the social structure more flexible is the decline in social integration. An index of this is the crime rate. In 1962 the number of crimes known to the police in England and Wales rose by 11 per cent over the previous year, and in Scotland by 8 per cent. Between 1938 and 1960 the incidence of larceny, breaking and entering, receiving, fraud and false pretences, sexual offences, violence against the person, and a small residue of other offences increased by 225 per cent. In the United States the crime rate for 1962 was 5 per cent above that for the previous year and 19 per cent above that for 1958, after adjustment for population growth.

As the problem of maintaining order becomes more severe, societies increasingly adopt formal controls, summarized by an anthropologist as 'courts, codes, constables, and central authority'. In the early days the parish constable was simply a citizen on duty. All able-bodied men were expected to give their services in turn, being elected for a year and serving without payment. By the eighteenth century this system had broken down completely in London and, after serious disorders, a permanent constabulary was created in 1829. But the authority that the new police exercised was still that of the citizen constable. Under English law every citizen is still technically bound to arrest anyone who commits a felony in his presence; this is his civic duty and he can be punished if he fails to perform it, though admittedly there is no record of anyone's being prosecuted for such a failure in recent times. Under both English and Scottish law a citizen must go to the assistance of a constable if called upon to do so. The policeman does have certain common law powers as acknowledged by judicial authorities, and he has since been given others by express direction of Acts of Parliament, but the core of his authority stems from his responsibilities as a citizen and the representative of citizens. Judicial decisions of both English and Scottish courts make it clear that the constable is not the employee of the local authority: he exercises his powers and discharges his duties as the independent holder of a public office. If he wrongly arrests and detains someone, then he is personally liable for his actions should the aggrieved party open civil proceedings against him. Nor would it be completely correct to regard the constable as a servant of the Crown: he does not have the immunities of the Crown servant and he cannot shelter behind the orders of a superior – as, for example, a soldier sometimes can. In this sense the constable is a professional citizen: he is paid to discharge obligations which fall upon all citizens, and his obligations are to the community as a whole.

In contrasting village society with the big industrial nation it is difficult not to convey a false impression. Even in the small-scale stable society consensus is never perfect; it is only relatively high. An even greater mistake would be to imply that consensus is absent under urban conditions. Certainly in some urban situations the moral controls are weak and the formal organization has to impose strict penalties, but there are many basic issues – such as ideas of duty to kinsfolk, work-mates, and neighbours –where popular morality remains powerful. In many urban residential neighbourhoods there is a very real sense of community even if informal social controls are less extensive than in the village. Policemen, being subconsciously aware of their dependence upon these other mechanisms of control, prefer to work as peace officers and to see their role in these terms. There is in Britain a current of opposition to specialization in police work and to the employment of civilian auxiliaries, which cannot easily be explained but which seems to rest upon this ideal of the policeman as a peace officer.

These same considerations apply to a considerable extent in

the United States as well, for the Americans inherited the British conception of the civilian constable. In the United States, as in Britain, the police officer is legally responsible for his actions and an aggrieved party may take out a civil suit against him. American police standards have in many places been depressed by local political control – in some municipalities the chief of police is still an elected official – but these arguments about changes in the policeman's role are nevertheless quite relevant to the American experience. The same contrast obtains between rural and urban areas in respect of social control, but, as might be expected with the volume of relatively recent immigration and the continuing internal population movement, social integration is lower than it would be in British communities of comparable size.

The Policeman in the Community

When the police officer's role is viewed, not from the standpoint of public order, but simply as an occupation, another major characteristic appears which is common to Britain and the United States, and indeed, perhaps to all the industrial democracies. The policeman is a member of the society whose laws and norms he is required to enforce. This simple proposition is in fact fundamental, for on the one hand his membership of the society has an important effect upon the way he performs his job and, on the other hand, his having to police his own community has a profound effect upon his off-duty role as a member of that community. Moreover, there is a basic inconsistency in his role in that he is called upon to be both the master and the servant of the public. The implications of this situation are particularly worthy of examination. Any analysis of the policeman's role must also be concerned with the likely impact upon it of future social changes. The ideal of the policeman as a peace officer is based upon conditions which are becoming less prevalent. When the average British household has a telephone and a motor car, the patrolman's pattern of activity will be significantly different.

In relations between people of similar status, when one party behaves in a fashion the other considers praiseworthy, the other is likely to reward him by expressing verbal approval or some mark of regard, whether it be a deferential tone of address or a more material acknowledgement. If a man fails to behave according to general expectation, the other person is likely to express disapproval; if the former continues in this deviant behaviour the latter may use what is normally the ultimate sanction of withdrawing completely from the relation. In relations between unequals, as between employee and employer, this sanction is normally available to both parties, though the personal cost of abandoning a job is usually greater to the worker than to the employer. But in relations between a policeman and a member of the public (let us, following American practice, call the latter a 'subject' for short) freedom to break off the relation is often absent. If a subject stops a policeman to ask him the way, he is free to withdraw when he wishes; but should his behaviour be suspicious, the policeman might detain him and he would have to offer an acceptable explanation of his conduct to win release. This element of constraint distinguishes police-public interaction from nearly all other forms of social relation.

It should not be thought, however, that subjects cannot control police behaviour. As a rule, people do not approach the police for assistance or with a complaint unless they have some idea of what action the police are likely to take. They do not wish to involve themselves in a relation that is going to be more trouble to them than benefit. A Scottish sergeant testified that in country districts people will rarely give you information about their neighbours' misdemeanours because they have to live with them. They will talk in a roundabout manner and drop the advice, 'It might be worth your while walking up so-and-so glen one of these evenings'. In such a situation the man is trying to control the policeman's behaviour by having him discover an offence without the speaker's being identifiable as the informer. He can do this because he knows how the policeman is likely to respond. At other times countrymen will go to very considerable trouble to get into touch with a police officer with whom they are acquainted. Trust, in this connexion, is frequently a matter of predictability. An American writer has concluded:

Probably the one single element which is responsible above all others for the unparalleled cooperation prevailing today between the police and the public in England is the complete integrity of the police under the law. They enjoy popular confidence and esteem because the people know they will not overstep the safeguards to individual liberty provided under the law and rigorously protected by the courts (Davies, 1954, p. 148).

This is a lawyer's view. The sociologist will emphasize that the public in Britain are able to trust the police because the actions of individual officers follow a common pattern so that the subject knows what to expect. Many studies of intergroup relations lay great stress upon this factor. For example, Negroes frequently assert that they would rather live in a society where racial discrimination is customary and open than in one where acts of discrimination are infrequent but unpredictable. In the former case, they say, they 'know where they stand'. In the latter, they may never meet discrimination, but they are continually wondering whether it is not going to hit them next time, or whether what happened to an acquaintance last week is not going to happen to them before the day is out. So it is, too, with policemen. The man who has once suffered bad treatment at the hands of an individual officer never knows whether the same or worse is not going to occur again next time.

The establishment of uniform and predictable modes of actions is not a matter for the police alone. They cannot respond in a standard fashion unless they know their behaviour will be correctly interpreted by subjects. The officer in the United States is less predictable than his British colleague partly because, in a heterogeneous population, common understandings are less inclusive. The American officer cannot rely upon the authority of his uniform, but in dealing with subjects must establish a personal authority by proving what a good guy he is, or what a dangerous one. For the relationships between the policeman and the non-criminal subject to serve both parties' ends, they must understand each other. They must both be members of a community, sharing values and modes of communication.

The effectiveness of the policeman as a peace officer lies in his participation in the life of the society he polices. This proposition has been reiterated earlier and to some readers it may seem self-evident. I do not believe that this is the case. On the contrary, there is evidence to suggest that the policeman's sense of participation varies considerably and that his performance of duties is related to these variations. The evidence comes from places where the gap between police and public is large, in colonies, in Northern United States cities, and from Negro communities in the Deep South, but there is every reason to suspect that the same factor is at work, usually to a milder degree, in all societies. Different police duties bring officers into contact with different sections of the public, and this is likely to influence both their attitudes and their behaviour on the job.

A writer with experience of colonial administration takes up the question of police-public relations to illustrate one of the causes of corruption. The African farmer, he says, is barefoot, but 'the policeman is wearing a pair of large, shiny boots, and this difference may stand as a symbol of their relative ability to protect themselves'. The policeman has knowledge of the law, contacts with government officials, and powers of arrest. The farmer does not understand the law very well and sooner or later he will infringe one of its provisions. If the policeman then demands a bribe, the farmer is relatively helpless. To complain to the constable's superior is likely to be ineffective. Even if he should spend a considerable sum to engage a strange lawyer from the city, and should win his case, he gets only temporary satisfaction, for he knows that all the police in the locality will be watching for his next mistake.[1] Only through a political movement does the farmer have any real control over the policeman; instead of the two men seeing infractions from one another's standpoints and responding to the same moral ideas, they see each other as belonging to different communities. There are few internal controls built into the relationship, and the chief constraints upon the policeman are those deriving from the discipline of his own organization. Where the farmer is weak the policeman is tempted to use his power to obtain money; where the farmer is wealthy it is he who is tempted to use his money to buy some of the policeman's power to shield his own activities. Thus one of the practices which arises to bridge the gap between the policeman and the community is corruption.

1. The position of a colonial-style police, trying to enforce laws unsupported by the local system of social control and seeking to have witnesses testify truthfully when they are subject to contrary community pressures, is the theme of Philip Mason's novel *Call the Next Witness*, 1945. Introducing his story, Mason maintains that the problem of the police in India is not that of finding their man so much as of getting honest witnesses to court.

Another is violence. In some of the cities in the Northern parts of the United States the police departments have been demoralized by political control, poor leadership, and low rates of pay. The life of many districts seems competitive and raw; individuals pursue their own ends with little regard for public morality, and the policeman sees the ugly underside of outwardly respectable households and businesses. Small wonder, then, that many American policemen are cynics.[2] 'After a while you don't believe that anyone tells you the truth', said one man. 'The favours that you do for people bounce back on you because the guy who came up with the sob story was lying' (Westley, 1953). Couple this experience of the public with the policeman's feeling that in his social life he is a pariah, scorned by citizens who are more respectable but no more honest, and it need surprise no one that the patrolman's loyalties to his department and his colleagues are often stronger than those to the wider society. The patrolman has little moral authority and he cannot identify himself with the entire community to the extent that his British colleague does. To make the public comply with their orders the policemen in such localities have to adopt a familiar manner, and when this is insufficient they feel obliged to employ violence in order to coerce an obstinate person into obedience or into evincing more respect for the police. William A. Westley, in a study made in a Mid-Western city at a time when police morale and standards seem to have been very low, asked policemen in what circumstances they thought officers were justified in 'roughing a man up'. Twenty-seven out of seventy-three men (37 per cent) replied that violence might be justified when a man showed disrespect for the police – no other set of circumstances received such frequent mention.

A gulf may arise between the police and the public where the police feel alienated from society. A comparable situation occurs where the police see a section of the population as not belonging to their own society. The results may be even more distressing. In words which quite clearly are chosen to describe cold facts rather than to express personal feelings, the President's Commission on Civil Rights concluded:

2. 'I do not know how police officers can escape from being cynics' (Holcomb, 1950, p. 10).

A comprehensive review of available evidence indicates that police brutality is still a serious and continuing problem. When policemen take the law into their own hands, assuming the roles of judge, jury, and, sometimes, executioner, they do so for a variety of reasons. Some officers take it upon themselves to enforce segregation or the Negro's subordinate status. Brutality of this nature occurs most often in those places where racial segregation has the force of tradition behind it.[3]

What struck me most forcibly when talking with ordinary white people in the American South was the way they would always refer to Negroes as 'they'; there seemed to be no situations in which White and Negroes belonged as 'we'. This observation is a commonplace in the sociological literature but its continuing validity can still impress the visiting European. Most Whites did not see Negroes and themselves as being members of the same community. At no time did I get the impression that white police officers felt the same involvement in the rights and wrongs of life in the Negro district as they did in the white districts. An officer who came across a Negro woman who had been badly beaten by her lover showed none of the feelings of indignation and sympathy he might have revealed had she been white. There were some exceptions, of course, as there usually are, but generally speaking the white policeman saw beatings and stabbings as customs of the Negro sections, like shooting craps. Many years earlier at the time of the First World War, a captain of detectives in a Southern town told a writer on police matters: 'In this town there are three classes of homicide. If a nigger kills a white man, that's murder. If a white man kills a nigger, that's justifiable homicide. If a nigger kills a nigger, that's one less nigger'. He was not saying that this was the way things should be, merely that it was the way things were. Something of this feeling that crimes between Negroes are no concern of the Whites and of white courts of justice remains in many parts of the South. The courts will give a Negro convicted of assaulting another Negro a sentence only a fraction of that which would have been imposed had the parties been white. If the courts take this view it is hard for the police officer not to follow suit.

The social separation of the police and the public is not, of

3. Justice (1960), *U.S. Commission on Civil Rights*, 1961, Report, Boole 5, Washington D.C.

course, the only factor giving rise to police brutality. Officers, both white and Negro, in an excellent Southern police department told me quite freely of occasions on which they had beaten prisoners. This was not a common occurrence. In one case the offender had tried to knife the officer, who had been behaving in a perfectly correct manner, and who felt quite shaken that anybody should try to do this to him when he had done nothing to provoke it. He lost control of himself. Another officer described how he, as a young policeman, had reacted similarly when prisoners had cursed him and spat on him. Illegal violence is apt to occur in this way when the police believe that the courts will not punish particular offences adequately and when senior officers fail to establish and enforce clear norms of what is expected of a police officer. In the Scottish city I have similarly heard stories from retired policemen and older officers of the use of illegal violence to punish offenders who the police thought would not receive a sufficiently severe sentence from the courts. Today, Scottish officers are inclined to insist that nowadays, illegal violence is never used.[4]

If the policeman patrolling a neighbourhood populated by people of another race feels no identification with them and performs his duties less well, may not the same be expected where the residents are distant from the policeman in terms of social class? In Britain there is indeed a suspicion in some quarters that the police side with the propertied classes and are the enemy of the working classes. Whatever the police may feel, the public apparently do not think this. To judge by the results of the Social Survey poll there is no distinctive variation between social classes in their approval of the police. Of respondents in the Registrar-General's social classes I and II (professional and managerial) 85·2 per cent said that they had great respect for the police; among social class III respondents (clerical and skilled manual) 81·8 per cent gave a similar reply; as did 81·9 per cent of social classes IV and V (semi-skilled and labouring). The most signifi-

4. Cf. Davies, 1954, p. 155. One aspect of this question which I have not seen mentioned is that offenders are more likely to try and goad policemen of shorter stature into a fight and, apparently, are more inclined to protest about any undue violence on their part – as if force from a big man were a fact of nature but from a small man an abuse of office.

cant variable seems to be age (older people expressing more respect for the police), though the distinction between motorists and non-motorists (79·7 per cent as against 84·1 per cent) merits some attention.[5] But even though they may not affect generalized public attitudes, class differences may be significant for police-public relations in other ways.

Probationers in a series of discussion groups at the Scottish Police College were asked if they had found any kind of people more difficult to handle than they had expected: they were unanimous in replying that upper-class people were more difficult to deal with than any other. Many of them cited instances,[6] though none perhaps as likely to draw a smile as that of the policeman who asked a woman driver for her licence, only to receive the reply: 'Don't you know who I am? I'm Lady So-and-so. You should stand to attention when you speak to me.' Nothing daunted, the officer replied: 'Well I'm PC 99 and I'm booking you for a parking offence.'

It seems likely that a working-class offender hits back at an intruding policeman in ways that the constable is prepared for. If a man tells the policeman to go to hell, this shows disrespect for the law as well as for the individual officer, and if he cautions or charges the offender he must feel that he is vindicating standards of proper conduct. In this way he reinforces his conception of

5. Geoffrey Gorer's survey, based on a self-selected sample of 4,983 readers of a popular newspaper, reported that three-quarters were in agreement in 'enthusiastic appreciation of the English police'. People earning less than £12 per week tended to be slightly more appreciative, but people who classed themselves as 'working class' were somewhat less favourable than those who considered themselves 'middle class'. Apart from the under 18s – who were enthusiastic – there was no association with respondents' age (Gorer, 1955, Table 80, p. 446).

6. An extreme case was reported in the *Guardian*, 7 November 1961: 'Lady (Barbara) Beaumont yesterday paid to a detective and a policewoman a fine and costs totalling £16 6s. after the police had waited outside her flat in Beaconsfield, Buckinghamshire, for five and a half hours. They had called at her home in the morning with a warrant for her arrest for non-payment of the fine, imposed on her in August, for failing to complete a census form. Soon after 11 a.m. Lady Beaumont called to the police officers through the locked door of her flat to say that she was dressing, but at midday they were still waiting outside. Three-quarters of an hour later, she called through the door again to say that she was having a bath. Finally, she opened the door and paid the fine.'

himself as an agent of the law. The upper-class offender – to judge from these discussions – hits back in a different way. He (or she) asserts that he is above the law (there is truth in this sometimes: not at all frequently, but often enough to appear as a threat to the young constable). Or he denies that the officer is really an independent agent of the law. 'I'm paying your wages', the offender says. 'You're not supposed to be doing this. You should be chasing criminals', etc. Such attacks are much more difficult for the constable to answer because they are more personal and tend to reduce any satisfaction he gets from doing his duty.

Quite apart, however, from any class differences in style of speech, the sorts of incidents which bring together policemen and middle-or upper-class people tend to be different from those which give rise to contacts between police and working-class people. If policemen meet members of any one social category chiefly in situations which spell trouble for the officer, they are likely to react by expressing disapproval of the whole category. This happens in many United States cities, where a disproportionate amount of crime is committed by Negroes and where many white people build up unfavourable stereotypes of Negroes on this account. Practitioners of any occupation are apt to be irritated by a group of people who give them extra trouble. However, 'trouble' requires definition. Most policemen would be acutely dissatisfied if they never had anything at all to do. Some tasks give them a sense of achievement and self-satisfaction, but if there were too many even of these they would lose their appeal. Beats, or patrol areas in middle-class districts tend to be much larger, and there are fewer policemen compared with the number of residents than there are in the poorer districts; but while there are relatively fewer cases in which middle-class residents have to be charged or warned by the patrol officer, there are not so many cases from which he is able to get the satisfaction that comes from helping someone who looked to the police for aid. All too often the calls which the beat man in a middle-class area receives concern lost dogs, cats stuck up trees, or other trivialities. Many policemen dislike having to work in such districts for this reason. On the other hand, the average middle-class resident shares more nearly the policeman's ideas about law enforcement, and in some respects is more ready to co-operate than the average working-class man.

Many of the calls which a policeman on duty in a poor neighbourhood receives are fairly easily settled and do not count as 'trouble'. They provide the satisfaction that comes from a worthwhile job well done without threatening the constable's person or involving him in difficulties with his superiors. Disputes between neighbours and minor requests for assistance can be settled without an officer's having to make detailed reports in writing about what action he took. There is less likelihood of these subjects going over his head to his superiors and causing them to put pressure on him in any way. So the beat man in such a locality can often establish a protective relationship with the law-abiding residents. One constable in a poor district asserted to the author that it was his responsibility to show particular consideration to people who had not had much opportunity in life, 'such as the people round here'. His attitude, though a little more vehement than most of his colleagues, was not atypical. A patrol officer in a poor district will probably get more tasks of an unpleasant character (e.g. searching bodies of persons several days dead, dealing with violent drunks or abusive juveniles) but he will also get more tasks that give his job meaning and may well advance his career. In a poor district the patrol officers have to give less attention to the protection of property and more to the supervision of the residents, because there is a much greater likelihood of breaches of the peace resulting from domestic disputes, drunkenness, etc., and probably less inclination on the part of the residents to report some kinds of offence to the police. The police become to a greater extent uniformed social workers as well as more active enforcers of the peace.

References
DAVIES, A. M. (1954), 'Police, the law and the individual', *Annals o, the American Academy of Political and Social Science*, no. 291.
GORER, G. (1955), *Exploring English Character*, Cresset.
HOLCOMB, R. D. (1950), *The Police and the Public*, C. C. Thomas, Springfield.
MYRDAL, G., *et al.* (1944), *An American Dilemma*, Harper, p. 1368.
WESTLEY, W. A. (1953), 'Violence and the Police', *American Journal of Sociology*, vol. 59, pp. 34–41.

13 Adam Podgórecki

Attitudes to the Workers' Courts

Excerpt from Adam Podgórecki, 'Socoiological analysis of the Legal Experiment Survey of Workers' Courts, *Polish Sociological Bulletin*, 1962, pp. 118–23.

A new institution for the administration of justice, namely Workers' Courts, was set up recently in a single voivodship (province) in Poland. These courts, the members of which are elected from among the workers by their colleagues, have no formal procedure, but make use solely of the pressure of public opinion within the given group. They deal with petty offences. The solution of a case by the Workers' Court may, although it does not necessarily, exclude it from being sent up to the civil court. So far, in this one voivodship alone, sixteen Workers' Courts in the same number of factories have dealt with seventy cases. The setting up of Workers' Courts in a single voivodship was intended as a social experiment, the aim of which was to see how they would function, before a law was passed setting up Workers' Courts throughout the whole country. An investigation was then set-on-foot to estimate the success or failure of the social experiment.[1]

In carrying out this research, efforts were made to collect information as diverse as possible to give a full picture of the subject of our study. Thus, both offenders and other workers were interviewed, and court documents examined, as well as statistical

1. The research was carried out by the Methodology Department of the Institute for Work Protection headed by Professor E. Modliński. The chief author of the research (plan, questionnaires and preliminary results) was Dr A. Podgórecki. The general premises were discussed with H. Borkowski, head of the Trade Unions Legal Bureau, Professor Ehrlich, head of the Theory of Law and State Department at Warsaw University and A. Turska from the same department, and Cz. Buczek from the Sociology Department in Wroclaw University contributed to the inquiry. The final report of the present stage of research was drawn up by Professor E. Modliński and Dr A. Podgórecki.

data on the work of the courts. The material at hand also included observers' notes and analyses of press discussions concerning the Workers' Courts. In choosing the objects of inquiry, factors such as the size of factory, the size of the town, the number and sex of workers, the type of factory and the qualifications of the workers, were taken into account. The quota sample method was used to select those to whom the questionnaires were given. They were divided into the following groups: administrative workers, technical personnel, skilled and unskilled manual workers. Another factor taken into account was: how far a given section in the factory was typical of the factory as a whole.

The people interviewed were divided into three basic categories (separate questionnaires being prepared for each category). These were (a) social activists, including: Party and trade union activists bearing a certain responsibility for the Workers' Courts on behalf of urban, district or voivodship Party or trade union committees; magistrates' court judges and public prosecutors; social activists, trade union and Party leaders of the given factory; representatives of the Workers' Councils and judges and secretaries of the Workers' Courts. In this group sixty-four interviews were conducted, using the questionnaires as a base; and several additional interviews without the use of the questionnaires; (b) employees of factories where there were Workers' Courts, (151 interviews); (c) offenders (eleven interviews).

The documents concerning the organization and work of the courts included: the regulations for the Workers' Courts, the 'guiding principles' laid down for the Workers' Courts by the Voivodship Court, a report of a conference of Wroclaw lawyers, information on the activity of the courts prepared for the use of the Voivodship Committee of the United Workers' Party, a draft Bill on Workers' Courts prepared by the Ministry of Justice, etc. But the reports of the trials constituted the main body of material. Out of the seventy trials dealt with by these Courts, the reports of forty-eight (all that were available for the researchers) were examined. Documents concerning the way the Courts were set up in some of the factories were also taken into account. In addition, the researchers were present at one of the trials. As another mean of inquiry, a questionnaire was sent to the management of all the factories where Workers' Courts operated. The managers were asked to give numerical data on the number of economic offences before and after the setting up of the courts.

A separate source of information was provided by reports of the members of the research team, who were sometimes able to give information reaching beyond the scope of the questionnaires and documents.

Did the Work of Workers' Courts Prove Effective?

Let us now examine the most important problems and the most interesting results brought to light by the research. Namely, are the Workers' Courts, and the fact that the worker has to face the judgement, and perhaps the condemnation, of his colleagues, an effective means of preventing petty offences?

The interviews showed that the majority of the workers considered the Workers' Courts an effective weapon against small thefts in factories. Of the 112 persons interviewed, eighty-three considered the courts an effective means, nine were of the opposite opinion, and twenty had no opinion. The statements made by social activists on the kind of cases which should be sent to the Workers' Courts (this problem is being discussed) may also be looked on as supporting the usefulness of the Workers' Courts.

The researchers also tried to make a numerical estimate of the Courts' effectiveness. Questionnaires were sent to sixteen factories asking the number of thefts committed during the six months before Workers' Courts were set up and during six months afterwards. As only four factories answered this questionnaire, there was not enough material for reliable conclusions to be drawn. It seems, however, that there was some decrease in such offences.

The effectiveness of the Worker's Court cannot be judged solely on the basis of the number of thefts which have been discovered (and of their supposed decrease), especially in such a short period. Some of the Workers' Courts examined not only thefts, but other cases as well, such as cases of hooliganism, or family disputes, in which it is even more difficult to measure the positive influence of the courts. The deterrent effect of the Workers' Courts is illustrated by the following: (a) in one of the factories the offender claimed he would commit suicide if his case was examined by the Workers' Court (this case was examined in camera), (b) a large number of the workers interviewed were of the opinion that the Workers' Courts had a strongly deterrent influence, through the workers' fear of being discredited in the eyes of their own colleagues. It is worth mentioning that while men are more strongly dismayed by public disgrace, women consider being fined as more painful as it affects the whole family.

Is the Existence of the Workers' Courts Justified?

Does the existence of the Workers' Courts not lead to the establishment of two kinds of justice – one for the population as a whole, and the other for those who work in places of employment which have Workers' Courts?

Up till now neither the authority nor the legality of the Workers' Courts has been questioned by the workers or by the offenders. According to the data available, none of the offenders left his work because of the verdict of that Court. One person did not come before the Court and another denied he was guilty. All the interviewed offenders (eleven persons) considered the verdict as basically just but only three of them accepted it without any reservations. The reservations expressed by the remaining eight may be divided into three categories: (1) 'why was it just my case that came up before the Workers' Court?'; (2) disproportion between the offence and the 'penalty' (i.e. public disgrace in the eyes of all the workers of the given factory for stealing an object worth 20 zlotys); (3) repetition of the same trial before the Workers' Court and a magistrates' court ('what is the authority of the Workers' Court if the case which has already been examined by the Workers' Court is once more directed to another court?' – there was one such case).

Social activists consider that, contrary to the regulations governing the Workers' Courts, the verdicts of these Courts are penalties, not merely judgements. Of sixty-four persons interviewed, fifty-three treated the decision of the Court as a penalty, not as a mere judgement. A similar question was posed to the workers. Among 151 persons interviewed the distribution of replies was as follows: 113 thought the Workers' Courts should have the right to pass sentences, twenty-one thought such Courts should only have the right of judgement, two said the Courts should have the right both to judge and to punish, and five persons had no opinion. Thus the workers would like to treat the verdict of their Courts as penalties, not just judgements.

The Degree of Social Acceptance

Are the Workers' Courts accepted by the workers employed in factories where such Courts exist?

Many factors show that Workers' Courts are socially accepted. Social workers asked whether punishment by means of public disgrace was 'right, just and effective', answered as follows: 110 said 'yes', two said 'no', and six had no opinion. The white-collar workers, asked whether their colleagues were in favour of Workers' Courts, in ninety-nine cases said 'yes' and in eight cases said 'no', the rest had no opinion. When asked their own opinion on the subject, 117 said 'yes' and nine said 'no'. The answers to the second question (the first being an indirect one) are more reliable. In spite of certain differences in the answers to the two questions they show a considerable degree of acceptance of the Workers' Courts.

When asked whether the Workers' Courts come up for criticism, 53 per cent of the social activists answered 'no', and 36 per cent answered 'yes'. Those who answered 'yes' gave the following explanations: they said that there was some criticism concerning the incompetence of the Workers' Courts, and some people criticized the Courts because they only examined cases against manual workers. Attention was called to the fact that trials before the Workers' Court are pointless if they are to be repeated in the public courts. Cases where the value of the object stolen was extremely small (2·47 zlotys in one case and 14 zlotys in another) were also criticized. The character of these criticisms shows that it is particular details concerning the functioning of the courts that are criticized rather than the institution itself. They also prompt the conclusion that positive answers concerning the acceptance of the Courts expressed thoughtful conviction and were not merely empty declarations. Analysis of the workers' answers to the question: 'Would you like to be elected as a judge of the Workers' Court?' confirms the sincerity of the other answers. Among 122 persons, twenty said 'yes', ninety-six answered 'no' and six had no opinion. It should be added that the high percentage of negative answers is easily explained by the fact that those who answered in such a way added that they did not have the qualifications necessary for being a judge. Another inquiry carried out by the Wroclaw centre showed that 95 per cent of the employees think that judges of the Workers' Courts should be chosen from among manual workers and only 5 per cent would be willing to admit management and executive personnel.

Among 139 persons, 102 thought the right candidates had been chosen as judges, six persons did not agree, and thirty-one had no opinion on the subject (thirty-five persons from among 141 interviewed had taken part in a trial before the Workers' Court while 106 had not).

Type of Cases Examined

What kind of cases are, and should be directed to the Workers' Courts with regard to type of offence, institution directing the case to the Court, or type of offender?

Among social activists 60 per cent thought that the Workers' Courts should deal with cases of theft (mainly petty thefts), 30 per cent thought they should deal with cases of hooliganism as well, and 10 per cent thought they should deal with petty disputes as well.

Of the forty-eight court reports examined more than a half (twenty-seven cases) concerned minor thefts, seventeen concerned breaches of the peace, and the rest (four) were other cases. Talks with the offenders did not point to the existence of any groups or factions within factories which would have an influence on directing cases to the Workers' Court, except in one instance. Of all the cases examined fourteen were directed to the Workers' Courts by the factory management, eleven by the police, eighteen by the Public Prosecutor, and five by tribunals.

The cases which come before the Workers' Courts are chosen because of their character. These are primarily cases where no doubt arises (cases that are straightforward and legally uncomplicated where the offender has confessed his guilt, and where the value of the object stolen is small) and where there is no controversy about whether or not the offender is to be condemned. The most important thing is to select simple offences which the newly created and inexperienced Court would have no difficulty in dealing with. In selecting these cases the social background of the offence is not always taken into account. From various data it is evident that offences do not usually come up before the Workers' Courts if they are committed by persons who are notoriously in trouble on the job, and who have a bad name among their fellow workers. The fact that cases are often selected according to the types of offence (those which are easier to deal with) and not according to their harmful public effects means that cases involving the managerial or executive personnel (and therefore comparatively more complicated cases) do not usually come before the Workers' Courts, which sometimes leads to the opinion that 'Workers' Courts are courts for workers.'

Legal Foundations of the Workers' Courts

What is the effect of the legal position of the Workers' Courts on their functioning? The lack of a settled legal foundation of Workers' Courts, in the form of codified general rules, leads to some scepticism, mainly on the part of lawyers. The workers themselves seem to doubt the stability of their courts; such an attitude was expressed in a number of questionnaires and in additional talks. There was a certain anxiety that the competence of the Courts might be questioned while a case was being examined (up till now no such case has occurred).

In a sense, the lack of legal standing diminishes the effectiveness of the Workers' Courts. However, it seems unavoidable in the present, experimental period and the negative effects of such a situation may be at least reduced by proper instructions.

Unintended Results

Were there any unintended, harmful effects of the Workers' Courts?

During the survey a number of such negative results were revealed: (1) It was established that in two cases certain persons not belonging to the bench were present at a session in camera. This could have given rise to gossip about pressure being used on members of the Court. (2) In one factory, the fact that the Workers'

Court had no clearly defined terms of reference, and that it referred a case for retrial in the public court resulted in a marked fall of attendance at the next session, and aroused criticism of the institution itself. Of the fifteen persons interviewed in this factory, only four expressed a favourable opinion on the Court, two were definitely against such Courts and the rest had criticisms to make.[2] The general picture of workers' opinions in all the factories investigated is as follows: among 149 persons interviewed, 117 were in favour of such Courts, nine were against, and the rest expressed various opinions. (3) The inquiry showed that, contrary to intentions of the founders, the interest in the cases examined by the Courts is very often limited to workers from the section in which the offence has been committed, and does not extend to all the workers. (4) Some workers make private use of factory goods (especially when they have no other means at their disposal, e.g. when they need a piece of wood or tin plate or want to make occasional use of the factory tools, etc.). Trials in such cases do not meet with approval in the eyes of the workers as a whole.

Conclusions

The experiment with Workers' Courts was based on the assumption that old means of mass repression are becoming obsolete, and are no longer sufficient to prevent certain forms of socially harmful behaviour; and that in such cases the pressure of opinion of the occupational groups is more effective than legal sanctions. On the whole, the inquiry confirmed these hypotheses. It was also established that the effectiveness of Workers' Courts depends on some additional factors, mainly on the uniformity of public opinion in the given occupational group. In the course of the research a number of unintended effects of this new type of Court were revealed.

2. We must make some reservations about this case in which the decreased approval of Workers' Courts might have been promoted by some additional factor. In this factory there existed a division among the workers and fairly widespread stealing; there was a kind of 'sentiment' for taking things out of the factory. Against this background the potentially negative attitude to the Workers' Courts may have found an easy rationalization in the above situation.

Part Three Law and Conflict Resolution

The topic of conflict resolution has brought to the surface a great diversity in the definition of law. Especially in anthropological analyses of conflict resolution one often meets with an emphasis upon the legal character of any ordered procedure aimed at the settlement of disputes. In this part I have found it advisable to include materials which cover a wide range of modes of conflict resolution. Comparisons between the various procedures, and the analysis of the structural conditions under which they arise, offers a fruitful field of research. The anthropologist Gluckman is included in this part so that the reader may see, through an example, how closely related are the anthropological and sociological studies of law when seen as a question of conflict resolution. Strictly speaking, Macaulay's article does not deal directly with conflict resolution, but is concerned with the preparatory steps in a contractual relationship that determine the forms of settlement in case a dispute arises.

14 Max Weber

Rational and Irrational Administration of Justice[1]

Excerpts from Max Rheinstein (ed.), *Max Weber on Law in Economy and Society*, Harvard University Press, 1954, pp. 349–56.

The decisive reason for the success of bureaucratic organization has always been its purely technical superiority over every other form. A fully developed bureaucratic administration stands in the same relationship to nonbureaucratic forms as machinery to nonmechanical modes of production. Precision, speed, consistency, availability of records, continuity, possibility of secrecy, unity, rigorous coordination, and minimization of friction and of expense for materials and personnel are achieved in a strictly bureaucratized, especially in a monocratically organized, administration conducted by trained officials to an extent incomparably greater than in any collegial form of administration or in any conducted by *honoratiores* or part-time administrators. As concerns the execution of complicated tasks, paid bureaucratic work is not only more exact but it is often cheaper in its results than the formally unpaid administration by *honoratiores*. *Honoratiores* administration is an avocational undertaking, and for that reason it is normally slower, less bound by rules, more amorphous and hence less exact, and it is less unified because it is less dependent on a superior; it is less continuous and, because of the almost inevitably more uneconomical utilization of the technical and clerical staff, it is often very expensive. This is particularly true when one takes into account not only the mere charges on the public purse, which are higher in bureaucratic than in *honoratiores* administration, but also the frequent economic losses of the ruled populace through loss of time and sloppiness. The possibility of

1. *Wirtschaft und Gesellschaft* pp. 660–65. In these pages Weber deals with certain aspects of sociology of law in general and of the interrelations between bureaucratic administration and the formal qualities of the law in particular. They form part of Chapter 6 (Bureaucracy), of Part 3 (Types of Domination) of *Wirtschaft und Gesellschaft*.

unpaid *honoratiores* administration normally exists in a stable way only where the business can be handled on a part-time basis. Its limits are reached with the qualitative intensification of the tasks with which the administration is confronted, as in contemporary England. Collegially organized work, on the other hand, produces frictions and delays, requires compromises between colliding interests and viewpoints, and hence takes place less exactly, more independently of superiors, and accordingly less unifiedly and more slowly. The progressiveness of the Prussian administrative system has been based, and will have to continue to be based, upon the ever-progressing elaboration of the bureaucratic, and particularly the monocratic, principle.

The utmost possible speed, precision, definiteness, and continuity in the execution of official business are demanded of the administration particularly in the modern capitalistic economy. The great modern capitalist enterprises are themselves normally unrivaled models of thoroughgoing bureaucratic organization. Their handling of business rests entirely on increasing precision, continuity, and especially speed of operation. This in its turn is conditioned by the nature of the modern means of communication, in which we include the news services. The extraordinary acceleration of the transmission of public announcements and of economic or political events exercises a steady and definite pressure in the direction of the maximum acceleration of the reaction of the administration to the given situation; this maximum can normally be reached only by thoroughgoing bureaucratic organization. Of course, the bureaucratic system can, and often does, produce obstacles to the appropriate handling of certain situations. These problems shall not be discussed at this point.

Above all, bureaucratization offers the optimal possibility for the realization of the principle of division of labor in administration according to purely technical considerations, allocating individual tasks to functionaries who are trained as specialists and who continuously add to their experience by constant practise. 'Professional' execution in this case means primarily execution 'without regard to person' in accordance with calculable rules. The consistent carrying through of bureaucratic authority produces a leveling of differences in social 'honor' or status, and, consequently, unless the principle of freedom in the market is simultaneously restricted, the universal sway of economic 'class position'. The fact that this result of bureaucratic authority has not always appeared concurrently with bureaucratization is based on the diversity of the possible principles by which political communities have fulfilled their tasks. But for modern bureaucracy, the element of 'calculability of its rules' has really been of decisive significance. The nature of modern civilization, especially its technical-economic substructure, requires this 'calculability' of consequences. Fully developed bureaucracy operates in a special sense *sine ira ac studio*.[2] Its peculiar character and with it its appropriateness for capitalism is the more fully actualized the more bureaucracy 'depersonalizes' itself, i.e., the more completely it succeeds in achieving that condition which is acclaimed as its peculiar virtue, namely, the exclusion of love, hatred, and every purely personal, especially irrational and incalculable, feeling from the execution of official tasks. In the place of the old-type ruler who is moved by sympathy, favor, grace, and gratitude, modern culture requires for its sustaining external apparatus the emotionally detached, and hence rigorously 'professional', expert; and the more complicated and the more specialized it is, the more it needs him. All these elements are provided by the bureaucratic structure. Bureaucracy provides the administration of justice with a foundation for the realization of a conceptually systematized rational body of law on the basis of 'laws', as it was achieved for the first time to a high degree of technical perfection in the late Roman Empire. In the Middle Ages the reception of this law proceeded hand in hand with the bureaucratization of the administration of justice. Adjudication by nationally trained specialists had to take the place of the older type of adjudication on the basis of tradition or irrational presuppositions.

Rational adjudication on the basis of rigorously formal legal concepts is to be contrasted with a type of adjudication which is guided primarily by sacred traditions without finding therein a clear basis for the decision of concrete cases. It thus decides cases either as charismatic justice, i.e., by the concrete 'revelations' of an oracle, a prophet's doom or an ordeal; or as khadi justice, non-formalistically and in accordance with concrete ethical or

2. Lat. = 'without bias or favor'.

other practical value-judgements; or as empirical justice, formalistically, but not by subsumption of the case under rational concepts but by the use of 'analogies' and the reference to and interpretation of 'precedents'. The last two cases are particularly interesting for us here. In khadi justice[3] there are no 'rational' bases of 'judgement' at all, and in the pure form of empirical justice we do not find such rational bases, at least in that sense in which we are using the term. The concrete value-judgement aspect of khadi justice can be intensified until it leads to a prophetic break with all tradition, while empirical justice can be sublimated and rationalized into a veritable technique. Since the non-bureaucratic forms of authority exhibit a peculiar juxtaposition of a sphere of rigorous subordination to tradition on the one hand and a sphere of free discretion and grace of the ruler on the other, combinations and marginal manifestations of both principles are frequent. In contemporary England, for instance, we still find a broad substratum of the legal system which is in substance khadi justice to an extent which cannot be easily visualized on the Continent.[4] Our own jury system, in which the reasons of the verdict are not pronounced, frequently operates in practise in the same way.[5] One should thus be careful not to assume that 'democratic' principles of adjudication are identical with rational, i.e., formalistic, adjudication. The very opposite is the truth, as we have shown in another place. Even American and British justice in the great national courts still is to a large extent empirical adjudication, based on precedent. The reason for the failure of all attempts to codify English law in a rational way as well as for the rejection of Roman law lay in the successful resistance of the great, centrally organized lawyers' guilds, a monopolistic stratum of *honoratiores*, who have produced from their ranks the judges

3. The term has been coined by R. Schmidt. (Weber's note.)

4. A. Mendelssohn-Bartholdy, *Imperium des Richters* (1908). Mendelssohn-Bartholdy vividly contrasts the refined and technical administration of justice in the Supreme Court of Judicature with the informal ways of the justices of the peace and those other inferior courts which serve the legal needs of the masses.

5. Written before the unpopular jury system was replaced in Germany, in 1924, by the system of the mixed bench, consisting of a majority of laymen and a minority of professional career judges deliberating jointly on all aspects of the case.

of the great courts. They kept legal education as a highly developed empirical technique in their own hands and combated the menace to their social and material position which threatened to arise from the ecclesiastical courts and, for a time, also from the universities in their attempts to rationalize the legal system. The struggle of the common-law lawyers against Roman and ecclesiastical law and against the power position of the church was to a large extent economically caused by their interest in fees, as was demonstrated by the royal intervention in this conflict. But their power position, which successfully withstood this conflict, was a result of political centralization. In Germany there was lacking, for predominantly political reasons, any socially powerful estate of *honoratiores* who, like the English lawyers, could have been the bearers of a national legal tradition, could have developed the national law as a veritable art with an orderly doctrine, and could have resisted the invasion of the technically superior training of the jurists educated in Roman law. It was not the greater suitability of substantive Roman law to the needs of emerging capitalism which decided the victory here. As a matter of fact, the specific legal institutions of modern capitalism were unknown to Roman law and are of medieval origin. No, the victory of the Roman law was due to its rational form and the technical necessity of placing procedure in the hands of rationally trained specialists, i.e., the Roman law-trained university graduates. The increasingly complicated nature of the cases arising out of the more and more rationalized economy was no longer satisfied with the old crude techniques of trial by ordeal or oath but required a rational technique of fact-finding such as the one in which these university men were trained. The factor of a changing economic structure operated, it is true, everywhere including England, where rational procedures of proof were introduced by the royal authority especially in the interests of the merchants. The main cause for the difference which nonetheless exists between the development of substantive law in England and Germany is not, as is already apparant, to be found here but rather in the autonomous tendencies of the two types of organization of authority. In England there was a centralized system of courts and, simultaneously, rule by *honoratiores*; in Germany there was no political centralization but yet there was bureaucracy. The first country of modern times to reach a high level of capitalistic development, i.e., England, thus preserved a less rational and less bureaucratic legal system. That capitalism could nevertheless make its way so well in England was largely because the court system and trial procedure amounted until well in the modern age to a denial of justice to the economically weaker groups. This fact and the cost in time and money of transfers of landed property, which was also influenced by the economic interests of the lawyers, influenced the structure of agrarian England in the direction of the accumulation and immobilization of landed property.

Roman adjudication in the time of the Republic was a peculiar mixture of rational, empirical, and even of khadi elements. The use of jurors as such as well as the original praetorian practise of granting *actiones in factum* only *ad hoc* and from case to case contains clear elements of khadi justice. The cautelary jurisprudence and all that grew out of it, including even a part of the *responsa* of the classical jurists, was 'empirical' in character. The decisive turn of jurisprudence toward rational procedures was first prepared in the technical form of the trial instructions contained in the formulae of the praetorian edicts which were expressed in legal concepts. Today, under the principle of fact pleading, under which recitation of the facts is decisive regardless of the legal concept under which the cause of action may arise, there no longer exists such a compulsion toward conceptualization as was produced by the peculiar technique of Roman law. We thus see that formalization in Roman law was largely due to procedural factors arising only indirectly from the structure of the state. But that peculiar rationalization of Roman law as a coherent, scientifically utilizable, conceptual system, by which it is distinguished from the products of the Orient and the Hellenistic cultures, was not completed before the bureaucratization of the state.

A typical instance of nonrational and yet 'rationalistic' and highly traditional empirical justice is to be found in the responses of the rabbis of the Talmud. Purely untraditional khadi justice is represented in every prophetic dictum of the pattern: 'It is written – but I say unto you.' The more the religious character of the khadi or of a similarly situated judge is emphasized, the freer he is in his treatment of individual cases within the sphere which is not bound by sacred tradition. The fact that the Tunisian ecclesiastical court (*Chara*) could decide in real property matters in accordance with its 'free discretion', as a European would say, remained a hindrance to the development of capitalism for a generation after the French occupation. But the sociological bases of all these older types of administration of justice shall be referred to another context.

Now it is perfectly clear that 'objectivity' and 'professionalism' are not necessarily identical with the supremacy of general abstract rules, not even in modern adjudication. The idea of a gapless system of law is, as we know, under heavy attack and there have been violent objections against the conception of the modern judge as a vending machine into which the pleadings are inserted together with the fee and which then disgorges the judgement together with its reasons mechanically derived from the Code. This attack has, perhaps, been motivated by the very reason that a certain approximation to that type of adjudication might actually result from the bureaucratization of the law. Even in the sphere of adjudication there are areas in which the bureaucratic judge is instructed by the legislators to arrive at his decision by 'individualizing' the case in its peculiar circumstances. But in the domain of administration proper, i.e., of governmental activity other than legislation and adjudication, the claim of freedom and of the decisiveness of the circumstances of the individual situation has been put forth, in the face of which general norms should play but a negative role as mere limits on the positive, unregulatable, and creative activity of the official. The full implications of this proposition will not be discussed here. The important point is that this 'freely' creative administration is not, as in pre-bureaucratic forms, a sphere of *free* discretion and grace, or of *personally* motivated favor and evaluation, but that it implies the supremacy of impersonal ends, their rational consideration, and their recognition as obligatory. Indeed, in the sphere of governmental administration in particular, that very proposition which does most to glorify the creative will of the official has put forward as his ultimate and highest guide the furtherance of the specifically modern and thoroughly impersonal idea of the *raison d'état*. To be sure, with this canonization of the abstractly impersonal there are fused the sure instincts of the bureaucracy for what is necessary to maintain their power in their own state, and, therewith, also as against other states. Finally, these power interests confer on the by no means unambiguous ideal of *raison d'état* a concretely applicable content and, in doubtful cases, the very decisive element. This point cannot be elaborated here. What is decisive for us is only that, in principle, behind every act of purely bureaucratic administration there stands a system of rationally discussable 'grounds', i.e., either subsumption under norms or calculation of means and ends.

Here, too, the attitude of every democratic movement, i.e., in this instance one aiming at the minimization of 'authority', must necessarily be ambiguous. The demands for 'legal equality' and of guarantees against arbitrariness require formal rational objectivity in administration in contrast to personal free choice on the basis of grace, as characterized the older type of patrimonial authority. The democratic ethos, where it pervades the masses in connexion with a concrete question, based as it is on the postulate of substantive justice in concrete cases for concrete individuals, inevitably comes into conflict with the formalism and the rule-bound, detached objectivity of bureaucratic administration. For this reason it must emotionally reject what is rationally demanded. The propertyless classes in particular are not served, in the way in which bourgeois are, by formal 'legal equality' and 'calculable' adjudication and administration. The propertyless demand that law and administration serve the equalization of economic and social opportunities *vis-à-vis* the propertied classes, and judges or administrators cannot perform this function unless they assume the substantively ethical and hence nonformalistic character of the Khadi. The rational course of justice and administration is interfered with not only by every form of 'popular justice', which is little concerned with rational norms and reasons, but also by every type of intensive influencing of the course of administration by 'public opinion', that is, in a mass democracy, that communal activity which is born of irrational 'feelings' and which is normally instigated or guided by party leaders or the press. As a matter of fact these interferences can be as disturbing as, or under circumstances even more disturbing than, those of the star chamber practises of an 'absolute' monarch.

15 Max Gluckman

The Judicial Process Among the Barotse of Northern Rhodesia

Excerpt from Max Gluckman, *The Judicial Process among the Barotse of Northern Rhodesia*, Manchester University Press, 1955, pp. 15–24.

Court hearings in Barotseland are marked by an elaborate etiquette in which rank is strongly stressed. Today, as one sits in a court, one can observe the obvious marks of differences in wealth between councillors and most other Barotse in their clothes alone, though some ordinary people are far wealthier than even senior councillors. Nevertheless, Barotse society is only beginning to differentiate into classes with different standards of living, which barely varied in the past. Chiefs, members of the royal family, councillors, and headmen possessed and handled far more property than commoners, and this was an important part of their power. But the economy remained basically egalitarian. Though the economy was fairly complex, it had certain limiting characteristics. Technological equipment in general was (and still is) restricted to tools which enable a man to produce little beyond what he could himself consume. Goods were all primary – simple food, simple clothes, simple dwellings, etc. – for the Lozi had few luxuries, so that no man, not even the king, could live markedly above the standard of his fellows. There was considerable internal trade for a Southern African society, and in the nineteenth century trade developed with the outside world, but the exchanges of these goods continued to take place within the limiting framework of the economy. Thus though Barotse society was ranked in chiefs and councillors and subjects, aristocrats and commoners, freemen and serfs, this ranking was not accompanied by any radical differences in standards of living. The king had greater security than his subjects, but lived at the same general level as they did. Tribute poured into his capital from the nation of 350,000 people of twenty-five tribes, but this tribute was given out again to the people. In this type of economy the wealthy man could not use his surplus land, cattle, or food in any enterprise which would produce a considerably higher standard of living for himself: all he could do with it was to use it to attract to himself many dependants, or to outface his rivals.

The nation as a whole was almost self-sufficient. The European goods introduced by traders in the nineteenth century were relatively few and were absorbed into the economy within old relationships. Today the nation exports labour, cattle, and fish: it imports food and large quantities of trade-goods.

Within the nation the people all lived in villages, each of which, with the kith and kin of its members, was largely self-sufficient. It co-operated in producing most of what its members consumed, and they shared their products. Therefore most of a Lozi's dealings in goods and services involved persons already related to him by kinship or political bonds. The Lozi who cultivated, fished, collected, and herded with his kin on his own and public land, and who shared with them the produce of his and their labour, entered into relations with outsiders to solve a few additional labour problems and to meet a few deficiencies, or to dispose of a limited surplus or skill. There were few specialists, and all of them derived their main subsistence directly from the land. A Lozi used part of his surplus for tribute and gifts to his overlords, and from them he obtained some goods to meet his additional wants. The remainder of his surplus he used to attract dependants and to feast his equals and subordinates. He would even deprive himself of food for these purposes. All these kinship, neighbourly, friendship, and political bonds were permanent, enduring through many years and indeed through generations. Even when Lozi entered into ephemeral transactions with strangers they tended to expand these to more permanent bonds of mutual help. A barter relationship became one of 'friendship' and then perhaps 'blood-brotherhood' – an unlimited exchange of goods and help between set partners. If a man deposited cattle to be herded by another, he ranked as a superior kinsman of the herder. A patient was mystically bound to the doctor who cured him of a serious disease.

Thus in the past, before the coming of the white man, practically all goods and services were held and disposed of in face-to-face relationships established by relative social position. A man was thrust into one set of these relationships, that of the kinship system, by birth: as he matured these relationships were extended by his and his kinsfolk's marriages. The other set of relationships was defined by the political structure and his links in it were dictated by its authorities. He could satisfy almost all his wants in these two sets of relationships.

The implications of this situation affect both the procedure and purpose of courts, and every doctrine of Lozi jurisprudence. In general terms, their courts aim at the same ends as courts in highly developed societies: the regulation of established and the creation of new relationships, the protection and maintenance of certain norms of behaviour, the readjustment of disturbed social relationships, and the punishing of offenders against certain rules. Their jurisprudence shares with other legal systems many basic doctrines: right and duty and injury; the concept of the reasonable man; the distinctions between statute and custom and between statute and equity or justice; responsibility, negligence, and guilt; ownership and trespass; etc. I shall establish the existence of these doctrines and examine how their particular character in Barotseland is determined by their setting within a social system in which most of the relationships between groups and individuals, and between these and land and chattels, are defined by position in the nation, in a village, and in kinship groupings. Since one of my main theses will be to demonstrate this, I emphasize its implications at the very beginning of my analysis.

In all societies men and women co-operate or struggle with one another in activities, organized or informal, which are directed to various ends. Sociologists classify these purposes as sexual, procreative, economic, educational, recreational, religious, political, and so on. The interactions between persons to serve each of these purposes constitute systems of social ties which are contained within the total social system and mutually influence one another. In more differentiated societies a person is linked to a variety of different persons, with many of whom his relationship is formally confined to a single interest, as, for example, that of a labourer with his employer, a bus traveller with the conductor, a housewife with a shopkeeper, even an invalid with a doctor or a churchgoer with a priest. It is chiefly in our simple family that we find the mixed ties that are typical of Barotse society. There nearly every social relationship serves many interests. Men live in villages with their kinsmen or quasi-kinsmen, and by virtue of kinship ties they acquire their rights and obligations. With his kin a man holds land and chattels; he produces goods in co-operation with them and shares with them in consuming these; he depends on them for insurance against famine, illness, and old age; he forms with them religious communities tending the same ancestors; they are responsible for the main part of his education; he seeks his recreation with them. He even ascribes the misfortunes which befall him to punishment inflicted on him by his ancestors for quarrelling with his kin, or to his kin's sorcery directed against him. He will be dominantly associated with the kin in whose village he resides. The family village is a group of kin which is defined by allegiance to a headman, a senior kinsman; the members of such a village are associated together by more important legal ties than those which link them to kin in other villages. Some Lozi live in royal villages, whose headmen are queens, princes, princesses, or councillors, with people of other kin-groups and even tribes. Then their bonds with their fellow-villagers are quasi-kinship bonds. This total set of relationships constitutes the village-kinship system. Its importance is shown in the widely extended system of classificatory kinship nomenclature, which groups distant kin with a few categories of close relatives – a system which all simple societies have.

But the village is also a basic political unit. The headman is related to his villagers by political as well as kinship bonds. By birth and by residence in a village a man acquires his civic status and is linked to a number of overlords. These political relationships also subsume a variety of ties. The state is not merely a political organization to maintain internal law and order and to wage defensive or aggressive war. As a subject, a man has the right to ask land from his king, and he works for and may beg help from his king. The nation is a religious community dependent on the king's ancestors for good fortune.

The network of links by which a man is attached to the king through councillors and stewards is intricate, but it usually originates in his headman, who occupies a crucial position in interlocking the political and kinship systems.

Political relationships are single-interest linkages far more than kinship relationships are, but the two sets of bonds are closely identified in their simplicity and common values. A chief is regarded as the parent of his people: he is called 'father and mother'. Every lord is a father to his underlings, and every father is a lord over his dependants. Therefore Lozi constantly use political terms like chief and councillor, as well as specific titles of councillors in kinship relations, and use kinship terms like father, mother, child, brother, in political relations. This identification expresses the manner in which face-to-face personal relations dominate Lozi life.

As we shall have constantly to refer to the consistency of Lozi law with these relationships which serve many interests, I propose, for brevity, to call them *multiplex* relationships. I require also a term to cover the structure of relationships in which a person tends to occupy the same position relative to the same set of other persons in all networks of purposive ties – economic, political, procreative, religious, educational. Professor Radcliffe-Brown has suggested I call this an *uncomplicated* structure, in contrast to Bouglé's defining our own social structure as *complicated*, since it links us with many different persons in various systems of ties. 'Complicated' and 'uncomplicated' are relative in in their connotation. Lozi social structure is uncomplicated when compared with our own; but it is complicated when compared with, say, Andamanese or Bushman structure. Degree of complication therefore defines relatively the degree of congruence in the links between the positions of persons in various systems of ties which make up the total social system.

But it is of fundamental importance to know that each Lozi man or woman is involved in more than one of these sets of multiplex ties. He or she belongs to several sets. Some of these sets of ties are of the same kind: a Lozi has rights in several different villages and several different kinship groupings. Villages and kinship groupings overlap but are distinctive and thus are examples of the different types of groupings of which a Lozi is a member. He is also linked in established relationships with neighbours and blood-brothers and friends, and in several different sets of political relationships and groups through stewards, councillors, and members of the royal family, and with fellow-tribesmen. This multiple membership of diverse groups and in diverse relationships is an important source of quarrels and conflict; but it is equally the basis of internal cohesion in any society (see Gluckman, 1954, and especially Colson, 1953).

With this brief survey of the structure of Lozi society, we may glance in a summary way at the problems we shall be considering. Most Lozi relationships are multiplex, enduring through the lives of individuals and even generations. Each of these relationships is part of an intricate network of similar relationships. Inevitably, therefore, many of the disputes which are investigated by Lozi kutas arise not in ephemeral relationships involving single interests, but in relationships which embrace many interests, which depend on similar related relationships, and which may endure into the future. This, at least, is usually the desire of the parties and the hope and desire of the judges and unbiased onlookers. The Lozi disapprove of any irremediable breaking of relationships. For them it is a supreme value that villages should remain united, kinsfolk and families and kinship groups should not separate, lord and underling should remain associated. Throughout a court hearing of this kind the judges try to prevent the breaking of relationships, and to make it possible for the parties to live together amicably in the future. Obviously this does not apply in every case, but it is true of a large number, and it is present in some degree in almost all cases. Therefore the court tends to be conciliating; it strives to effect a compromise acceptable to, and accepted by, all the parties. This is the main task of the judges, which I shall describe in the next chapter of the book. This task of the judges is related to the nature of the social relationships out of which spring the disputes that come before them. In order to fulfil their task the judges constantly have to broaden the field of their inquiries, and consider the total history of relations between the litigants, not only the narrow legal issue raised by one of them. Since the kuta is an administrative body, as well as a law-court, it may take varied action to achieve its aim, or convert a 'civil suit' into a 'criminal hearing' in the public interest. The result is that in cases of this sort the court's conception of 'relevance' is very wide, for many facts affect the settlement of the dispute. This applies particularly to cases between blood-kin and between fellow-villagers. The relationship of husband and wife is more ephemeral, and in disputes between them the court concentrates more on the immediately relevant facts. When a contract between strangers, or an injury by a man on a stranger, is involved, the court narrows its range of relevance yet further.

Lozi, like all Africans, appear to be very litigious. Almost every Lozi of middle age can recount dispute after dispute in which he has been involved: most of these have been debated in family and village 'courts' but many have also gone to political courts. Many Lozi are ever ready to rush to court where they dispute with great bitterness and determination. In cases where they clearly cannot win they will proceed from court to court. Their bitterness must be understood from the way in which a dispute provoking a lawsuit precipitates ill-feeling about many trifling incidents in the past both between the parties and among their kin, incidents which may go back over many years. Men may sue knowing they will lose, but that they thus bring to the kuta a kinsman who has slighted them and who will be rebuked. Or a man will commit an offence to induce another to sue him, with the same end in view.

The kuta should not achieve a reconciliation without blaming those who have done wrong. The litigants in coming to court have appealed for a public hearing of their grievances, and these are examined against the norms of behaviour expected of people. The judges therefore upbraid all the parties where they have departed from these norms: judgements are sermons on filial, parental, and brotherly love. This is not inappropriate since the kuta is the central administrative chapter for national religious affairs. People involved indirectly as well as the litigants themselves are admonished on how to behave.

When we assemble the norms which are stated in this exemplary way, we shall see that they form that figure which is so prominent in all legal systems – the reasonable man. This figure is also used by the judges as the basis of their cross-examination to arrive at the truth: therefore I pause in my argument to consider the problem of evidence (the significance of direct, circumstantial, and hearsay evidence; the use of oath and ordeal, etc.) before investigating the nature of the reasonable man in Lozi society. Here we shall find that he is highly specified, in accordance with the specific social positions which the parties occupy. Following up this point we shall find that many disputes, apparently over gardens or chattels, are in fact suits by the plaintiff to have the kuta state that the defendant has not behaved reasonably in accordance with the norms of their relationship.

It will have already emerged from this summary account that in assessing whether behaviour is reasonable the judges lay blame on those who have erred. Implicit in the reasonable man is the upright man, and moral issues in these relationships are barely differentiated from legal issues. This is so even though the Lozi distinguish 'legal' rules which the kuta has power to enforce or protect, from 'moral' rules it has not power to enforce or protect. But the judges are reluctant to support the person who is right in law, but wrong in justice, and may seek to achieve justice by indirect, and perhaps administrative, action.

In the course of this account of Lozi trials we shall also cover a number of other problems. I indicate a few here. First, since almost all a man's relationships exist in his positions in the political and kinship systems, a litigant in many cases arising from these multiplex relationships comes to court not as a right-and-duty bearing *persona*, but in terms of his total social personality. That is, in most disputes a person is not involved merely as buyer, seller, lessor, lessee, landowner, the injured party and the wrongdoer – briefly, the plaintiff and the defendant, the complainant and the accused – but he is involved as an individual in specific relationships with a whole set of other people. In administering the law the judges consider these total relationships, not only the relations between right-and-duty bearing units. But concepts of these units exist as nuclei for the substantive law.

I conclude this section of the analysis by surveying the relation of the judicial process to 'law' as a whole among the Lozi, and find that it is in essence similar to that process in Western law. The judges have to apply certain normative rules to a particular set of circumstances in dispute. These rules, known somewhat vaguely as 'the law', are contained in customary usages; in statutes; in institutions common to all tribes of the region and in some institutions which they believe are common to all humanity and derive from God; in general equity and justice; in judicial precedent; and in the regular processes of the natural world (in our sense). Customary usage – ritual and secular – is one of the sources of Lozi law, as it has been in all systems; and the Lozi have the same other sources as those other systems.

Theoretically, this total body of law is known and certain and the judges are supposed only to pronounce it, abide by it, and apply it. However, since the law has only recently and barely begun to be recorded, the judges do not make a systematic survey of all the sources and decide what rules are applicable. Generally they tend to form a moral and equitable judgement on the case and then state – and amend – the law to accord with this judgement. Often they cannot do this, and must abide by some well-known statutory law or customary rule. But especially in cases between kinsmen they are generally able to satisfy their ethical view of the facts. This process emerges notably in the fact that judges refer less often to judicial precedents in previous disputes than to precedents of people behaving morally in circumstances similar to those of the case they are trying.

This process of judicial reasoning begins with the pleadings of the parties and the judges' examination of the evidence, which at every point is evaluated against moral norms. Nevertheless, the process is controlled by logical reasoning, which proceeds from premises of fact and premises of law ('reasons' as the Lozi call them) to certain conclusions, and the Lozi have a developed vocabulary to evaluate the skill or clumsiness of judicial analysis. Judges also try to develop the law by reasoning by analogy and logical development to meet new situations. Thus they employ Cardozo's methods of philosophy, evolution, and tradition. They also employ his so-called 'method of sociology', by which they import equity, social welfare and public policy into their applications of the law. They are able to do so because the main certainty of the law consists in certain general principles whose constituent concepts are 'flexible' – as law itself, right and duty, good evidence, negligence, reasonableness. The judges' task is to define these concepts for a particular set of circumstances, and in this process of specification they introduce into judgement through the flexible concepts all sorts of social values and prejudices, and indeed personal prejudices and values.

Finally, I conclude by making bold to submit that Western jurists, in maintaining or attacking the myth of law's certainty, have not fully explored the flexible 'uncertainty' of legal concepts; and have particularly failed to arrange these concepts in order either of flexibility or of moral implication. I suggest that this ordering is necessary if we are to understand the relation between law and ethics; for I see the judicial process as the attempt to specify legal concepts with ethical implications according to the structure of society, in application to the great variety of circumstance of life itself. In this process the judges are able to develop the law to cope with social changes.

References
COLSON, E. (1953), 'Social control and vengeance in plateau Tonga society', *Africa*, vol. 23, no. 3.
GLUCKMAN, M. (1954), 'Political institutions', in *The Institutions of Primitive Society*, Blackwell, Oxford.

16 Torstein Eckhoff

The Mediator and the Judge

Excerpt from Torstein Eckhoff, 'The mediator, the judge and the administrator in conflict-resolution', *Acta Sociologica*, vol. 10 (1966), pp. 158–66.

Mediation consists of influencing the parties to come to agreement by appealing to their own interests. The mediator may make use of various means to attain this goal. He may work on the parties' ideas of what serves them best, for instance, in such a way that he gets them to consider their common interests as more essential than they did previously, or their competing interests as less essential. He may also look for possibilities of resolution which the parties themselves have not discovered and try to convince them that both will be well served with his suggestion. The very fact that a suggestion is proposed by an impartial third party may also, in certain cases, be sufficient for the parties to accept it (cf. Schelling, 1960, pp. 62, 63, 71 and 143 ff.). The mediator also has the possibility of using promises or threats. He may, for instance, promise the parties help or support in the future if they become reconciled or he may threaten to ally himself with one of them if the other does not give in. A mediator does not necessarily have to go in for compromise solutions, but for many reasons he will, as a rule, do so. The compromise is often the way of least resistance for one who shall get the parties to agree to an arrangement. As pointed out by Aubert (1963, p. 39) it may also contribute to the mediator's own prestige that he promotes intermediate solutions. Therewith he appears as the moderate and reasonable person with ability to see the problem from different angles – in contrast to the parties who will easily be suspected of having been onesided and quarrelsome since they have not managed to resolve the conflict on their own.

In order that both parties should have confidence in the mediator and be willing to co-operate with him and listen to his advice, it is important that they consider him impartial. This gives him an extra reason to follow the line of compromise (Aubert, 1963, p. 39, and Eckhoff, 1965, pp. 13–14). For, by giving both parties some support, he shows that the interests of one lie as close to his heart as those of the other. Regard for impartiality carries with it the consequence that the mediator sometimes must display caution in pressing the parties too hard. That the mediator, for instance, makes a threat to one of the parties to ally himself with the opponent unless compliance is forthcoming, may be an effective means of exerting pressure, but will easily endanger confidence in his impartiality. This can reduce his possibilities for getting the conflict resolved if threats do not work and it can weaken his future prestige as a mediator.

The conditions for mediation are best in cases where both parties are interested in having the conflict resolved. The stronger this common interest is, the greater reason they have for bringing the conflict before a third party, and the more motivated they will be for co-operating actively with him in finding a solution, and for adjusting their demands in such a way that a solution can be reached.

If the parties, or one of them, is, to begin with, not motivated for having the conflict resolved, or in any case not motivated to agree to any compromise, such motives must be *created* in him, for instance with the help of threats or sanction. Cases may occur where the parties (or the unwilling one of them), may have a mediator forced upon them, and under pressure of persuasion from him or from the environment agree to an arrangement. But mediation under such circumstances presents difficulties, among other reasons, because it demands a balancing between the regard for impartiality and the regard for exertion of sufficient pressure. If the conditions for resolving the conflict by a judgement or administrative decision exist these will, as a rule, be more effective procedures than mediation in the cases described here.

That normative factors are considered relevant for the solution, can in certain cases be helpful during mediation. By referring to a norm (e.g. concerning what is right and wrong) the mediator may get the parties to renounce unreasonable demands so that their points of view approach each other. Even if the parties do not feel bound by the norms, it is conceivable that others consider it important that they be followed and that the mediator can therefore argue that a party will be exposed to disapproval if he does not accommodate.

The norms will be of special support for the mediator if the parties are generally in agreement on their content and are willing to submit to them, so that the reason that there is a conflict at all can be traced back to the fact that the norms do not cover all aspects of the difference. The remainder which is not covered will then have the features of a fairly pure conflict of interests where the norms have brought the points of departure nearer one another than they would otherwise have been.

If, however, the parties consider the norms as giving answers to the questions being disputed, but disagree on what the answers are, the possibilities for mediation will, as a rule, be weakened. In the first place, the probability that the conflict will at all be made the object of mediation is reduced, among other reasons, because bringing it before a judge will often be possible and more likely in these cases. Secondly, mediation which has been begun may be made difficult because of the parties' disagreement concerning the norms or the relevant facts. This is the more true the more inflexibly the opinions are opposed to each other and the more value-laden they are. The parties' resistance to compromising on questions of right or truth makes itself felt also when the mediator appears in the arena. Perhaps the presence of a third party will make the parties even more set on asserting their rights than they otherwise would have been. The mediator can try to 'de-ideologize' the dispute by arguing that it is not always wise to 'stand on one's right' and that one should not 'push things to extremes', but go the 'golden middle road'.[1] Sometimes he succeeds in this and manages to concentrate attention on the interest-aspects, so that the usual mediation arguments will have an effect. But it may also go the other way. The mediator lets himself be influenced by the parties to see the normative aspects

1. Confucius considered this as one of the conflict-resolver's most important tasks. His teaching that the parties tending to assert their rights must be dampened, so that one could get them to compromise, has left deep marks in the East-Asiatic ideology of conflict-resolution. This is probably one of the reasons that the idea of the Rule of Law has had such difficulty in winning support in the East. Cf., *The Dynamic Aspects of the Rule of Law in the Modern Age*, issued by the International Commission of Jurists, 1965, pp. 31–2.

as the most important, and ends up by judging instead of mediating. And even if he does not go so far, his opinions concerning norms and facts may inhibit his eagerness to mediate. In any case, it may be distasteful for him to work for a compromise if he has made up his mind that one of the parties is completely right and the other wrong.

Hoebel's survey (1954) of conflict-resolution in various primitive cultures confirms the impression that conditions are, generally speaking, less favourable for mediation than for other forms of conflict-resolution when the conflicts are characterized by disagreements about normative factors. Most of the third party institutions he describes have more in common with what I in this article call judgemental and administrative activity than with mediation. The only example in Hoebel's book of the development of a pure mediation institution for the resolution of disputes which have a strongly normative element, is found among the Ifugao-people in the northern part of Luzon in the Philippines. This is an agricultural people without any kind of state-form but with well developed rules governing property rights, sale, mortgage, social status (which is conditional on how much one owns), family relations, violation of rights, etc. Conflicts concerning these relations occur often. If the parties do not manage to solve them on their own they are regularly left to a mediator, who is called a *mokalun*. This is not a permanent office that belongs to certain persons but a task to which the person is appointed for the particular case. In practice the *mokalun* is always a person of high rank and generally someone who has won esteem as a headhunter. He is chosen by the plaintiff, but is regarded as an impartial intermediary, not as a representative for a party. The parties are obligated to keep peace so long as mediation is in progress and they may not have any direct contact with each other during this period. The *mokalun* visits them alternately. He brings offers of conciliation and replies to these offers, and he tries, with the help of persuasion, and also generally with threats, to push through a conciliation. If he attains this he will receive good pay and increased prestige. If the mediation is not successful the conflict will remain unresolved and will perhaps result in homicide and blood feuds, for the *mokalun* has no authority to make decisions which are binding on the parties.

It is easy to point to features in the Ifugao culture which can have favoured the growth of such a method of conflict-resolution. On the one hand, there has obviously been a strong need to avoid open struggle within the local society, among other reasons, because the people were resident farmers who had put generations of work into terraces and irrigation works. On the other hand, there was no political leadership and no organized restraining power, and the conditions were therefore not favourable for conflict-resolution by judgement or coercive power. Nevertheless, it is noteworthy that the mediation arrangement functioned so well as it did, considering that it was applied to conflicts where divergent opinions of right and wrong were pitted against each other. It is natural to make a comparison with our present international conflicts, where the conditions are parallel to the extent that the danger for combat actions and the absence of other kinds of third party institutions create a strong need for mediation, but where the mediation institutions so far developed have been far less effective.

The *judge* is distinguished from the mediator in that his activity is related to the level of norms rather than to the level of interests. His task is not to try to reconcile the parties but to reach a decision about which of them is right. This leads to several important differences between the two methods of conflict-resolution. The mediator should preferably look forward, toward the consequences which may follow from the various alternative solutions, and he must work on the parties to get them to accept a solution. The judge, on the other hand, looks back to the events which have taken place (e.g. agreements which the parties have entered into, violations which one has inflicted on the other, etc.) and to the norms concerning acquisition of rights, responsibilities, etc. which are connected with these events. When he has taken his standpoint on this basis, his task is finished. The judge, therefore, does not have to be an adaptable negotiator with ability to convince and to find constructive solutions, as the mediator preferably should be. But he must be able to speak with authority on the existing questions of norms and facts in order to be an effective resolver of conflicts.

The possibility for judging in a dispute presupposes that the

175

norms are considered relevant to the solution. The norms may be more or less structured. They may consist in a formal set of rules (e.g. a judicial system, the by-laws of an organization or the rules of a game), in customs or only in vague notions of what is right and just. The normative frame of reference in which a decision is placed does not have to be the same – and does not even have to exist – for all those who have something to do with the conflict. What one person perceives as a judgement another may perceive as an arbitrary command, If, however, *none* of those involved (the parties, the third party, the environment) applies normative considerations to the relationship because all consider it a pure conflict of interests, decision by judgement is excluded.

A decision may be a 'judgement' (in the sense in which the term is used here) even if the parties do not comply with it. But the greater the possibility that a judgement will be lived up to, the more suitable judgement will be as a method for conflict-resolution, and the better reason will the person who desires a solution have for preferring that procedure. It is therefore of significance to map out the factors which promote and hinder compliance to judgements.

The parties' interests in the outcome play an important role in this connexion. If the main thing for them is to have the dispute settled, and it is of secondary importance what the content of the solution is, it will require very little for them to comply with the judgement. If, on the other hand, there are strong and competing interests connected with the outcome, so that submission to the judgement implies a great sacrifice for one or both of the parties, the question of compliance is more precarious.

That one party (voluntarily or by force) submits to a judgement in spite of the sacrifice it means for him, may be due in part to norms and in part to the authority of the judge. There may be many reasons for the parties' respect for those *norms* on which the judge bases his decision; for instance, they may be internalized, or one fears gods' or people's punishment if one violates them, or one finds it profitable in the long run to follow them (e.g. because it creates confidence in one's business activities if one gains a reputation for law-abidance or because it makes the game more fun if the rules are followed). If the parties are sufficiently motivated to comply with the norms and give exhaustive answers to the question under dispute, then relatively modest demands are made on the *judge's* authority. If he is regarded as having knowledge of the norms and as having ability to find the facts, this will be sufficient to assure that his judgements are respected. Sometimes this is a simple assignment which many can fulfil. We may, for instance, take the case of two chess players who have not yet completely learned the rules of the game and who disagree as to whether it is permissible to castle in the present position. They ask a more experienced player who is present and comply without question to his decision because they consider it obvious that the rules should be followed and know that he is acquainted with them. But there are also cases where insight into norms, and perhaps also ability to clarify the factual relations in the matter, presuppose special expertise which only a few have. The kind of expertise required varies with the nature of the normative ideas. It may be, for instance, that contact with supernatural powers is considered to provide special prerequisites for finding out what is true and right, or it may be life-experience or professional studies. Monopolizing of insight may be a natural consequence of the fact that a norm system is large and cannot be taken in at a glance, but there are also many examples of systematic endeavours on the part of experts to prevent intruders from acquiring their knowledge.

If the parties are not sufficiently strongly motivated to comply with the norms which regulate their mutual rights and duties, or if they do not regard these as giving exhaustive answers to the matter of dispute, the judgement must appear as something more than a conveyance of information in order to command respect. The parties must, in one way or another, be bound or forced to adhere to it. One condition which may contribute to this is that, in addition to the primary norms which define the parties' mutual rights and obligations, there is also a set of secondary norms of adjudication which single out the judge as the proper person to settle the dispute and which possibly also impose upon the parties the duty to abide by his decision. That the judge is in this way equipped with *authority* is in many cases sufficient reason for the parties to consider themselves bound to live up to his decision. But the establishment of authority often presupposes power, and

177

even if the authority-relationship is established, it may sometimes be necessary to press through a decision by force. The power can reside with the judge, with someone he represents (e.g. the state) or with others who are interested in the decision being respected (e.g. the winning party or his relatives or friends). And it can have various bases: physical or military strength, control of resources on which the parties are dependent, powers of sorcery, etc. How *much* power is necessary depends partly on what other factors promote and hinder compliance, and partly upon the relative strength of the enforcing authority and the disobedient party.

That the parties and others have confidence in the judge's impartiality promotes compliance to judgements. It strengthens the belief that the decisions he makes are right and it facilitates enforcement by making the application of force more legitimate. As mentioned before, it is also important for the mediator to appear impartial, but the manner of showing impartiality is different for the two kinds of third parties.[2] To a certain extent the judge can display that he gives equal consideration to both parties, for instance, by giving both the same possibilities for arguing and for presenting evidence. But he cannot, like the mediator, systematically endeavour to reach compromises, because the norms sometimes demand decision in favour of one of the parties. If he finds that one party is completely right he must judge in his favour, and the outcome of the case will not in itself be a testimony to his giving equal consideration to both.

But the judge has other possibilities for appearing impartial. Sometimes his person gives sufficient guarantee. He is, for instance, because of his high rank, his contact with supernatural powers or his recognized wisdom and strength of character regarded as infallible, or at least freed from suspicion of partisanship. The privilege of the judge to assume a retired position during the proceedings and not to engage in argumentation with the parties makes it easier to ascribe such qualities to him than to the mediator. Another significant factor is that there are, as a rule, small possibilities for checking the rightness of a judgement because this presupposes knowledge of both the system of norms and the facts of the particular case. To maintain a belief that

2. Cf. Eckhoff (1965, pp. 12 ff.), where there is a survey of various ways in which conflict-resolvers can show their impartiality.

certain persons are infallible can, nevertheless, present difficulties, especially in cultures characterized by democratization and secularization. To reduce or conceal the human factor in decision-making will therefore often be better suited to strengthening confidence in the decisions. Letting the judge appear as a 'mouthpiece of the law', who cannot himself exert any influence worth mentioning on the outcome of the cases, tends to remove the fear that his own interests, prejudices, sympathies and antipathies may have impact on his rulings.

Tendencies to overestimate the influence of the norms and underestimate the influence of the judge may also have other functions than strengthening confidence in the judge's impartiality. Firstly, these tendencies contribute to the transmission of authority from the norm system to the individual decisions. Secondly, the conditions are favourable for a gradual and often almost unnoticeable development of a norm system through court practice, so that the resistance to change is reduced. And thirdly, the judge will be less exposed to criticism and self-reproach when he (both in his own and others' eyes) avoids appearing as personally responsible for his decisions. This is important because it might otherwise involve great strain to make decisions in disputes where the parties' contentions are strongly opposed to each other, where there are perhaps great interests at stake for both, and where it may be extremely doubtful who is right (cf. Eckhoff and Jacobsen, 1960, especially pp. 37 ff.). It is therefore not surprising that many techniques have been used in the various judicial systems for the purpose of eliminating, limiting or concealing the influence of the judge. The use of ordeals and drawing of lots in the administration of justice (cf. Eckhoff, 1965, pp. 16–17; and Wedberg, 1935) may be mentioned as examples of this, and the same is true for the technique of judicial argumentation which gives the decisions the appearance of being the products of knowledge and logic, and not of evaluation and choice.

Judicial activity and formation of norms serve to support each other mutually. On the one hand, the judge is dependent on normative premises on which he can base his decisions. The greater the relevance attributed to them, and the stronger the ideological anchoring of the norm system, the more favourable

179

are the conditions for conflict-resolution by judgement. On the other hand, the activity of judges can contribute to the spreading of knowledge about norms, to their increased recognition and authority, and to a gradual extension of the norm system to cover new types of conflict situations.

The activity of judging is in these respects quite different from the activity of mediating. As mentioned before, the task of the mediator becomes more difficult the more emphasis the parties place on the normative aspects of the conflict (presupposing that there is disagreement about these, as there usually will be in conflict situations). The mediator, therefore, must try to 'de-ideologize' the conflict, for instance, by stressing that interests are more important than the question of who is right and who is wrong, or by arguing that one ought to be reasonable and willing to compromise. The use of mediation in certain types of disputes may tend to create or reinforce the norm that willingness to compromise is the proper behaviour in conflict situations, and thereby to reduce the significance of such norms as judges base their decisions on.

The contrasts between the two types of third-party intervention make it difficult to combine the role of the judge and the role of the mediator in a satisfactory way. Indeed it does happen that a third party first tries to mediate between the parties and if that does not succeed, passes judgement.[3] Also the reverse is conceivable: that a third part first passes judgement and then proceeds to mediate when he sees that the judgement will not be respected. But in both cases attempts to use one method may place hindrances in the way of the other. By mediating one may weaken the normative basis for a later judgement and perhaps also undermine confidence in one's impartiality as a judge; and by judging first one will easily reduce the willingness to compromise of the party who was supported in the judgement, and will be met with suspicion of partiality by the other.

When the establishment of new third-party institutions is sought, for instance, by a legislator who is looking for new ways of settling labour conflicts, or by those who are working for the

3. The Norwegian Civil Procedure Act (of 13 August 1915, p. 99) provides that the judge may, at any stage of the case, attempt to mediate between the parties.

peaceful adjustment of international conflicts, there may be a dilemma about which way to go. Should one go in for building up the norm system, and for strengthening the normative engagement with the aim of having as many conflicts as possible decided by judgement? Or ought one rather rely on 'de-ideologization' and mediation? In considering such questions it is important not to let oneself be led by superficial analogies but to take account of all the relevant factors. Regarding international conflicts, for instance, one must consider that there is no superior instance which is powerful enough to force a powerful state to obedience. This has the consequence that courts can hardly be effective organs for the resolution of conflicts where substantial interests are at stake. Mediation also presents difficulties, among other reasons because the parties often place great emphasis on the moral and legal aspects of the conflict, and have strongly divergent opinions concerning both norms and (perhaps especially) the relevant facts. But there is good reason to believe that the difficulties in mediation are, after all, easier to overcome and that endeavours should therefore go in the direction of reducing the normative engagement.

References

AUBERT, V. (1963), 'Competition and dissensus: two types of conflict and of conflict resolution', *Journal of Conflict Resolution*, vol. 7.

ECKHOFF, T. (1965), 'Impartiality, separation of powers and judicial independence', *Scandinavian Studies in Law*, vol. 9.

ECKHOFF, T., and JACOBSEN, D. (1960), 'Rationality and responsibility in administrative and judicial decision-making', *Interdisciplinary Studies from the Scandinavian Summer University*, Copenhagen.

HOEBEL, E. A. (1954), *The Law of Primitive Man*, Cambridge, Mass.

SCHELLING, T. C. (1960), *The Strategy of Conflict*, Cambridge, Mass.

WEDBERG, B. (1935), *Tärningkast om liv och död*, Stockholm.

17 Takeyoshi Kawashima

Dispute Resolution in Japan

Excerpt from Takeyoshi Kawashima, 'Dispute resolution in contemporary Japan', in Arthur Taylor von Mehren (ed.), *Law in Japan: The Legal Order of a Changing Society*, Harvard University Press and Charles F. Tuttle Co., Tokyo, 1964, pp. 41–52.

There is probably no society in which litigation is the normal means of resolving disputes. Rarely will both parties press their claims so far as to require resort to a court; instead, one of the disputants will probably offer a satisfactory settlement or propose the use of some extrajudicial, informal procedure. Although direct evidence of this tendency is difficult to obtain, the phenomena described below offer indirect support for the existence of these attitudes among the Japanese people.

Formal Means of Dispute Resolution: Lawsuits

During the last years of the First World War, when the housing shortage became critical, active speculations in real estate existed and there arose a large number of disputes regarding land and leases, both residential and farm. Because of the patriarchal nature of the traditional lease in Japan, tenants had not previously dared to dispute the terms or meaning of a lease. Thus when tenants began to press these disagreements, the choice of a method for resolution was influenced almost entirely by the advantages and disadvantages of the alternatives. Although the increase of litigation regarding these contracts threatened the government so seriously that the institution of *chōtei* (mediation) was hastily legalized,[1] in the following years the volume of litigation was relatively small when we take into account the seriousness of the housing shortage and the social unrest caused by it. This suggests

1. By the Leased Land and Leased House Mediation Law, Law No. 41 of 1922.

that only a small portion of the disputes were brought to the courts. Furthermore, if we compare the number of mediation cases regarding leases and farm tenancies after mediation was legalized with the lawsuits of the same type, we note that the latter figure is considerably smaller, showing the extent to which mediation was preferred to litigation.

Similarly, a comparison of the number of lawsuits and mediation cases regarding leases during the years immediately after the Japanese surrender in 1945, when the complete destruction of housing by air raids in most of the cities had produced a serious housing shortage, suggests that litigation was resorted to in only a relatively small number of cases. Mediation was vastly preferred.

It is also indicative in this connexion that during the years of economic depression after the panic of 1927 – in Japan the depression started two years earlier than in the United States – the statistics do not show any significant increase in the number of lawsuits, although a large number of debtors became insolvent. The judicial statistics of the same period of some states in the United States, on the other hand, show a remarkable increase in the number of lawsuits. The fairly small number of lawyers in Japan relative to the population and the degree of industrialization suggests that people do not go to court so frequently as in Western countries and that the demand for lawyers' services is not great (Hattori, 1963).

Finally, it is of significance that, according to a survey conducted by this writer, extremely few claims arising from traffic accidents involving railroads and taxis were brought to court, and almost all of the cases were settled by extrajudicial agreements. A railroad was involved in a total of 145 traffic accidents which caused physical injury during the period from April 1960 to September 1960; but not a single case was brought to court, and only two cases were handled by attorneys. Of all the accidents of the same company which caused physical injury during the past seven years, only three cases were brought to court, and all three were settled during the course of the litigation. Of the total of 372 accidents which caused physical injury and involved another railroad in 1960, not a single case was brought to court, and only one case was handled by an attorney.

The volume of litigation arising in 1960 from traffic accidents caused by taxis is as follows.[2]

Company	Personal injury	Property damage	Total	Litigation
A	221	2,041	2,262	1
B	10	195	205	1
C	4	54	58	0
D	0	appr. 42	appr. 42	0

There are several possible explanations of this relative lack of litigation. On the one hand, litigation takes time and is expensive, but this seems to be true in almost all countries having modern judicial systems and can hardly account for the specifically strong inclination of the Japanese public to avoid judicial procedures. Or one might point out that monetary compensation awarded by the courts for damage due to personal injury or death in traffic accidents is usually extremely small. In a large number of cases the damages awarded by the courts for a death caused by a traffic accident were said to be less than 300,000 yen (approximately 833 dollars); thus the Automobile Damage Compensation Security Law[3] when originally enacted provided that the compulsory insurance for a death need cover only 300,000 yen.[4] A more decisive factor is to be found in the social-cultural background of the problem. Traditionally, the Japanese people prefer extra-judicial, informal means of settling a controversy. Litigation

2. The following figures from a study by M. A. Franklin, R. G. Chanin, and I. Mark (Columbia University Project for Effective Justice) suggest the significance of these Japanese figures. 'Each year in New York City some 193,000 accident victims seek to recover damages for injuries ascribed to someone else's fault. For about 154,000 of these claimants the first step is retaining an attorney, while 39,000 proceed without aid of counsel. Theoretically, a claim is but the first step on the road to the courthouse, but in fact very few of the 193,000 claims ever got that far. Approximately 116,000 are closed without suit, leaving 77,000 that are actually sued. Almost all claimants who have been unable to recover without suit, and who wish to continue, retain an attorney.' *Accidents, Money, and the Law: A Study of the Economics of Personal Injury Litigation*, 61 *Colum. L. Rev.* I, at 10 (1961).

3. Law No. 97 of 1955.

4. Automobile Damage Compensation Security Law, art. 13; Automobile Damage Compensation Law Enforcement Order, Cabinet Order No. 86 of 1955, art. 2.

presupposes and admits the existence of a dispute and leads to a decision which makes clear who is right or wrong in accordance with standards that are independent of the wills of the disputants. Furthermore, judicial decisions emphasize the conflict between the parties, deprive them of participation in the settlement, and assign a moral fault which can be avoided in a compromise solution.

This attitude is presumably related to the nature of the traditional social groups in Japan, which may be epitomized by two characteristics. First, they are hierarchical in the sense that social status is differentiated in terms of deference and authority. Not only the village community and the family, but even contractual relationships have customarily been hierarchical. From the construction contract arises a relationship in which the contractor defers to the owner as his patron; from the contract of lease a relationship in which the lessee defers to the lessor; from the contract of employment a relationship in which the servant or employee defers to the master or employer; from the contract of apprenticeship a relationship in which the apprentice defers to the master; and from the contract of sale a relationship in which the seller defers to the buyer (the former being expected, in each case, to yield to the direction or desire of the latter). At the same time, however, the status of the master or employer is patriarchal and not despotic; in other words, he is supposed, not only to dominate, but also to patronize, and therefore partially to consent to the requests of his servant or employee. Consequently, even though their social roles are defined in one way or other, the role definition is precarious and each man's role is contingent on that of the other. Obviously this characteristic is incompatible with judicial decisions based on fixed universalistic standards.[5]

Second, in traditional social groups relationships between people of equal status have also been to a great extent 'particularistic' and at the same time 'functionally diffuse'. For instance, the relationship between members of the same village community who are equal in social status is supposed to be 'intimate'; their social roles are defined in general and very flexible terms so that

5. The terms 'universalistic', 'particularistic', and 'functionally diffuse' are used here in the sense of the 'pattern variables' scheme of Parsons (1951, pp. 62–5); Parsons and Shils (1962, pp. 82–4).

they can be modified whenever circumstances dictate. In direct proportion with the degree to which they are dependent on or intimate with each other, the role definition of each is contingent upon that of the other. Once again, role definition with fixed universalistic standards does not fit such a relationship.

In short, this definition of social roles can be, and commonly is, characterized by the term 'harmony'. There is a strong expectation that a dispute should not and will not arise; even when one does occur it is to be solved by mutual understanding. Thus there is no *raison d'être* for the majority rule that is so widespread in other modern societies; instead the principle of rule by consensus prevails.[6]

It is obvious that a judicial decision does not fit and even endangers relationships. When people are socially organized in small groups and when subordination of individual desires in favor of group agreement is idealized, the group's stability and the security of individual members are threatened by attempts to regulate conduct by universalistic standards. The impact is greater when such an effort is reinforced by an organized political power. Furthermore, the litigious process, in which both parties seek to justify their position by objective standards, and the emergence of a judicial decision based thereon, tend to convert situational interests into firmly consolidated and independent ones. Because of the resulting disorganization of traditional social groups, resort to litigation has been condemned as morally wrong, subversive, and rebellious.

On the other hand there were, even in the traditional culture, disputes in which no such social relationship was involved. First, disputes arising outside of harmonious social groups, namely *between* such social groups, have a completely different background. Such disputes arise, so to speak, in a social vacuum.

6. This principle is still observed today in village communities with regard to a 'right of common' in land. To bring about any alteration of rights respecting 'common', the mores require unanimous consent of the villagers, and majority rule is not admitted. This traditional principle is recognized as customary law by article 2 of the Law for the Application of Laws, Law No. 10 of 1898. Legal recognition of the unanimity rule makes it extremely difficult for villagers to introduce innovations in the use of common, so that vast areas of common lands are left uncultivated despite a serious shortage of agricultural land.

Since amicable behavior from the other party is not to be expected in such a context, both parties to the dispute tend to become emotionally involved to a great extent, and the traditional culture contains no fixed rules of behavior to indicate the acceptable course of action. Yet, even in the absence of a specific tradition of harmony and in spite of strong emotional antagonism, disputes of this type are often settled by reconciliation. If one disputant apologizes, it is postulated by traditional culture that the other party must be lenient enough to forgive him, and, as a matter of fact, emotional involvement is usually quite easily released by the apology of an enemy. Occasionally disputes, usually antagonisms of long standing, are settled because the disadvantage of continuing disagreement outweighs the price of concession. These agreements are usually achieved through the mediation of third parties and are similar in nature to peace treaties. Until and unless such a peaceful settlement is made, sheer antagonism and the rule of power, very often of violence, prevail. Disputes of this kind are also settled when one party can impose a *fait accompli* by force. In other words, superiority in power establishes a new social order. The only way in which the weaker party can escape from this rule of power is through the lawsuit. For this reason, a large number of suits relating to the 'right of common' (*iriaiken*) in land recorded in the law reports of the prewar period were disputes between village communities.

A second class of disputes, those between a usurer and his debtor, lacks from the very beginning a harmonious relationship comparable to that normally found between lessor and lessee or master and servant. Usurers never fail to be armed not only with nonlegal means with which to enforce the factual power situation, but also with means founded upon law that enable them to resort to the courts. Since the Meiji era (1867–1912), long before industrialization was under way, official statistics have shown a surprisingly large number of cases involving claims of this sort.

In short, a wide discrepancy has existed between state law and the judicial system on the one hand, and operative social behavior on the other. Bearing this in mind we can understand the popularity and function of mediation procedure as an extra-judicial informal means of dispute resolution in Japan.

This attitude is also reflected in the customary characteristics of contracts. Parties to a contractual agreement are not expected to become involved in any serious differences in the future. Whenever they enter such a relationship they are supposed to be friendly enough not to consider eventual disputes, much less preparation for a lawsuit. Parties do not, or at least pretend that they do not, care about an instrument or other kinds of written evidence and rather hesitate to ask for any kind of written document, fearing that such a request might impair the amicable inclination of the other party. Even when written documents are drawn up, they do not provide machinery for settling disputes.[7] The contracting parties occasionally insert clauses providing that in case of dispute the parties 'may' (instead of 'must') negotiate with each other. [. . .]

The contractual relationship in Japan is by nature quite precarious and cannot be sustained by legal sanctions. If the disputants seek to continue their relationship some agreement is worked out, even if this means, in rare cases, that one party accepts the *status quo* imposed by the other. This rarely happens, however, because business and social custom forbids one to terminate a harmonious social tie by selfishly insisting on one's own interests. Usually it is clear that the unilaterally imposed solution is totally inadmissible when no agreement can be reached and the wronged party is then supported by the moral opinion of of the community, leaving the contract breaker in an untenable position. Thus what seems at first glance to be an absurd and serious deficiency in the contractual concept is in actuality only a reflection of the normal way of conducting business transactions. A similar reliance on custom may be seen in the American practise of buying and selling corporate stock through verbal orders.

This emphasis on compromise has produced its own abuses. A special profession, the *jidan-ya* or makers of compromises, has arisen, particularly in the large cities. Hired by people having difficulty collecting debts, these bill collectors compel payment

7. Von Mehren (1958, pp. 1486, 1494), points out 'there are still very large areas of Japanese life in which it is difficult to predict whether a dispute will be settled by reference to legal standards (applied either in court or in an out-of-court settlement) or in terms of quite different conceptions. It is often impossible to know in advance whether a party will seek to enforce his legal rights.'

by intimidation, frequently by violence. This is of course a criminal offense (*Penal Code*, arts. 249–50), and prosecution of the *jidan-ya* is reported from time to time in the newspapers. But their occupation is apparently flourishing. Furthermore, public opinion seems to be favorable or at least neutral concerning this practise; even intimidated debtors thus compelled to pay seem to acquiesce easily and do not indicate strong opposition. This attitude is doubtlessly due to some extent to the delay and expense of litigation, but at the same time the traditonal frame of mind regarding extrajudicial means of dispute resolution undoubtedly has had some influence on public opinion toward the *jidan-ya*. The common use of the term *jidan-ya* seems to suggest that extrajudicial coercion and compromise are not distinctly differentiated in the minds of people.

Finally, the specific social attitudes toward disputes are reflected in the judicial process. Japanese not only hesitate to resort to a lawsuit but are also quite ready to settle an action already instituted through conciliatory processes during the course of litigation. With this inclination in the background, judges also are likely to hesitate, or at least not seek, to expedite judicial decision, preferring instead to reconcile the litigant parties. Complaint about delay in reaching judicial decisions is almost universal, particularly in recent years, and the reasons for the delay are diverse. But one reason may be this judicial hesitancy to attribute clear-cut victory and defeat to the respective parties.[8] It is, though, interesting to note that the percentage of judicial decisions has tended to rise since 1952, while the percentage of judicial proceedings terminated by compromise and successful mediation has tended to fall. It would be incautious to conclude hastily that these

8. In this connexion another aspect of this judicial attitude should be pointed out: because of the inclination to avoid attributing to one party clear-cut victory or defeat, judges are apt to attribute some fault to both parties. For instance, in case of a suit for damages based on tort, in which a truck driver, ignoring the right of way of another car, crossed a street and collided with the latter, the court declared that the victim was also negligent in not slowing down his speed, and reduced the amount of damages for personal injury and property damage to 30.000 yen (approximately 83 dollars). *Yamaki* v. *Yūgen Kaisha Kubota Shōji* (*Kubota Commercial Limited Liability Co.*), Tokyo District Court, 24 March 1959, 10 *Kakyū Saibansho Minji Saiban Reishū* (A Collection of Civil Cases in the Inferior Courts) 545.

figures indicate a popular shift from the traditional attitude to a more individualistic one, but the beginning of such a tendency may be suggested.

Furthermore, it seems that judges are rather commonly inclined to attach importance to the *status quo* or to a *fait accompli*. The legal adage, *pereat mundus, fiat justitia*, is apparently alien to the Japanese public as a whole and to Japanese lawyers in particular. Once a certain situation is set, especially when it has been in existence for some time, people are inclined to accept it even if it is not legally permissible. The courts reflect this attitude of the people and then attempt to rationalize the result. Such a tendency also seems to be related to the traditional popular conception of social relationships, which sees them not as something controlled by objective fixed standards but as something precarious depending on and changing with actual situations. [. . .]

Considering these facts, parties in dispute usually find that resort to a lawsuit is less profitable than resort to other means of settlement. A lawsuit takes more time and more expense, terminates the harmonious relationship between the parties, and gives the plaintiff just as little as, or quite often less than, what he would obtain through extrajudicial means. Who would resort to a lawsuit in view of these disadvantages except pugnacious, litigious fellows?

Jerome Frank has noted that an overwhelmingly large number of lawsuits in the United States are not appealed to a higher court and that nearly 95 per cent of the cases come to an end in the trial court (Frank, 1950, p. 33). Such finality is in striking contrast to the comparatively large number of cases appealed to a higher court in Japan. Presumably this reflects the reluctance of litigants to accept a court decision rendered and imposed upon them without being convinced of the righteousness of its content; in the traditional ways of settling a dispute the solution was, in principle, reached through agreement by both parties. The notion that a justice measured by universal standards can exist independent of the wills of the disputants is apparently alien to the traditional habit of the Japanese people. Consequently, distrust of judges and a lack of respect for the authority of judicial decisions is widespread throughout the nation.

Informal Means of Dispute Resolution: Reconcilement and Conciliation

The prevailing forms of settling disputes in Japan are the extra-judicial means of reconcilement and conciliation. By *reconcilement* is meant the process by which parties in the dispute confer with each other and reach a point at which they can come to terms and restore or create harmonious relationships. As stated above, social groups or contractual relationships of the traditional nature presuppose situational changes depending on their members' needs and demands and on the existing power balance; the process of conferring with each other permits this adjustment. Particularly in a patriarchal relationship the superior (*oyabun*) who has the status of a patriarch is expected to exercise his power for the best interests of his inferior (*kobun*), and consequently his decision is, in principle, more or less accepted as the basis for reconcilement even though the decision might in reality be imposed on the inferior. Reconcilement is the basic form of dispute resolution in the traditional culture of Japan. *Conciliation*, a modified form of reconcilement, is reconcilement through a third person.

In the legal systems of Western countries as well as of Japan, dispute resolution through a third person as intermediary includes two categories: mediation and arbitration. In mediation a third party offers his good offices to help the others reach an agreement; the mediator offers suggestions which have no binding force. In contrast, a third party acting as arbitrator renders a decision on the merits of the dispute. In the traditional culture of Japan, however, mediation and arbitration have not been differentiated; in principle, the third person who intervenes to settle a dispute, the go-between, is supposed to be a man of higher status than the disputants. When such a person suggests conditions for reconcilement, his prestige and authority ordinarily are sufficient to persuade the two parties to accept the settlement. Consequently, in the case of mediation also, the conditions for reconcilement which he suggests are in a sense imposed, and the difference between mediation and arbitration is nothing but a question of the degree of the go-between's power. Generally speaking, the higher the prestige and the authority of the go-between, the stronger is the actual influence on the parties in dispute, and in the same proportion conciliation takes on the coloration of arbitration or of mediation. The settlement of a dispute aims to maintain, restore, or create a harmonious 'particularistic' relationship, and for that purpose not only mediation but also arbitration must avoid the principles implicit in a judicial settlement: the go-between should not make any clear-cut decision on who is right or wrong or inquire into the existence and scope of the rights of the parties. Consequently the principle of *kenka ryō-seibai* (both disputants are to be punished) is applied in both mediation and arbitration.

If a dispute is very likely to arise and the parties thereto are more or less equal in their status (in other words, the power balance is not sufficient to settle an eventual dispute), they normally agree in advance on a third person as mediator or arbitrator. For example, when marriage takes place, it is a common custom in Japan to have a go-between (sometimes each of the marrying families appoints its respective go-between) witness the marriage and play the role of mediator or arbitrator if serious troubles arise later. Or when a man is employed (not only as a domestic servant, or apprentice of a carpenter, painter, or merchant, but also as a clerk in such business enterprises as steel mills, chemical plants, and banks), it is still common practise for the employer to demand from the employee an instrument of surety signed by a *mimoto hikiukenin* or *mimoto hoshōnin* (literally translated, a person who ensures the antecedents of the employee). Originally this man had to undertake the role of mediator or arbitrator in case of sickness, breach of trust of the employee, or other eventual troubles; in recent years he simply undertakes the obligation as a surety. The reason that a very small portion of disputes are brought to court is to be found, as stated above, in the fact that most of the disputes are settled through these informal means.

References

FRANK, J. P. (1950), *Courts on Trial*, Princeton University Press.
HATTORI, T. (1963), 'The legal profession in Japan: its historical development and present state', in A. T. von Mehren (ed.), *Law in Japan*, Harvard University Press.
MEHREN, A. T. VON (1958), 'Some reflections on Japanese law', *Harvard Law Review*, vol. 7.

PARSONS, T. (1951), *The Social System*, The Free Press.
PARSONS, T., and SHILS, E. A. (1962), 'Categories of the orientation and organization of action', in *Toward a General Theory of Action*, Harper Torchbooks, New York.

18 Stewart Macaulay

Non-Contractual Relations in Business

Abridged from Stewart Macaulay, 'Non-contractual relations in business: a preliminary study', *American Sociological Review*, vol. 28 (1963), pp. 55–66.

What good is contract law? Who uses it? When and how? Complete answers would require an investigation of almost every type of transaction between individuals and organizations. In this report, research has been confined to exchanges between businesses, and primarily to manufacturers. Furthermore, this report will be limited to a presentation of the findings concerning when contract is and is not used and to a tentative explanation of these findings.

This research is only the first phase in a scientific study. The primary research technique involved interviewing sixty-eight businessmen and lawyers representing forty-eight companies and six law firms. [. . .]

All but two of the companies had plants in Wisconsin; seventeen were manufacturers of machinery but none made such items as food products, scientific instruments, textiles or petroleum products. Thus the likelihood of error because of sampling bias may be considerable.[1] [. . .]

This study represents the effort of a law teacher to draw on sociological ideas and empirical investigation. It stresses, among other things, the functions and dysfunctions of using contract to solve exchange problems and the influence of occupational roles on how one assesses whether the benefits of using contract outweigh the costs.

To discuss when contract is and is not used, the term 'contract' must be specified. This term will be used here to refer to devices for conducting exchanges. Contract is not treated as synonymous

1. However, the cases have not been selected because they *did* use contract. There is as much interest in, and effort to obtain, cases of nonuse as of use of contract. Thus, one variety of bias has been minimized.

with an exchange itself, which may or may not be characterized as contractual. Nor is contract used to refer to a writing recording an agreement. Contract, as I use the term here, involves two distinct elements: (a) Rational planning of the transaction with careful provision for as many future contingencies as can be foreseen, and (b) the existence or use of actual or potential legal sanctions to induce performance of the exchange or to compensate for non-performance. [...]

The creation of exchange relationships. In creating exchange relationships, businessmen may plan to a greater or lesser degree in relation to several types of issues. Before reporting the findings as to practises in creating such relationships, it is necessary to describe what one can plan about in a bargain and the degrees of planning which are possible.

People negotiating a contract can make plans concerning several types of issues: (1) They can plan what each is to do or refrain from doing; e.g. S might agree to deliver ten 1963 Studebaker four-door sedan automobiles to B on a certain date in exchange for a specified amount of money. (2) They can plan what effect certain contingencies are to have on their duties; e.g. what is to happen to S and B's obligations if S cannot deliver the cars because of a strike at the Studebaker factory? (3) They can plan what is to happen if either of them fails to perform; e.g., what is to happen if S delivers nine of the cars two weeks late? (4) They can plan their agreement so that it is a legally enforceable contract – that is, so that a legal sanction would be available to provide compensation for injury suffered by B as a result of S's failure to deliver the cars on time. [...]

Most larger companies, and many smaller ones, attempt to plan carefully and completely. Important transactions not in the ordinary course of business are handled by a detailed contract. For example, recently the Empire State Building was sold for $65 million. More than 100 attorneys, representing thirty-four parties, produced a 400-page contract. [...]

More routine transactions commonly are handled by what can be called standardized planning. A firm will have a set of terms and conditions for purchases, sales, or both printed on the business documents used in these exchanges. Thus the things to be sold

195

and the price may be planned particularly for each transaction, but standard provisions will further elaborate the performances and cover the other subjects of planning. Typically, these terms and conditions are lengthy and printed in small type on the back of the forms. For example, twenty-four paragraphs in eight-point type are printed on the back of the purchase order form used by the Allis Chalmers Manufacturing Company. [. . .]

While businessmen can and often do carefully and completely plan, it is clear that not all exchanges are neatly rationalized. Although most businessmen think that a clear description of both the seller's and buyer's performances is obvious common sense, they do not always live up to this ideal. The house counsel and the purchasing agents of a medium size manufacturer of automobile parts reported that several times their engineers had committed the company to buy expensive machines without adequate specifications. The engineers had drawn careful specifications as to the type of machine and how it was to be made but had neglected to require that the machine produce specified results. An attorney and an auditor both stated that most contract disputes arise because of ambiguity in the specifications.

Businessmen often prefer to rely on 'a man's word' in a brief letter, a handshake, or 'common honesty and decency' – even when the transaction involves exposure to serious risks. Seven lawyers from law firms with business practises were interviewed. Five thought that businessmen often entered contracts with only a minimal degree of advance planning. They complained that businessmen desire to 'keep it simple and avoid red tape' even where large amounts of money and significant risks are involved. One stated that he was 'sick of being told, "We can trust old Max", when the problem is not one of honesty but one of reaching an agreement that both sides understand'. Another said that businessmen when bargaining often talk only in pleasant generalities, think they have a contract, but fail to reach agreement on any of the hard, unpleasant questions until forced to do so by a lawyer. Two outside lawyers had different views. One thought that large firms usually planned important exchanges, although he conceded that occasionally matters might be left in a fairly vague state. The other dissenter represents a large utility that commonly buys heavy equipment and buildings. The supplier's employees come onto the utility's property to install the equipment or construct the buildings and they may be injured while there. The utility has been sued by such employees so often that it carefully plans purchases with the assistance of a lawyer so that suppliers take this burden.

Moreover, standardized planning can break down. In the example of such planning previously given, it was assumed that the purchasing agent would use his company's form with its twenty-four paragraphs printed on the back and that the seller would accept this or object to any provisions he did not like. However, the seller may fail to read the buyer's twenty-four paragraphs of fine print and may accept the buyer's order on the seller's own acknowledgment-of-order form. Typically this form will have ten to fifty paragraphs favouring the seller, and these provisions are likely to be different from or inconsistent with the buyer's provisions. The seller's acknowledgment form may be received by the buyer and checked by a clerk. She will read the *face* of the acknowledgment but not the fine print on the back of it because she has neither the time nor ability to analyse the small print on the 100 to 500 forms she must review each day. The face of the acknowledgment – where the goods and the price are specified – is likely to correspond with the face of the purchase order. If it does, the two forms are filed away. At this point, both buyer and seller are likely to assume they have planned an exchange and made a contract. Yet they have done neither, as they are in disagreement about all that appears on the back of their forms. This practise is common enough to have a name. Law teachers call it 'the battle of the forms'.

Ten of the twelve purchasing agents interviewed said that frequently the provisions on the back of their purchase order and those on the back of a supplier's acknowledgment would differ or be inconsistent. Yet they would assume that the purchase was complete without further action unless one of the supplier's provisions was really objectionable. Moreover, only occasionally would they bother to read the fine print on the back of supplier's forms. [...]

Sixteen sales managers were asked about the battle of the forms. Nine said that frequently no agreement was reached on which set of fine print was to govern, while seven said that there was no problem. Four of the seven worked for companies whose major customers are the large automobile companies or the large manufacturers of paper products. These customers demand that their terms and conditions govern any purchase, are careful generally to see that suppliers acquiesce, and have the bargaining power to have their way. The other three of the seven sales managers who have no battle of the forms problem, work for manufacturers of special industrial machines. Their firms are careful to reach complete agreement with their customers. [. . .]

A large manufacturer of packaging materials audited its records to determine how often it had failed to agree on terms and conditions with its customers or had failed to create legally binding contracts. Such failures cause a risk of loss to this firm since the packaging is printed with the customer's design and cannot be salvaged once this is done. The orders for five days in four different years were reviewed. The percentage of orders where no agreement on terms and conditions was reached or no contract was formed were as follows:

1953	75·0%
1954	69·4%
1955	71·5%
1956	59·5%

It is likely that businessmen pay more attention to describing the performances in an exchange than to planning for contingencies or defective performances or to obtaining legal enforceability of their contracts. Even when a purchase order and acknowledgment have conflicting provisions printed on the back, almost always the buyer and seller will be in agreement on what is to be sold and how much is to be paid for it. The lawyers who said businessmen often commit their firms to significant exchanges too casually, stated that the performances would be defined in the brief letter or telephone call; the lawyers objected that nothing else would be covered. Moreover, it is likely that businessmen are least concerned about planning their transactions so that they are legally enforceable contracts.[2] For

2. Compare the findings of an empirical study of Connecticut business practises in Comment, 'The Statute of Frauds and the Business Community: A Re-Appraisal in Light of Prevailing Practises', *Yale Law Journal*, vol. 66 (1957), pp. 1038–71.

example, in Wisconsin requirements contracts – contracts to supply a firm's requirements of an item rather than a definite quantity – probably are not legally enforceable. Seven people interviewed reported that their firms regularly used requirements contracts in dealings in Wisconsin. None thought that the lack of legal sanction made any difference. Three of these people were house counsel who knew the Wisconsin law before being interviewed. [. . .]

Thus one can conclude that (1) many business exchanges reflect a high degree of planning about the four categories – description, contingencies, defective performances and legal sanction – but (2) many, if not most, exchanges reflect no planning, or only a minimal amount of it, especially concerning legal sanctions and the effect of defective performances. As a result, the opportunity for good faith disputes during the life of the exchange relationship often is present.

The adjustment of exchange relationships and the settling of disputes. While a significant amount of creating business exchanges is done on a fairly noncontractual basis, the creation of exchanges usually is far more contractual than the adjustment of such relationships and the settlement of disputes. Exchanges are adjusted when the obligations of one or both parties are modified by agreement during the life of the relationship. For example, the buyer may be allowed to cancel all or part of the goods he has ordered because he no longer needs them; the seller may be paid more than the contract price by the buyer because of unusual changed circumstances. Dispute settlement involves determining whether or not a party has performed as agreed and, if he has not, doing something about it. For example, a court may have to interpret the meaning of a contract, determine what the alleged defaulting party has done, and determine what, if any, remedy the aggrieved party is entitled to. Or one party may assert that the other is in default, refuse to proceed with performing the contract and refuse to deal ever again with the alleged defaulter. If the alleged defaulter, who in fact may not be in default, takes no action, the dispute is then 'settled'.

Business exchanges in non-speculative areas are usually adjusted without dispute. Under the law of contracts, if B orders

1,000 widgets from S at $1·00 each, B must take all 1,000 widgets or be in breach of contract and liable to pay S his expenses up to the time of the breach plus his lost anticipated profit. Yet all ten of the purchasing agents asked about cancellation of orders once placed indicated that they expected to be able to cancel orders freely subject to only an obligation to pay for the seller's major expenses such as scrapped steel.[3] All seventeen sales personnel asked reported that they often had to accept cancellation. One said, 'You can't ask a man to eat paper (the firm's product) when he has no use for it.' [. . .]

Disputes are frequently settled without reference to the contract or potential of actual legal sanctions. There is a hesitancy to speak of legal rights or to threaten to sue in these negotiations. Even where the parties have a detailed and carefully planned agreement which indicates what is to happen if, say, the seller fails to deliver on time, often they will never refer to the agreement but will negotiate a solution when the problem arises apparently as if there had never been any original contract. One purchasing agent expressed a common business attitude when he said:

If something comes up, you get the other man on the telephone and deal with the problem. You don't read legalistic contract clauses at each other if you ever want to do business again. One doesn't run to lawyers if he wants to stay in business because one must behave decently.

Or as one businessman put it: 'You can settle any dispute if you keep the lawyers and accountants out of it. They just do not understand the give-and-take needed in business.' All of the house counsel interviewed indicated that they are called into the dispute settlement process only after the businessmen have failed to settle matters in their own way. Two indicated that after being called in house counsel at first will only advise the purchasing agent, sales manager or other official involved; not even the house counsel's letterhead is used on communications with the other side until all hope for a peaceful resolution is gone.

Law suits for breach of contract appear to be rare. Only five of the twelve purchasing agents had ever been involved in even a negotiation concerning a contract dispute where both sides were

3. See the case studies on cancellation of contracts in *Harvard Business Review*, vol. 2 (1923–4), pp. 238–40, 367–70, 496–502.

represented by lawyers; only two of ten sales managers had ever gone this far. None had been involved in a case that went through trial. A law firm with more than forty lawyers and a large commercial practise handles in a year only about six trials concerned with contract problems. Less than 10 per cent of the time of this office is devoted to any type of work related to contracts disputes. Corporations big enough to do business in more than one state tend to sue and be sued in the federal courts. Yet only 2,779 out of 58,293 civil actions filed in the United States District Courts in fiscal year 1961 involved private contracts.[4] During the same period only 3,447 of the 61,138 civil cases filed in the principal trial courts of New York State involved private contracts.[5] The same picture emerges from a review of appellate cases.[6] [. . .]

At times relatively contractual methods are used to make adjustments in ongoing transactions and to settle disputes. Demands of one side which are deemed unreasonable by the other occasionally are blocked by reference to the terms of the agreement between the parties. The legal position of the parties can influence negotiations even though legal rights or litigation are never mentioned in their discussions; it makes a difference if one is demanding what both concede to be a right or begging for a favor. Now and then a firm may threaten to turn matters over to its attorneys, threaten to sue, commence a suit or even litigate and carry an appeal to the highest court which will hear the matter. Thus, legal sanctions, while not an everyday affair, are not unknown in business.

One can conclude that while detailed planning and legal sanctions play a significant role in some exchanges between businesses, in many business exchanges their role is small.

4. *Annual Report of the Director of the Administrative Office of the United States Courts*, 1961, p. 238.

5. State of New York, The Judicial Conference, Sixth Annual Report' 1961, pp. 209–11.

6. My colleague Lawrence M. Freidman has studied the work of the Supreme Court of Wisconsin in contracts cases. He has found that contracts cases reaching that court tend to involve economically-marginal businesses and family economic disputes rather than important commercial transactions. This has been the situation since about the turn of the century. Only during the Civil War period did the court deal with significant numbers of important contracts cases, but this happened against the background of a much simpler and different economic system.

Tentative Explanations

Two questions need to be answered: (a) How can business successfully operate exchange relationships with relatively so little attention to detailed planning or to legal sanctions, and (b) Why does business ever use contract in light of its success without it?

Why are relatively non-contractual practises so common? In most situations contract is not needed. Often its functions are served by other devices. Most problems are avoided without resort to detailed planning or legal sanctions because usually there is little room for honest misunderstandings or good faith differences of opinion about the nature and quality of a seller's performance. Although the parties fail to cover all foreseeable contingencies, they will exercise care to see that both understand the primary obligation on each side. Either products are standardized with an accepted description or specifications are written calling for production to certain tolerances or results. Those who write and read specifications are experienced professionals who will know the customs of their industry and those of the industries with which they deal. Consequently, these customs can fill gaps in the express agreements of the parties. Finally, most products can be tested to see if they are what was ordered; typically in manufacturing industry we are not dealing with questions of taste or judgement where people can differ in good faith.

When defaults occur they are not likely to be disastrous because of techniques of risk avoidance or risk spreading. One can deal with firms of good reputation or he may be able to get some form of security to guarantee performance. One can insure against many breaches of contract where the risks justify the costs. Sellers set up reserves for bad debts on their books and can sell some of their accounts receivable. Buyers can place orders with two or more suppliers of the same item so that a default by one will not stop the buyer's assembly lines.

Moreover, contract and contract law are often thought unnecessary because there are many effective non-legal sanctions. Two norms are widely accepted. (1) Commitments are to be honored in almost all situations; one does not welsh on a deal.

(2) One ought to produce a good product and stand behind it. Then, too, business units are organized to perform commitments, and internal sanctions will induce performance. For example, sales personnel must face angry customers when there has been a late or defective performance. The salesmen do not enjoy this and will put pressure on the production personnel responsible for the default. If the production personnel default too often, they will be fired. At all levels of the two business units personal relationships across the boundaries of the two organizations exert pressures for conformity to expectations. Salesmen often know purchasing agents well. The same two individuals occupying these roles may have dealt with each other from five to twenty-five years. Each has something to give the other. Salesmen have gossip about competitors, shortages and price increases to give purchasing agents who treat them well. Salesmen take purchasing agents to dinner, and they give purchasing agents Christmas gifts hoping to improve the chances of making sale. The buyer's engineering staff may work with the seller's engineering staff to solve problems jointly. The seller's engineers may render great assistance, and the buyer's engineers may desire to return the favor by drafting specifications which only the seller can meet. The top executives of the two firms may know each other. They may sit together on government or trade committees. They may know each other socially and even belong to the same country club. The inter-relationships may be more formal. Sellers may hold stock in corporations which are important customers; buyers may hold stock in important suppliers. Both buyer and seller may share common directors on their boards. They may share a common financial institution which has financed both units.

The final type of non-legal sanction is the most obvious. Both business units involved in the exchange desire to continue success-fully in business and will avoid conduct which might interfere with attaining this goal. One is concerned with both the reaction of the other party in the particular exchange and with his own general business reputation. Obviously, the buyer gains sanctions in so far as the seller wants the particular exchange to be completed. Buyers can withhold part or all of their payments until sellers have performed to their satisfaction. If a seller has a great deal of money tied up in his performance which he must recover quickly, he will go a long way to please the buyer in order to be paid. Moreover, buyers who are dissatisfied may cancel and cause sellers to lose the cost of what they have done up to cancellation. Furthermore, sellers hope for repeat orders, and one gets few of these from unhappy customers. Some industrial buyers go so far as to formalize this sanction by issuing 'report cards' rating the performance of each supplier. The supplier rating goes to the top management of the seller organization, and these men can apply internal sanctions to salesmen, production supervisors or product designers if there are too many 'Ds' or 'Fs' on the report card.

While it is generally assumed that the customer is always right, the seller may have some counterbalancing sanctions against the buyer. The seller may have obtained a large downpayment from the buyer which he will want to protect. The seller may have an exclusive process which the buyer needs. The seller may be one of the few firms which has the skill to make the item to the tolerances set by the buyer's engineers and within the time available. There are costs and delays involved in turning from a supplier one has dealt with in the past to a new supplier. Then, too, market conditions can change so that a buyer is faced with shortages of critical items. The most extreme example is the post Second World War grey market conditions when sellers were rationing goods rather than selling them. Buyers must build up some reserve of goodwill with suppliers if they face the risk of such shortages and desire good treatment when they occur. Finally, there is reciprocity in buying and selling. A buyer cannot push a supplier too far if that supplier also buys significant quantities of the product made by the buyer.

Not only do the particular business units in a given exchange want to deal with each other again, they also want to deal with other business units in the future. And the way one behaves in a particular transaction, or a series of transactions, will color his general business reputation. Blacklisting can be formal or informal. Buyers who fail to pay their bills on time risk a bad report in credit rating services such as Dun and Bradstreet. Sellers who do not satisfy their customers become the subject of discussion in the gossip exchanged by purchasing agents and salesmen, at meetings of purchasing agents' associations and trade associations or even at country clubs or social gatherings where members of top management meet. The American male's habit of debating the merits of new cars carries over to industrial items. Obviously, a poor reputation does not help a firm make sales and may force it to offer great price discounts or added services to remain in business. Furthermore, the habits of unusually demanding buyers become known, and they tend to get no more than they can coerce out of suppliers who choose to deal with them. Thus often contract is not needed as there are alternatives.

Not only are contract and contract law not needed in many situations, their use may have, or may be thought to have, undesirable consequences. Detailed negotiated contracts can get in the way of creating good exchange relationships between business units. If one side insists on a detailed plan, there will be delay while letters are exchanged as the parties try to agree on what should happen if a remote and unlikely contingency occurs. In some cases they may not be able to agree at all on such matters and as a result a sale may be lost to the seller and the buyer may have to search elsewhere for an acceptable supplier. Many businessmen would react by thinking that had no one raised the series of remote and unlikely contingencies all this wasted effort could have been avoided.

Even where agreement can be reached at the negotiation stage, carefully planned arrangements may create undesirable exchange relationships between business units. Some businessmen object that in such a carefully worked out relationship one gets performance only to the letter of the contract. Such planning indicates a lack of trust and blunts the demands of friendship, turning a cooperative venture into an antagonistic horse trade. Yet the greater danger perceived by some businessmen is that one would have to perform his side of the bargain to its letter and thus lose what is called 'flexibility'. Businessmen may welcome a measure of vagueness in the obligations they assume so that they may negotiate matters in light of the actual circumstances.

Adjustment of exchange relationships and dispute settlement by litigation or the threat of it also has many costs. The gain anticipated from using this form of coercion often fails to outweigh these costs, which are both monetary and non-monetary. Threatening to turn matters over to an attorney may cost no more money than postage or a telephone call; yet few are so skilled in making such a threat that it will not cost some deterioration of the relationship between the firms. One businessman said that customers had better not rely on legal rights or threaten to bring a breach of contract law suit against him since he 'would not be treated like a criminal' and would fight back with every means available. Clearly actual litigation is even more costly than making threats. Lawyers demand substantial fees from larger business units. A firm's executives often will have to be transported and maintained in another city during the proceedings if, as often is the case, the trial must be held away from the home office. Top management does not travel by Greyhound and stay at the Y.M.C.A. Moreover, there will be the cost of diverting top management, engineers, and others in the organization from their normal activities. The firm may lose many days work from several key people. The non-monetary costs may be large too. A breach of contract law suit may settle a particular dispute, but such an action often results in a 'divorce' ending the 'marriage' between the two businesses, since a contract action is likely to carry charges with at least overtones of bad faith. Many executives, moreover, dislike the prospect of being cross-examined in public. Some executives may dislike losing control of a situation by turning the decision-making power over to lawyers. Finally, the law of contract damages may not provide an adequate remedy even if the firm wins the suit; one may get vindication but not much money.

Why do relatively contractual practises ever exist? Although contract is not needed and actually may have negative consequences, businessmen do make some carefully planned contracts, negotiate settlements influenced by their legal rights and commence and defend some breach of contract law suits or arbitration proceedings. In view of the findings and explanation presented to this point, one may ask why. Exchanges are carefully planned when it is thought that planning and a potential legal sanction will have more advantages than disadvantages. Such a judgement may be reached when contract planning serves the internal needs of an organization involved in a business exchange. For example, a fairly detailed contract can serve as a communication device within a large corporation. While the corporation's sales manager and house counsel may work out all the provisions with the customer, its production manager will have to make the product. He must be told what to do and how to handle at least the most obvious contingencies. Moreover, the sales manager may want to remove certain issues from future negotiation by his subordinates. If he puts the matter in the written contract, he may be able to keep his salesmen from making concessions to the customer without first consulting the sales manager. Then the sales manager may be aided in his battles with his firm's financial or engineering departments if the contract calls for certain practises which the sales manager advocates but which the other departments resist. Now the corporation is obligated to a customer to do what the sales manager wants to do; how can the financial or engineering departments insist on anything else?

Also one tends to find a judgement that the gains of contract outweigh the costs where there is a likelihood that significant problems will arise. One factor leading to this conclusion is complexity of the agreed performance over a long period. Another factor is whether or not the degree of injury in case of default is thought to be potentially great. This factor cuts two ways. First, a buyer may want to commit a seller to a detailed and legally binding contract, where the consequences of a default by the seller would seriously injure the buyer. For example, the airlines are subject to law suits from the survivors of passengers and to great adverse publicity as a result of crashes. One would expect the airlines to bargain for carefully defined and legally enforceable obligations on the part of the airframe manufacturers when they purchase aircraft. Second, a seller may want to limit his liability for a buyer's damages by a provision in their contract. For example, a manufacturer of air conditioning may deal with motels in the South and Southwest. If this equipment fails in the hot summer months a motel may lose a great deal of business. The manufacturer may wish to avoid any liability for this type of injury to his customers and may want a contract with a clear disclaimer clause.

Similarly, one uses or threatens to use legal sanctions to settle disputes when other devices will not work and when the gains are thought to outweigh the costs. For example, perhaps the most common type of business contracts case fought all the way through to the appellate courts today is an action for an alleged wrongful termination of a dealer's franchise by a manufacturer. Since the franchise has been terminated, factors such as personal relationships and the desire for future business will have little effect; the cancellation of the franchise indicates they have already failed to maintain the relationship. Nor will a complaining dealer worry about creating a hostile relationship between himself and the manufacturer. Often the dealer has suffered a great financial loss both as to his investment in building and equipment and as to his anticipated future profits. A cancelled automobile dealer's lease on his showroom and shop will continue to run, and his tools for servicing, say, Plymouths cannot be used to service other makes of cars. Moreover, he will have no more new Plymouths to sell. Today there is some chance of winning a law suit for terminating a franchise in bad faith in many states and in the federal courts. Thus, often the dealer chooses to risk the cost of a lawyer's fee because of the chance that he may recover some compensation for his losses.

An 'irrational' factor may exert some influence on the decision to use legal sanctions. The man who controls a firm may feel that he or his organization has been made to appear foolish or has been the victim of fraud or bad faith. The law suit may be seen as a vehicle 'to get even' although the potential gains, as viewed by an objective observer, are outweighed by the potential costs.

The decision whether or not to use contract – whether the gain exceeds the costs – will be made by the person within the business unit with the power to make it, and it tends to make a difference who he is. People in a sales department oppose contract. Contractual negotiations are just one more hurdle in the way of a sale. Holding a customer to the letter of a contract is bad for 'customer relations'. Suing a customer who is not bankrupt and might order again is poor strategy. Purchasing agents and their buyers are less hostile to contracts but regard attention devoted to such matters as a waste of time. In contrast, the financial control department – the treasurer, controller or auditor – leans toward more contractual dealings. Contract is viewed by these people as an organizing tool to control operations in a large organization. It tends to define precisely and to minimize the risks to which the firm is exposed. Outside lawyers – those with many clients – may share this enthusiasm for a more contractual method of dealing. These lawyers are concerned with preventive law – avoiding any possible legal difficulty. They see many unstable and unsuccessful exchange transactions, and so they are aware of, and perhaps overly concerned with, all of the things which can go wrong. Moreover, their job of settling disputes with legal sanctions is much easier if their client has not been overly casual about transaction planning. The inside lawyer, or house counsel, is harder to classify. He is likely to have some sympathy with a more contractual method of dealing. He shares the outside lawyer's 'craft urge' to see exchange transactions neat and tidy from a legal standpoint. Since he is more concerned with avoiding and settling disputes than selling goods, he is likely to be less willing to rely on a man's word as the sole sanction than is a salesman. Yet the house counsel is more a part of the organization and more aware of its goals and subject to its internal sanctions. If the potential risks are not too great, he may hesitate to suggest a more contractual procedure to the sales department. He must sell his services to the operating departments, and he must hoard what power he has, expending it on only what he sees as significant issues.

The power to decide that a more contractual method of creating relationships and settling disputes shall be used will be held by different people at different times in different organizations. In most firms the sales department and the purchasing department have a great deal of power to resist contractual procedures or to ignore them if they are formally adopted and to handle disputes their own way. Yet in larger organizations the treasurer and the controller have increasing power to demand both systems and compliance. Occasionally, the house counsel must arbitrate the conflicting positions of these departments; in giving 'legal advice' he may make the business judgement necessary regarding the use of contract. At times he may ask for an opinion from an outside law firm to reinforce his own position with the outside firm's prestige.

Part Four Judicial Behaviour

The statistical studies of court decisions and judicial opinion can be viewed as an attempt to test the empirical validity of the legal model of decision-making. The selections included here demonstrate that judicial personnel vary in their decisions also when confronted with similar cases. Schubert, following in the steps of Pritchett, shows from the point of view of a political scientist how dissents in the U.S. Supreme Court are linked to the ideological commitments of the justices. Kalven and Zeisel find the reasons for disagreements between judge and jury in general differences in outlook between professional jurists and laymen. Hood's study is more purely descriptive. Stone's comment raises philosophical and political issues arising out of the attempts to predict – or even to programme – judicial decisions.

19 Glendon Schubert

Judicial Policy-Making

Excerpts from Glendon Schubert, *The Political Role of the Courts: Judicial Policy-Making*, Scott, Foresman and Co., 1965, pp. 113–25.

The conversion structure is central in the judicial policy-making process. Conversion is the process by means of which issues are recognized and decided as a result of group interaction and the integration of the values of the individual justices. The conversion structure consists of the values of the individual justices and the issues – their shared perceptions about the policy and factual questions raised by cases before them for a decision. In a formal sense, conversion as a process occurs when individual justices cast their votes on the disposition of a case at the group conference; and strictly speaking, the subsequent announcement both of the voting division of the Court, and of the opinions of the Court and of individual justices, are among the *outputs* of the conversion process. Conversion consists, therefore, of both psychological and social processes. When each justice decides how he will vote, that is a psychological process; but when he announces his vote, in a fixed order of articulation, as a contributor to a group decision that depends upon an integration of the preferences of the individual participants, that is a social process. Analysis of the interrelation between individual decisions and the group decision in a case involves us in sociopsychological study. [. . .]

Although the values and issues are shared, the means by which each justice acquires his values is a very individual matter. An individual's values are a product of socialization, and his socialization experience results from a combination of chance considerations operating within the political culture in which he has been reared. Supreme Court justices acquire their values in part as a consequence of having been born into a particular family at a particular place and time; nationality, race, family, and early as well as later education all have some influence in building the political character of each justice, as do marriage, law school training, and subsequent professional experience. Table I presents a summary of three classes of judicial attributes (experience, appointing President, and partisan affiliation) and two classes of judicial values. Of course, it is not to be assumed that a mature man can be completely described by a handful of labels designated as 'attribute' or 'attitudinal' variables. His values, like his attributes, have been moulded by a lifetime of experience. Nevertheless, it is quite possible that when we ask why he votes as he does in a particular case or series of cases (raising, for him, the same policy issue), a small number of variables may approximate *what is most relevant about him* closely enough to be useful in analysing decision-making. If such a focusing of attention, for analytical purposes, were not possible, then we could say nothing of scientific value about the causes of the behavior of judges (or of any other complex living organisms, for that matter).

A tabulation such as that of Table I illustrates some of the kinds of relationships that are investigated in studies of the effect of socialization upon judicial policy-making. This table implies a set of hypotheses about the relationship among the attribute variables (i.e., appointing President and partisan affiliation), or between an attribute variable and one or both of the attitudinal variables. The sample of data presented in this table, which relates only to the justices incumbent during the 1963 term, is too small for any statistically significant relationships to be apparent; but studies of larger samples of judges indicate that there are meaningful and important correlations among these (and similar) attribute variables and these (and other) attitudinal variables (Nagel, 1962, and Schmidhauser, 1962).

Attributes

Supreme Court justices invariably have been white males, whose average age (at the time of appointment) has ranged from forty-seven to fifty-seven years of age. Nine out of ten (86 per cent) have been of British ethnic origin, and of the others only two (Cardozo, Iberian; Goldberg, Slavic) were not descended from emigrants from north-western Europe; no Asians, Africans, or

Table 1
Status, Selected Attributes, and Attitudinal Orientations of Supreme Court Justices (1963 term)

Seniority status	Name	Major legal and/or political experience	Appointed by:	Political party affiliation	Attitudinal orientation	
					Political	Economic
1	Warren	SA (governor, state attorney general)	Eisenhower	Rep.	Liberal	Liberal
2	Black	SJ NL (municipal judge, US senator)	Roosevelt	Dem.	Liberal	Liberal
3	Douglas	P. NA (law professor, chairman of S.E.C.)	Roosevelt	Dem.	Liberal	Liberal
4	Clark	NA (U.S. Attorney General)	Truman	Dem.	Conservative	Moderate
5	Harlan	P. NJ (corporation lawyer: U.S. circuit judge for 1 year)	Eisenhower	Rep.	Conservative	Conservative
6	Brennan	SJ (state judge)	Eisenhower	Dem.	Liberal	Liberal
7	Stewart	P. NJ (corporation lawyer: U.S. circuit judge for 2 years)	Eisenhower	Rep.	Moderate	Conservative
8	White	NA (U.S. Deputy Attorney General)	Kennedy	Dem.	Conservative	Moderate
9	Goldberg	P. NA (union lawyer : U.S. Secretary of Labour)	Kennedy	Dem.	Liberal	Moderate

*Key to abbreviations for experience categories
P=private N=national S=state A=administrative J=judicial
L=legislative

even Italians ever have been appointed to the Supreme Court. Nine out of ten (88 per cent) have been Protestant; during the first century of the Court's existence, only one Catholic (Taney) was appointed out of a total of fifty justices, and although one Jew was offered a nomination to the Court, none was appointed prior to 1916; among the forty-four appointees since 1890 there have been five more Catholics and four Jews. Among the eighty-three Protestants, about nine out of ten (86 per cent) were affiliated with high social-status denominations (Episcopalian, Presbyterian, Unitarian, Congregational). During the first few decades after the establishment of the Court, most justices were born into the landed aristocracy; since then, they have been drawn primarily from the professional upper middle classes. As a group, they have been exceptionally well educated (in relation to the standards of the period in which they served), even in terms of non-legal education; five sixths of them either attended a law school of high standing or studied as an apprentice under a prominent lawyer or judge. Moreover, they were born into politically active families, as a consequence of which the justices, as young men, were both encouraged and aided in their own quests for political careers (Schmidhauser, 1959, pp. 22–3). [. . .]

Table I shows that only one of the incumbent justices (Brennan) was affiliated with a political party different from that of the President who appointed him. One out of nine is about the usual proportion of 'nonpartisan' appointees; there have been eleven other instances, and during the half century spanned by the Taft and Eisenhower administrations, every President (with the solitary exception of Coolidge) crossed party lines in at least one of his appointments to the Court. But the usual practise has recognized that Supreme Court positions are among the most important sources of patronage available to an administration. Presidents expect to advance preferred policy goals in making such appointments, and a record of political party or administrative (and, as Schmidhauser has argued, of prior judicial [Schmidhauser, 1959, pp. 41–4, 47]) service provides what are assumed to be important clues to the ideological orientation of appointees. Nagel has demonstrated that, in general, Republican justices have supported the use of judicial review of national statutes when the effect has been to advance economic conservatism, while Democratic justices have supported judicial review when the effect has been to further political liberalism (Nagel, 1963, p. 340). Moreover many of the justices have remained so intensely involved in the liberal-conservative ideological struggle that they have not hesitated to attempt to influence Presidents who were in the process of selecting new colleagues for them; indeed, for a justice to behave otherwise is politically irrational. [. . .]

Interaction and Leadership

There is consensus among many scholars using different methods of analysis that the justices of the Supreme Court, at least during the past four decades (upon which research thus far has tended to focus), have been divided consistently into subsets of relatively liberal justices and of relatively conservative justices, with one or more moderate justices who have given consistent support to neither of the more extreme groups of ideological partisans (Pritchett, 1941 and 1948; Thurstone and Degan, 1951; Bernard, 1955; Snyder, 1958; Schubert, 1959, pp. 77–172; Ulmer, 1960; Schubert, 1965). During the middle 1930s, for example, there was a liberal subgroup consisting of Brandeis, Cardozo and Stone; a conservative subgroup consisting of Butler, McReynolds, Sutherland and Van Devanter; and two justices, Hughes and Roberts, who gave somewhat greater support to the conservative bloc *before*, and to the liberal bloc *after*, President Roosevelt's attack on the Court in February 1937. During the 1940s, the liberal bloc consisted of Black, Douglas, Murphy and Rutledge; the conservatives included Vinson, Burton and Reed; while the other two justices, Frankfurter and Jackson, were even more conservative than the Vinson group on economic issues but more liberal than the Vinson group on issues of civil liberty. (As Table I indicates.) The 1963 Court again contained a bloc of four liberals; but the retirement (at the end of 1961) of Frankfurter and Whittaker left only one consistent conservative, Harlan. Of the other four incumbent justices, Stewart was a moderate on civil liberty issues but a conservative on economic issues; Goldberg was a liberal on civil liberty issues but a moderate on economic issues; and Clark and White were conservative on civil liberty issues but moderate on economic issues. [. . .]

217

Certain aspects of the role of the Chief Justice thrust him into a position of formal leadership. Among the most important of his formal functions that facilitate his leadership of the group is his assignment of the opinion of the Court. (The Chief Justice makes this assignment when he votes with the majority; if he dissents, then the senior associate justice voting with the majority determines who will write the opinion.) The assignment to speak for the Court can be used to stake out a relatively extreme policy position, as when Warren has Douglas or Black write in a pro-civil liberty decision; but when such a decision is five to four, the opinion is likely to be assigned to the moderate judge who is the marginal member of the majority, because to do otherwise might result in losing the majority and hence control over the decision.

Recent research indicates that it is useful to distinguish between two kinds of group leadership: 'task' and 'social' (Danelski, 1961). In leading the justices through the decision-making of the weekly conference, for example, one essential function is to get decisions made, so that the Court will not fall so far behind in its docket that criticism from outside will be attracted. To get decisions made, group discussion must be focused and to some extent limited, and this requires task leadership. But the discussion involves nine men – a relatively large 'small group' – all of whom are quite independent of each other in their life tenure and among whom there are complex patterns of relationships of ideological affinity and conflict, depending upon the issue under discussion. Their attitudes toward public policy issues tend to be reinforced by their attitudes toward each other: some are close personal friends, and others are involved in what at times have been notorious 'feuds'. In other words, social leadership is necessary to control the level of emotional relationships in the discussions if decision-making is to proceed in an efficient manner.

Some Chief Justices, such as Hughes, have been outstanding in both leadership roles. Others have done well in one role and poorly in the other. Taft, for example, was a good social leader, but he depended upon Van Devanter to function as the effective foreman in constructing the Court's majorities for decision-making. Stone, on the other hand, was so much a democrat that he was not an effective task leader, and he was so much an ideological partisan that he was also ineffective in the social leadership role. An analysis of the level of consensus in the Court's decision-making under all seven of the Chief Justices between 1888–1958 has demonstrated that the justices were more deeply and variously divided in their voting under Stone than at any other time during the seven decades (Ulmer, 1961a). Efficiency in getting decisions made, however, is not the only relevant standard of effective leadership, nor is it necessarily the best criterion. It has been argued that in comparison with Hughes' autocratic management, Stone encouraged full and open discussion of the issues. If a major aspect of the Supreme Court's role is to educate its audience, then open articulation of value and policy disagreements among the justices is preferable to their being smothered under a spurious mantle of togetherness and contrived consensus (Schubert, 1960, pp. 123–5; Frank, 1957, p. 629n).

Attitudes

Sociometric analysis of interagreement in voting behavior, which focused upon a pool of all of the votes of all of the justices, in cases decided on the merits during a stipulated period, showed (as reported above) that the Court characteristically divided into a liberal bloc and a conservative bloc. But bloc analysis also showed that there were usually some justices who did not seem to affiliate with either bloc, and there seemed to be a considerable amount of inconsistent voting, even among the bloc members – inconsistent, that is, in the sense that in some decisions one or more justices would vote with members of the 'opposing' bloc rather than with members of their own bloc. The latter findings were perplexing, and it was not until the introduction of more powerful research tools that they were understood. At first through linear cumulative scaling and subsequently through factor analysis and multidimensional scaling, studies of the voting behavior of Supreme Court justices have shown that there are three major attitudinal components of judicial liberalism and conservatism. In order better to distinguish among them, we shall henceforth refer to the three components as 'attitudes', and we shall designate as 'ideologies' the more general concepts of liberalism and conservatism.

The three major attitudes are (1) *political* liberalism and conservatism; (2) *economic* liberalism and conservatism; and (3) *social* liberalism and conservatism (Ulmer, 1961b, pp. 195–204 [the political scale]; Spaeth, 1963, pp. 79–108, especially pp. 79–84 [the economic scale]; Schubert, 1962a, pp. 90–107, especially pp. 97–101 [both the political scale and the economic scale]). Here it is sufficient to say that political liberalism is the belief in and the support of civil rights and liberties; political conservatism is the upholding of law and order and the defense of the *status quo* – no matter what may be the pattern of accepted values that the *status quo* happens to represent. Economic liberalism is the belief in and the support of a more equal distribution of wealth, goods, and services; the economic conservative defends private enterprise, vested interests, and broad differentials in wealth and income between the owners of property and laborers. A social liberal is a person who is liberal in both of the other two attitudes and who therefore upholds individual personal rights (political liberalism) but collective property rights (economic liberalism); a social conservative upholds collective personal rights but individual property rights. The social liberal favors change – disequilibrium – in regard to both personal and property rights; the social conservative favors the *status quo* – homeostasis – in regard to both. It is easy to see, however, that it is quite possible for a judge to feel that he is being consistent in his ideology if he favors political liberalism and economic conservatism, for this combination of attitudes means to uphold both the personal and the property rights of the individual. Similarly, a justice who consistently upholds the necessarily collectivized interests represented by the government will be politically conservative and economically liberal in his attitudes.

Let us assume that the attitude of social liberalism defines a position that is the core of a broader range of attitudes extending from political liberalism through economic liberalism, which together span the range of the liberal ideology (see Figure 1). Similarly, we can define an opposing conservative ideology. The range from economic conservatism to political liberalism defines the ideology of individualism; the opposite range defines collectivism.

We find Supreme Court justices in all four categories of

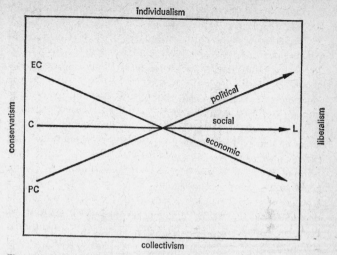

Figure 1. A Paradigm of the relationship between Judicial types and Output Norms.

ideological type: some are liberals, some are conservatives, some are individualists, some are collectivists. Among the incumbents, we can see from Table I that there are four liberals (Douglas, Black, Warren, and Brennan), one conservative (Harlan), two individualists (Goldberg and Stewart), and two collectivists (Clark and White). None of the last four justices fits the ideological types perfectly – Goldberg, Clark, and White because of their economic moderation, and Stewart because of his political moderation.

The attitudinal issues to which the justices respond are not necessarily manifest in either their opinions or the records of the cases. *Prima facie*, for example, no question of law is raised for decision by the Court when it reviews the decisions of lower courts (state or national) in Federal Employers' Liability Act evidentiary cases. The statutory law, presumably, is clear, or at least, to the extent that it is not, it was clarified long ago by interpretative decisions of the Supreme Court. The question at issue always is whether, given the unique set of facts that have been 'found' by the trial court in the particular case, the evidence of employer

221

negligence was sufficient to support a jury verdict of damages in favor of the injured railroad worker.

Conservative critics have castigated the Court throughout the past decade for its perverse persistence in wasting its time in hearing such appeals; the precious time of the Court, the critics insist, should be reserved for the decision of more important policy issues. (As Frankfurter again and again reminded his colleagues, it is not their role to play God; they cannot note the fall of every sparrow and attempt to correct all the mistakes of judgement of lower courts – if, indeed, they be mistakes.) But the issue is not exclusively 'what really happened when the employee was injured'; the latent policy issue is: who should bear the economic costs of industrial accidents, when the system for allocation consists of a right to a lawsuit instead of a workmen's compensation schedule? Should the economic as well as the physical injury be borne exclusively by the worker (or his widowed family), or should at least the economic cost be collectively shared? Of course, the Supreme Court has no 'legal right' to decide any such question, since the Congress presumably answered it primarily in the negative when it enacted the statute more than half a century ago. Consequently, the opinions of the justices tend to be confined to ostensibly legal questions of 'contributory negligence' and the 'weight of the evidence'. Nevertheless, the latent question, which taps the justices' attitudes and to which they respond in their voting, is: where do your basic sympathies lie – with economic underdogs or with their employers? In case after case, no matter what the variation in the 'facts', economic liberals vote to uphold the claims of workers, and economic conservatives vote against them (Schubert, 1962b).

Prediction

In analysing the prediction of judicial decision-making, it is possible to work with various classes of variables. The broadest and most diffuse class consists of 'The Political Environment'. The cultural variables define the range of variation for attribute variables, which include the kinds of personal background factors discussed above. Attributes, in turn, affect attitudes, which determine decisions. We expect, therefore, that prediction will be most likely to succeed between adjacent classes of variables: between cultural and attribute variables; between attribute and either cultural or attitudinal variables; between attitudinal and either attribute or decisional variables; and between decisional and attitudinal variables. This implies that the prediction of judicial decision-making behavior will be most successful if it is based upon the observation and measurement of judicial attitudes.

In their search for rationality in decision-making, lawyers have sought to find it in the patterns of policy norms, in the decisions and opinions that are the outputs of the conversion process (see Llewellyn, 1960; Wasserstrom, 1961). One of the problems that they have encountered is that the norms appear to be continuously in flux, no doubt reflecting changes both in the composition of the Court and in the socio-economic bases of the issues presented to it. There is a high degree of rationality in judicial decision-making, but it consists primarily of the *psychological* rationality of consistency in the structuring of attitudes in the minds of individual judges, rather than of the *logical* rationality of consistency in the structuring of the rationalizations for outcomes found in their written opinions. If judges did decide present cases in particular ways *because* their predecessors have so decided 'similar' cases, then the principle of *stare decisis* would explain the conversion process. We should not then need to be concerned about judges' personal beliefs and individual attitudes, which would, in any event, be irrelevant to the outcomes of decisions and therefore to the outputs of courts. If this were true, *stare decisis* ought to operate, of course, only in phase with a 'natural' chronology – that is, judges ought to decide present cases on the basis of past precedents; we should not expect to find them deciding cases, at some time in the past, on the basis of future 'precedent' decisions that have not yet been established! Nevertheless, the recent work of a scholar who was seeking to validate – to prove that judges really do follow – the principle of *stare decisis* shows that in several different policy areas and with different courts, it was possible for him to predict the outcomes of decisions just as well (and in some instances, better) working *backwards* rather than *forwards* through time (Kort, 1963, pp. 133–97, especially pp. 177–8). In short, the 'legal precedents' could be predicted just as well from the 'future decisions' as the latter from the former. What this suggests, of course, is that the underlying consistency was very high but that this consistency was in the attitudes of the judicial decision-makers toward the policy issues, not in cause-and-effect relationships among either the decisions or the output norms that the decisions are presumed to imply.

Attempts to improve the accuracy with which outcomes can be predicted have constituted an important research activity in recent years. Naturally, this is a question of considerable interest to, and with important practical consequences for, practising lawyers. The usual approach to prediction of outcomes, which is highly qualitative and intensely personal and subjective, is well illustrated by the success with which a Yale law professor predicted the outcome in the Supreme Court's first major reapportionment decision, *Baker* v. *Carr* (Rodell, 1962, pp. 707-8). With this should be compared, however, the equally successful prediction, by a practising lawyer who made his forecast using Boolean algebra and a computer (Lawlor, 1963, pp. 337-44, especially pp. 343-4), of a recent major civil rights decision of the Court (*Gideon* v. *Wainwright*, 372 U.S. 335 (1963)). The important difference between these two types of prediction is that the latter represents a technique that is communicable and transferable to other researchers and that can be replicated by them; the former does not. In the same research, the computer analyst found it necessary to distinguish among what he designated as three different types of *stare decisis*: traditional, local, and personal. By traditional *stare decisis* he meant the obligation of a lower court to follow the policy norms output by a higher court, or the obligation of the Supreme Court to follow its own precedents; by local *stare decisis* he meant the obligation of one panel of a court of appeals to follow the precedents established by other panels of the same court; and by personal *stare decisis* he meant the consistency of the individual justices with their own earlier voting behavior on similar issues. Evidently, in his analysis of personal *stare decisis* he was measuring the consistency of the attitudes of individual justices toward the defined sub-issue of political liberalism. His attempt to predict the Supreme Court's decision in *Gideon* v. *Wainwright* on the basis of traditional *stare decisis* was unsuccessful; but when he programmed his computer in terms of the personal attitudes of the then incumbent justices of the Supreme Court, he did very well indeed.

The research on outcomes focuses upon the particular decisions in individual cases; a different but at least as important recent emphasis has been upon statistical prediction – that is, upon sets of aggregate outcomes, which characterize the Court's decision-making behavior in grosser but more comprehensive terms than does the prediction of individual case outcomes. One such study has analysed the Supreme Court's jurisdictional decision-making in order to specify the attributes of cases that the Court is most likely to accept for decision-making on the merits (Tannenhaus, Schick, Muraskin and Rosen, 1963). Another recent venture attempted, with only partial success, to extrapolate from various quantitative indices of the Court's output in several recent terms to the equivalent indices for the term that was then getting under way (Schubert, 1963, pp. 137–42, and 1964, pp. 579–87). The most fruitful and probably the most fundamental work done to date, however, has been the prediction of pattern relationships in voting behavior on the basis of the assumption of stability in individual attitudes. The rank-order relationships of the justices, on scales of political and economic liberalism, are highly stable from term to term. As techniques for the analysis of the content of issue inputs become more refined, it may be possible to predict both the outcomes and other aspects of the decision-making behavior of the Supreme Court (and of other courts as well) on a systematic basis and with considerable accuracy. Prediction would thus serve to validate the construction of theory about judicial behavior, which in turn might have important implications for understanding the behavior of persons other than judges.

References

BERNARD, J. (1955), 'Dimensions and axes of Supreme Court decisions: a study in the sociology of conflict', *Social Forces*, vol. 34, pp. 19–27.

DANELSKI, D. J. (1961), 'The influence of the Chief Justice in the decisional process', in W. F. Murphy and C. H. Pritchett (eds.), *Courts, Judges and Politics*, Random House, pp. 497–508.

FRANK, J. P. (1957), 'Harlan Fiske Stone: an estimate', *Stanford Law Review*, vol. 9.

KORT, F. (1963), 'What computers can do: analysis and prediction of judicial decisions', *American Bar Association Journal*, vol. 49.

LAWLOR, R. C. (1963), 'What computers can do: analysis and prediction of judicial decisions', *American Bar Association Journal*, vol. 49, pp. 337–43.

LLEWELLYN, K. N. (1960), *The Common-Law Tradition: Deciding Appeals*, Little, Brown and Co.

NAGEL, S. S. (1962), 'Judicial backgrounds and criminal cases', *Journal of Criminal Law, Criminology, and Police Science*, vol. 53, pp. 333–9.

NAGEL, S. S. (1963), 'Political parties and judicial review in American history', *Journal of Public Law*, vol. 11.

PRITCHETT, C. H. (1941), 'Division of opinion among Justices of the United States Supreme Court, 1939–41', *American Political Science Review*, vol. 35, pp. 990–98.

PRITCHETT, C. H. (1948), *The Roosevelt Court: A Study in Judicial Politics and Values, 1937–47*, Macmillan.

RODELL, F. (1962), 'For every justice, judicial deference is a sometime thing', *Georgetown Law Journal*, vol. 50.

SCHUBERT, G. (1959), *Quantitative Analysis of Judicial Behavior*, The Free Press of Glencoe.

SCHUBERT, G. (1960), *Constitutional Politics*, Holt, Rinehart and Winston, Inc.

SCHUBERT, G. (1962a), 'The 1960 term of the Supreme Court: a psychological analysis', *American Political Science Review*, vol. 56.

SCHUBERT, G. (1962b), 'Policy without law: an extension of the Certiorari Game', *Stanford Review*, vol. 14, pp. 284–327.

SCHUBERT, G. (1963), 'Judicial attitudes and voting behavior: the 1961 term of the United States Supreme Court', *Law and Contemporary Problems*, vol. 28, pp. 100–142.

SCHUBERT, G. (1964), *Judicial Behavior*, Rand McNally.

SCHUBERT, G. (1965), *The Judicial Mind: The Attitudes and Ideologies of Supreme Court Justices, 1946–1963*, Northwestern University Press.

SCHMIDHAUSER, J. R. (1959), 'The Justices of the Supreme Court: a collective portrait', *Midwest Journal of Political Science*, vol. 3.

SCHMIDHAUSER, J. R. (1962), '*Stare decisis*, dissent, and the background of the Justices of the Supreme Court of the United States', *University of Toronto Law Journal*, vol. 14, pp. 194–212.

SNYDER, E. C. (1958), 'The Supreme Court as a small group', *Social Forces*, vol. 36, pp. 232–8.

SPAETH, H. J. (1963), 'Warren Court attitudes toward business: the "13" scale', in G. Schubert (ed.), *Judicial Decision-Making*, The Free Press of Glencoe.

TANENHAUS, J., SCHICK, M., MURASKIN, M., and ROSEN, D. (1963), 'The Supreme Court's certiorari jurisdiction: cue theory', in G. Schubert (ed.), *Judicial Decision-Making*, The Free Press of Glencoe, pp. 111–32.

THURSTONE, L. L., and DEGAN, J. W. (1951), 'A factrial study of the

Supreme Court, *Proceedings of the National Academy of Science*, vol. 37, pp. 628–35.

ULMER, S. S. (1960), 'The analysis of behavior patterns on the United States Supreme Court', *Journal of Politics*, vol. 22, pp. 629–53.

ULMER, S. S. (1961a), 'Homeostatic tendencies in the United States Supreme Court', in S. S. Ulmer (ed.), *Introductory Readings in Political Behavior*, Rand McNally, pp. 167–88.

ULMER, S. S. (1961b), 'A note on attitudinal consistency in the United States Supreme Court', *Indian Journal of Political Science*, vol. 22.

WASSERSTROM, R. A. (1961), *The Judicial Decision: Toward a Theory of Legal Justification*, Stanford University Press.

20 Roger Hood

Sentencing in Magistrates' Courts

Excerpt from Roger Hood, *Sentencing in Magistrates' Courts*, Stevens and Sons, 1962, pp. 118–27.

The detailed examination of the samples of offenders taken at the courts, and the consideration of the characteristics of communities and benches, has thrown some interesting light on the nature of the sentencing policies at magistrates' courts.

A summary of the main findings of this research is presented in the first part of this excerpt. The final section will discuss some conclusions which emerge about the way in which imprisonment is used; and some of the factors which are most likely to act as barriers to any attempt to reform the policies of the courts.

Summary

1. There are large disparities in the proportions of men aged twenty-one and over convicted of indictable offences who are imprisoned by different borough courts.

2. The courts which have the greatest disparities between their imprisonment rates have some differences in the types of offenders appearing before them. However, there are no consistent differences in the distributions of various characteristics of offenders between *all* courts with a high imprisonment rate (over 30 per cent) and the two with a low rate (under 15 per cent). Any variations, therefore, in the types of offenders appearing before these courts are not highly correlated with variations in the use of imprisonment.

3. The courts with similar imprisonment rates have, on the whole, offenders with similar distributions of characteristics appearing before them.

4. It was examined whether there were any differences between the types of men actually imprisoned by different courts.

Any variations in the proportions of men with certain characteristics (for example, with long criminal records), did not account for the differences in the imprisonment rates between Highness, Selbury, and Regbury on the one hand and the courts in Group D on the other. The proportion of men imprisoned at each court was compared with the proportion with similar characteristics imprisoned out of the total sample. This analysis showed that the courts in Group A consistently imprisoned far more offenders than could be explained by the types of men appearing before them; Railton and Oldchester far fewer than could be expected. But the courts in Group A used imprisonment more frequently for all types of offenders, and not simply for those with bad records. Offenders were imprisoned at these courts who would have received a different sentence at most other courts in the sample. At the other extreme, Railton and Oldchester failed to imprison offenders who would most likely have been imprisoned elsewhere. Only at Selbury was the high imprisonment rate explained by the types of offenders with which the magistrates had to deal.

5. The courts imprisoning similar proportions of offenders, in the main, imprison only those who share certain characteristics (the great majority had relatively long criminal records, had unsteady work habits, or had been charged with more than one offence). There is some evidence here, at least of 'equality of consideration'. This does not mean, however, that all men possessing any of these characteristics were imprisoned. It is clear that many men with similar backgrounds received an alternative sentence.

6. The imprisonment policies of the magistrates appear to be related to the social characteristics of the area they serve, the social constitution of the bench, and its particular view of the crime problem: factors which are themselves highly associated. The last of these factors may well in general be the most important, but in cases where there is a particularly high imprisonment rate the areas have similar social compositions and benches with comparable social backgrounds. Other courts with comparable communities and benches with similar social backgrounds (Ashlake and Tolville) have magistrates who clearly differ in their attitudes to short-term imprisonment. There is some evidence

in favour of the hypothesis that middle-class magistrates dealing with working-class offenders, in relatively small and stable middle-class communities, are likely to be relatively severe. The material at least gives an indication that the type of community served by the court, and the social composition of the bench, may influence sentencing policy. A study of the crime rates of the areas showed no consistent connexion between this factor and sentencing policy, although the most lenient courts had the highest crime rate (by one measure).

7. Two of the four courts using imprisonment in over 30 per cent of cases also impose longer sentences than other courts. Only three courts imprisoning under 30 per cent sent more men to the sessions for sentence than the courts in Groups A and B.

8. On the whole, little use is made of probation for adult offenders, but there are considerable variations between the extent to which orders are made. Perhaps surprisingly, there is no correlation between the use of imprisonment by courts and their use of probation: Selbury in Group B makes the most orders, Railton in Group D almost the least, but other variations are more randomly distributed among the courts. The probation service also appeared to be used infrequently for making pre-sentence inquiries. In some courts the tradition that probation is only for juveniles is still strong. Where probation officers are consistently dealing with juveniles they have little chance to build up a relationship of confidence with the magistrates in the adult court. But probation is a personal service. In small boroughs much will probably depend on the personal qualities and contacts of the individual officer.

9. There are large variations in the use made of fines. This method of dealing with offenders is in many courts the main alternative to imprisonment. The courts using imprisonment the least, and fines the most, do not impose more severe fines than the courts using imprisonment most frequently.

10. There are few differences between the cases chosen for probation and those for conditional discharge. Some courts using probation infrequently use discharges as the alternative. Absolute discharge is ordered only for the least serious cases.

11. The analysis of indecent assault on young children under sixteen suffered from the small number of cases in the sample

when comparisons were made between courts. All courts were as severe, or more severe, with indecent assault cases than they were with larceny cases. Probation was used more frequently, and fines were heavier. As with the larceny cases, the courts using imprisonment most were not less severe in the sentences which they passed, and the courts using fines most did not impose fines of larger amounts.

Conclusions

The use of imprisonment

The research has shown that some courts are using prison sentences far more frequently than are others and that this cannot be fully explained by the fact that they have a larger proportion of men appearing before them who are more likely to be imprisoned by *any* court. On the other hand, there are other courts which imprison far fewer men than can be explained by the type of offender coming before them. The great majority of the courts, however, imprison a proportion of men somewhere between these limits, and a small sample of these courts has shown that they imprison similar types of men. The courts with the high imprisonment rates imprison some offenders who have characteristics which would not make them liable for imprisonment if they were dealt with by courts in Groups C or D.

There is no evidence to show that short-term imprisonment meets with more success (i.e. non-reconviction) than does fining or probation for the majority of offenders. In any case it is doubtful whether many magistrates know to what extent their sentences have been a 'success' or a 'failure'. The Advisory Council on the Treatment of Offenders in the publication *Alternatives to Short Terms of Imprisonment* states that in a 'substantial number of cases a short term of imprisonment does no good and may do some harm' (H.M.S.O., 1957, p. 4). It seems that a higher proportion of such cases is likely to be found among those committed by the courts which use imprisonment most frequently. On the other hand the short sentence as such cannot be completely condemned; there may be cases where it appears inevitable. Possibly the two courts which use imprisonment very infrequently should use it more often. At least one of these courts

231

was criticized by the police and press because of its leniency. But where courts were using imprisonment as frequently as in about 20 per cent of the cases there was no evidence to suggest that there was any feeling of uneasiness in the community or widespread criticism of the bench. It seems reasonable to suppose that the courts with the high imprisonment rates could make their policy more lenient without causing very much of a local stir if they so wished. There is no evidence to show, in fact, that very much interest is taken in the day-to-day activities of the local bench, especially in the larger towns.

In the absence of any theoretical framework or empirical evidence to suggest that any other method of dealing with particular types of offenders is just as successful as imprisonment, we cannot make any general recommendations. However, the little use made of probation suggests that more experiments in this direction could be tried. It is possible that a choice of punishment or treatment would be made easier for the court if more information was made available about the defendant through the more frequent use by courts of their powers to order inquiries.

There is little doubt that the courts which use imprisonment relatively frequently, have in many instances no reason to do so, if the experience of other courts is any criterion. In using imprisonment frequently, and perhaps unnecessarily, harm may be done by giving the offender contact with other criminals. Resentment may also be roused where an offender can read that others, with similar offences and records to his own, have not been imprisoned. Also, prisoners from the four courts in the sample which imprisoned over 30 per cent of offenders are sent to prisons to which committals are made by courts which imprison much less frequently. The fact that prisoners from three of these former courts had better records than those committed from the other courts may be an additional source of resentment to some men (see Jayne, 1956).

Equality of treatment may be desirable from the point of view of reclaiming offenders, but it is also a problem in moral and legal philosophy. It is evident that some offenders' chances of being imprisoned are far higher in certain parts of the country than in others. Admittedly, the type of community is a legitimate factor to take into consideration. However, it has yet to be proved that differences in local attitudes are so large and potent that they necessitate wide disparities in sentencing policies.

Basic hindrances to reform of sentencing policy

Two basic hindrances to gaining more equality in sentencing practices emerged from this study. One lies in the differences in the attitudes of the justices themselves; the other, in the difficulty of reaching more consistent decisions.

The first difficulty is due to variations in the philosophy of punishment held by justices and in their belief in the abilities of particular methods of treatment or punishment to achieve the results desired. It could be that differences in sentencing policy are not so much a reflection of opposing views on the aims of punishment, but a reflection of different beliefs on how to achieve these aims. One court may think that deterrence can only be achieved by imprisonment; another may think that a similar aim can be reached just as well through the imposition of a fine. The fact that courts which use imprisonment least do not use probation shows that the main emphasis in sentencing at these courts is still upon punitive measures. The court using probation most frequently is also one which makes ample use of imprisonment: these two measures are clearly not incompatible. It is impossible to judge these differing viewpoints. It has yet to be proved that one method of treatment is more likely to reach a desired end than another.

Other difficulties include the influence of one magistrate, or small group of magistrates, on the court's policy; the infrequency of meetings and the splitting into groups; the influence of tradition, including the system of training; and the attitude towards permissive legislation, especially section 14 of the Magistrates' Courts Act. It has been shown that in some courts the Chairman sits regularly and has a great deal of influence in the sentencing decisions of the court; because of the practice made of not retiring for deliberation in a number of cases, it may be difficult for the other members of the bench to make their opinions known. In view of the stress that is placed upon the value of experience, magistrates of long standing may have a disproportionate say in the decisions of the court, and their personal attitudes and opinions may hold too great a sway. In some other courts the rota system leads to the individual magistrate becoming identified with one particular group which sits together regularly but which has little contact with other groups. This means that there may be considerable day-to-day or week-to-week variations in sentences, and little agreement reached between the total body of justices about the type of sentences which should be imposed. It is not suggested of course that a rigid scale should be made out, but just that a decision should be made on the circumstances which should be present before imprisonment is imposed.

Traditional practices sometimes appear to hamper any change in policy. The method of training justices by placing them under the 'tutorship' of a chairman, who is supposedly endowed with greater insight, means that only the non-conformist magistrate with strong views will attempt to alter radically the policy of the bench. The use of probation is an example of the influence of the traditional element. In the areas where little use is made of the service it is largely looked upon as an agency which should help the juveniles; the service has always been connected with the juvenile court, and little effort has been made to introduce its benefits for the treatment of adult offenders. Probation is a personal service, and so quite naturally the personal element is a strong factor in influencing the use made of it. However, the initial stimulus must come from the justices; for in the areas where probation is mainly used for younger offenders the officer has no chance to build up a strong relationship of confidence with the magistrates sitting in the adult court. They must provide the initial stimulus by using the service more frequently, even if only for the purpose of making inquiries. When this has been done it is certainly true that much will depend upon the personality and work of the officer in encouraging the justices to make further experiments with probation. If the probation officer at a small court is well known in the borough and mixes socially with the justices it seems that the service is likely to benefit. In the large cities, however, where each probation officer cannot possibly be known by the many justices, the main factor may well be that of the 'probation-mindedness' of the magistrates. This was also certainly true of the stipendiary magistrates. In one city the probation department was efficient and the chief officers well known, but the service little used for

adults, whereas in another a change in the person of the stipendiary brought about a rapid increase in the use of probation
without any alteration in the efficiency of the service having first
taken place.

The inertia in making use of permissive legislation can be seen
in the very small number of cases into which inquiries are made
at all but one of the courts. It is a lesson of social history that
very little is done when permissive legislation is passed. The
bodies which act are those few which are more progressive, but
the majority do nothing. This happened in the period between
1907 and 1925, when, in the words of the *Handbook of Probation*,
there was 'ample evidence that many courts were failing to
avail themselves of the facilities given them by the existing law,
and made no attempt to appoint probation officers' (Le Mesurier,
1935, p. 27), and such appointments had to be made mandatory
by the Criminal Justice Act, 1925. This is what may have happened
in recent years with the sections of the Criminal Justice Act,
1948, and the Magistrates' Courts Act, 1952, which empower the
courts to remand cases in order for inquiries to be made. In the
experience of this study inquiries were made usually only to
make sure that an officer considered the defendant suitable for
probation. Most magistrates appeared to think that decisions
could be made perfectly well with the minimum amount of
information about the offender. This may be the case if their
only consideration is deterrence, but it may be desirable for
sentencing policy to keep more in line with the ideas embodied in
the Criminal Justice Act, 1948, and in such Government publications as the Advisory Council's report, *Alternatives to Short Terms
of Imprisonment*, in which evidence given by the Magistrates'
Association calls for more inquiries to be made into the background of offenders (H.M.S.O., 1957, p. 18).

Only if more is known about the offenders will it be possible to
devise some kind of scheme whereby sentencing decisions could
be made more consistent. The difference between receiving a
sentence of imprisonment and being fined or placed on probation
is so great for the offender both in its immediate, and probably in
its later, consequences, that it is important that the choice should
not be haphazard.

It is hoped that sentencing policy will be influenced by the

235

results of research projects such as the present study, which show that some of the reasons put forward for local differences in sentences are based on an incorrect interpretation or misunderstanding of the actual situation. Research can also make known to justices the disparities which occur, of which many seem unaware, and the experience of other courts in dealing with similar types of offenders. Discussion may perhaps be stimulated by previously unknown facts. Benches may possibly be encouraged to consider the problem of equality of consideration in sentencing; make more use of their powers to order inquiries on which to base their decisions; and most important of all, attempt to carry out policies which are more in line with modern penological thought.

This particular piece of research has been largely fact-finding. But it has also been possible to point out some ways in which more consistent sentencing policies between magistrates' courts may be reached. One of the most important of these is through the training of justices. Perhaps more could be done to provide them with information on the problems of sentencing, the objects of punishment, and the chances of success. This could be achieved without interfering in any way with the independence of the magistracy. If more emphasis were put on the sentencing process, new magistrates would become more independent. The supposed superior sentencing ability of the older magistrates based on experience would be regarded more critically. This experience in sentencing has no scientific basis and no validity. Magistrates, as yet, do not know the degree of their 'success'.

References

ADVISORY COUNCIL ON THE TREATMENT OF OFFENDERS (1957), *Alternatives to Short Terms of Imprisonment*, H.M.S.O.

JAYNE, I. W. (1956), 'The purpose of the sentence', *National Probation and Parole Association Journal*, vol. 2, p. 316.

LE MESURIER, L. (ed.) (1935), *A Handbook of Probation and Social Work of the Courts*, National Association of Probation Officers.

21 Harry Kalven Jr and Hans Zeisel

Disagreement between Jury and Judge

Excerpts from Harry Kalven Jr and Hans Zeisel, *The American Jury*, Little, Brown, 1966, pp. 55–65, 104–17.

This study seeks to answer two basic questions: First, what is the magnitude and direction of the disagreement between judge and jury? And, second, what are the sources and explanations of such disagreement? [. . .]

Although any distinctive function of the jury must be found in the possibility of disagreement between judge and jury, there is something curious in the question how much judge and jury agree and disagree. No prior expectations exist either among the legal profession or in legal tradition as to what a proper amount of disagreement between judge and jury should be. We lack a pre-existing context in which to place the measurements. You may find it amusing to make your own private guess and to see whether it overestimates or underestimates the amount of actual disagreement.

Table 1 reports for the full sample of 3576 cases the actual verdict of the jury and the matching hypothetical verdict of the judge. Since the jury may acquit, convict, or hang, where realistically the judge may only acquit or convict, the verdicts distribute in six cells.

Table 1 thus furnishes the basic measure of the magnitude of judge–jury disagreement. Reading the two shaded cells first, we obtain the percentage of cases in which judge and jury agree. They agree to acquit in 13·4 per cent of all cases and to convict in 62·0 per cent of all cases, thus yielding a total agreement rate of 75·4 per cent.

Looking next at the four unshaded cells, we see that the total disagreement, 24·6 per cent of all cases, consists of (16·9+2·2=) 19·1 per cent of cases in which judge and jury disagree on guilt, and (1·1+4·4=) 5·5 per cent of cases in which the jury hangs.

Table 1
Verdict of Jury and Judge (Per Cent of All 3576 Trials)

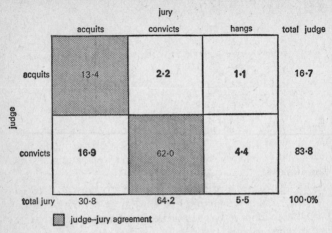

| | jury | | | |
	acquits	convicts	hangs	total judge
judge acquits	13·4	2·2	1·1	16·7
convicts	16·9	62·0	4·4	83·8
total jury	30·8	64·2	5·5	100·0%

☐ judge–jury agreement

It is not easy to know what to make of these figures. To some, no doubt, the fact that judge and jury agree some 75 per cent of the time will be read as a reassuring sign of the competence and stability of the jury system; to others the fact that they disagree 25 per cent of the time will be viewed as a disturbing sign of the anarchy and eccentricity of the jury. We would suggest that the significance of these figures for any judgement about the jury must depend on the reasons for these disagreements and must wait upon the detailed examination of those reasons.

The inclusion of hung juries makes Table 1 somewhat awkward to handle. At times it will prove useful to employ the following convention in the counting of hung juries: a hung jury will be considered as in effect half an acquittal. Accordingly in Table 2, Table 1 is rewritten by redistributing the hung juries half to the acquittals and half to the convictions and rounding off to integers.[1]

1. This distribution is predicated on the experience that, as a practical matter, roughly half the hung jury cases end up having the same consequences for the defendant as an acquittal, either because his prosecution is dropped or because he is acquitted in a subsequent trial.

Compare the English practise: 'There is ... no compulsion upon the

Table 2
Verdict of Jury and Judge – Consolidated
(Per Cent of All 3576 Trials)

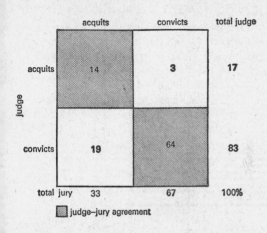

	acquits	convicts	total judge
acquits	14	**3**	**17**
convicts	**19**	64	83
total jury	33	67	100%

judge–jury agreement

It is immediately apparent in Table 2 that the jury's disagreement with the judge is massively in one direction, and the direction is the expected one. The jury has long been regarded as a bulwark of protection for the criminal defendant, and Table 2 can be taken to retell this story. There is some puzzle, however, as to how best to state the extent of this imbalance in favor of the defendant. After considerable deliberation over the point, we now conclude that the most meaningful statement is the simplest. The jury is less lenient than the judge in 3 per cent of the cases and more lenient than the judge in 19 per cent of the cases. Thus, the jury trials show on balance a net leniency of 16 per cent. This means that in the cases which the defendant decides to bring before the jury, on balance, he fares better 16 per cent of the time than he would have in a bench trial.

Crown to re-indict a man, after the disagreement of the jury, but it is the usual practise to re-indict once, and then, if the jury disagrees a second time, to enter a *nolle prosequi* or consent to a directed acquittal. Sometimes, for special reasons, the Crown abandons a case after a single disagreement of the jury' (Williams, 1955, p. 283).

But this figure must not be made the basis for a general probability calculus by *any* defendant, because the cases to which this 16 per cent applies have been selected for jury trial *because* they are expected to evoke pro-defendant sentiments.

Tables 1 and 2 summarize the most important area of disagreement between judge and jury, namely disagreement on acquittal and conviction. There are, however, further ways in which judge and jury can disagree in criminal cases, and, to round out the picture, we look now at the possibilities of disagreements on charge and on penalty. Such subsidiary disagreements arise from special characteristics of the case and from special provisions of the law which vary from one jurisdiction to another.

In a fair number of cases more than one charge is presented to the jury; hence, judge and jury can agree to convict but may disagree as to the charge. Again, in some jurisdictions the jury is given the power to set the penalty, as in many southern states with respect to all crimes, and in almost all states with respect to the death penalty. Here, judge and jury may agree to convict and even agree on the charge (if there is more than one) but still disagree as to the level of penalty. In Tables 1 and 2 both these subsidiary disagreements are concealed as agreements to convict.

Table 3 provides the relevant data for disagreements on charge.

Table 3
Jury and Judge Agree to Convict, May Disagree on Charge
(Per Cent of All 3576 Trials)

Verdict	Single charge Cases	Multiple charge Cases	Total
Judge more lenient*	—	0·7	0·7
Both agree	38·2	18·6	56·8
Jury more lenient†	—	4·5	4·5
Total	38·2	23·8	62·0**

*Judge, in disagreement with the jury, would have found for lesser charge.

†Jury, in disagreement with the judge, finds for lesser charge.

** This 62·0 per cent appears in Table 1 and represents the trials in which judge and jury agreed to convict.

While the picture is somewhat complicated by the circumstance that almost 40 per cent of the cases offer no possibility of disagreement on charge, nevertheless in these disagreements the jury once again shows a marked imbalance (4·5 per cent to 0·7 per cent) in favour of the defendant.

In an important sense, the 5·2 per cent enlarges the amount of disagreement between jury and judge and hence will be added to the universe of disagreement cases which it is the central objective of this study to analyse. For almost all purposes hereafter disagreements on charge will be considered as full units of disagreement.

The final opportunity for disagreement between judge and jury arises in those cases where the law allows the jury to set the penalty. To trace disagreements on penalty we need carry forward from Table 3 only the 56·8 per cent of all cases in which there was agreement on charge as well as on guilt; it is only in these cases that an independent disagreement on penalty can arise. Table 4 provides the relevant data. While the directionality is the same, the ratio of jury leniency to severity is more evenly balanced for disagreements on penalty than for those on guilt or charge.

Table 4
Jury and Judge Agree on Conviction and Charge,
May Disagree on Penalty (Per Cent of All 3576 Trials)

	Per cent
Judge gives more lenient penalty	1·5
Jury and judge agree on penalty	5·4
Jury gives more lenient penalty	2·5
Total	9·4*

* In 47·4 per cent of all trials, judge and jury convict on the same charge, but since the judge sets the penalty no penalty disagreement can occur. Adding to these 47·4 per cent the 9·4 per cent penalty disagreement and the 5·2 per cent charge disagreement, we obtain the 62·0 per cent of all trials in which judge and jury agree to convict. See Table 1.

The disagreements on penalty will not be included in the later analysis of disagreements, although we devote a separate chapter to the death penalty. Table 5 gives one last view of the full range of disagreement between judge and jury. Beginning with the disagreements on guilt and hung juries, it separates out from the agreements to convict the disagreements on charge, and finally from the agreements to convict on the same charge, the disagreements on penalty.

Table 5
Summary View of Judge–Jury Disagreement
(Per Cent of All 3576 Trials)

Disagreement on *guilt*		19·1
Judge acquits	2·2	
Jury acquits	16·9	
Jury *hangs* while judge –		5·5
would have acquitted	1·1	
would have convicted	4·4	
Disagreement on *charge* only		5·2
Judge for lesser offense	0·7	
Jury for lesser offense	4·5	
Disagreement on *penalty* only		4·0
Judge more lenient	1·5	
Jury more lenient	2·5	
Total disagreement		33·8%*
Judge more lenient	5·5%	
Jury more lenient	28·3%	

*The figures for disagreements on guilt and for the hung juries are taken from Table 1. The figures for disagreements on charge from Table 3 and those on penalty from Table 4. The figure which complements the 33·8 per cent disagreement for 100·0 per cent is 66·2 per cent; it represents the number of trials in which there is no disagreement between jury and judge, neither on guilt nor on charge nor on penalty.

This then is the summary report on the magnitude and direction of judge–jury disagreement in criminal cases, in all its dimensions. Table 5 shows that even when hung juries, disagreements on charge, and disagreements on penalty are included, the general impression left by Table 1 is not substantially altered.

It may be illuminating to set the data on the criminal jury in another perspective by placing it into a complementary context.

We can compare the results in criminal cases with the parallel data from the study of civil jury trials.

Table 6
Judge–Jury Disagreement in Civil Cases
(Per Cent of All Trials)

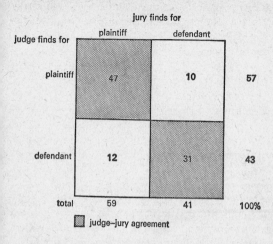

judge–jury agreement

Once again, reading the diagonal of agreement, one notes that the over-all magnitude of agreement of 78 per cent is exactly the same as the 78 per cent for the criminal cases in Table 2. In some 47 per cent of all cases judge and jury find in favor of the plaintiff on liability, and in some 31 per cent find for the defendant, producing the over-all agreement on liability of 78 per cent. It is quite striking then that the over-all level of agreement between jury and judge is roughly the same whether the business is criminal or civil.

In one important respect, however, the disagreement patterns in criminal and in civil cases are in sharp contrast. In civil cases the disagreement is distributed evenly in the two directions. In 12 per cent of the cases it is the jury that will be more favorable to the plaintiff, and in 10 per cent of the cases it is the judge who would be more favorable to the plaintiff. This finding is in the teeth of the popular expectation that the jury in personal injury cases favors the plaintiff, at least if that expectation is taken to mean that the jury is more likely to favor the plaintiff than is the judge.

243

Undoubtedly this contrast indicates something profound about the values, attitudes, and functions of the jury in its criminal and civil spheres. There is, however, a line of explanation suggested by our study of jury waiver in criminal cases which should be noted here. To some degree the difference in the directionality of the disagreements must be a function of the difference in the waiver practise in civil and criminal cases. As we have seen, the defendant in a criminal case in law and in practise tends to have the option between jury and bench trial. He therefore chooses the jury in cases where he thinks it will be favorable to him and waives the jury in cases where he thinks it will be unfavorable. If the defendant were completely knowledgeable there would be only normal disagreements and no cross-overs, since he would have withdrawn the cross-over possibilities from the jury trial universe by waiving the jury.

In the civil case the matter stands differently. The jury cannot be waived unless both parties consent, and wherever there is an expectation that jury trial may favor one side, that side is going to insist on a jury trial. Thus in civil cases the waiver rules do not operate to screen out any one class of disagreements. The marked lack of directionality in judge–jury disagreement in civil cases must at least in part be the result of this situation.

This brief comparison of the criminal and civil jury has been made simply to underscore the directionality of the disagreement of the criminal jury and will have to suffice here. [. . .]

We shall now give an over-all summary of the reasons found for disagreements. In a sense this complements in summary form the report on the magnitude and direction of disagreement, so as to bring us to the answer to our two major questions: how much disagreement is there between judge and jury in criminal cases? And, what are the reasons or sources of this disagreement?

We begin with the content of the reason code. The coding operation involved assigning highly specific reasons to the individual instances of disagreement. As the coding developed, it became possible to group the individual reasons into narrow sub-categories and those into larger categories. In the final stage of the coding process the reasons were subsumed into five generic categories: [. . .]

Evidence factors
Facts only the judge knew
Disparity of counsel
Jury sentiments about the individual defendant
Jury sentiments about the law

Since these labels are not self-explanatory, a brief description of each is provided. It should be stressed that, in each instance, the category locates a generic source of disagreement, without regard to whether it is the judge or the jury who is the more lenient.

Evidence factors. Although the traditional view of the jury is that it is largely concerned with issues of fact, it turns out to be surprisingly difficult to give a thumbnail sketch of evidence as a category of judge–jury disagreement. At times the jury may evaluate specific items of evidence differently; at other times the jury might simply require a higher degree of proof. Frequently evidentiary disagreement, in our usage, refers simply to the closeness of the case, which liberated the jury to respond to non-evidentiary factors. Under these special circumstances, issues of evidence, as we were able to handle them, are properly speaking not so much a cause for disagreement as a condition for it.

Facts only the judge knew. Here the concern is with the occasional circumstance that, during or prior to the trial, an important fact will become available to the judge but not to the jury, such as whether the defendant had a prior specific criminal record or not. Whenever the judge notes such special knowledge on his part in a disagreement case, it has been taken as a reason for his disagreement. The rationale is that judge and jury were, in fact, trying different cases, and had the jury known what the judge knew, it would have agreed with him.

Disparity of counsel. It was possible to collect data systematically on how evenly counsel for prosecution and for defense were matched. This category covers the instances in which the superiority of either defense or prosecution counsel was given as one of the reasons for the jury's disagreement with the judge.

Jury sentiments about the individual defendant. The type of defendant involved in a criminal case can vary across the entire spectrum of human personality and background, from the crippled war veteran who evokes intense sympathy to the loud mouth who alienates the jury. In this category are included all reasons for judge–jury disagreement attributable to the personal characteristics of the defendant.

Jury sentiments about the law. This category includes particular instances of 'jury equity', reasons for disagreement that imply criticism of either the law or the legal result. For example, the jury may regard a particular set of facts inappropriately classified as rape, because it perceives what might be called contributory negligence on the part of the victim. A similar notion may operate in fraud cases in which the victim first hoped for an improper gain. Thus, a broader concept, contributory fault of the victim, evolves as a defense to a crime. This general category of jury sentiments about the law includes roughly a dozen subcategories of such jury sentiments.

There must remain, of course, a certain blandness and ambiguity about the major categories for the present. Since the purpose here is only to provide an over-all summary view of the explanations for judge–jury disagreement, these sketches will have to suffice. At this point the categories simply provide a handy device for summarizing the data. [. . .]

To say that the reason code fell into these five major categories is to make more than a point about coding technique. It is to state a theory. In its most general and also its least exciting form, the theory is that all disagreement between judge and jury arises because of disparity of counsel, facts that only the judge knew, jury sentiments about the defendant, jury sentiments about the law, and evidentiary factors, operating alone or in combination with each other; and as a corollary, that the judge is less likely to be influenced by these factors than is the jury. There is some gain in emphasis if we invert the statement: unless at least one of these factors is present in a case, the jury and the judge will not disagree.

We are now ready to quantify the explanations for judge–jury disagreement. We begin with a revised version of the basic table of disagreement.

Table 7
Judge–Jury Disagreements in the 3576 Trials

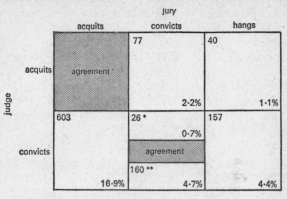

** jury convicts of *major* offense; judge of lesser
* jury convicts of *lesser* offense; judge of major

The universe of disagreement can now be defined with precision. It comprises the disagreements on guilt, disagreements on charge, and the cases in which the jury hangs. Reading off the relevant figures from Table 7, it can be seen that this total universe of disagreement consists of 1063 instances that fall conveniently into six groups as follows. With Table 8 we establish a

Table 8
Type and Direction of Disagreement

	Per cent	*Number*
Normal disagreements on		
Guilt	57	*603*
Charge	15	*160*
Hung Jury	15	*157*
Cross-over disagreements on		
Guilt	7	*77*
Charge	2	*26*
Hung Jury	4	*40*
Total disagreements	100%	*1063*

usage already adverted to which it will be convenient to follow henceforth. Cases of disagreement where *the jury is more lenient* than the judge will be called *normal* disagreements; cases where, in the less frequent situation, *the judge is more lenient* will be called *cross-over* disagreements.

The precise quest of this study then is to explain what caused the disagreements in these 1063 instances, constituting 30 per cent of all trials.

We must adjust now for the circumstance that it was not possible to find an explanation for every case of disagreement. Table 9 presents the basic tabulation of success and failure in obtaining explanations.

Table 9
Percentage of Unexplained Disagreements

| Normal disagreements on | | | Cross-overs on | | | Total |
Guilt	Charge	Hung	Guilt	Charge	Hung	Disagreements
7%	11%	19%	3%	4%	15%	10%

No explanation was forthcoming in 101 out of 1063 cases, or about 10 per cent of all disagreements. The percentage is smallest for the disagreements on guilt and largest, as might be expected, for hung juries. The percentage of failures is, on the average, smaller for the cross-over cases than it is for the normal disagreements, suggesting that the reversal of the jury's normal response is so exceptional that explanations for it are easier to see. Subtracting 101 from 1063 leaves 962 instances, or 90 per cent of all disagreement for which we have an explanation.

An exhaustive comparison of the 101 unexplained cases with the 962 explained cases revealed no marked differences between the two groups such as would suggest any peculiarities in the unexplained cases. We will therefore disregard these cases in future discussion, on the assumption that even if we knew the answers, they would not represent new sources of disagreement but would have satisfied someone of the established categories of explanation without changing their relative frequency (Zeisel, 1957, chapter 3).

In the future discussion, then, the relevant universe will be the

962 disagreements for which it proved possible to find an explanation. Table 10 reports the basic data for these cases in terms of the five basic reason categories.

Table 10
Summary Explanation of Disagreement

	Normal disagreements on			Cross-overs on			Total disagreements
	Guilt %	Charge %	Hung %	Guilt %	Charge %	Hung %	%
Sentiments on the law	53	59	32	49	72	26	50
Sentiments on the defendant	23	27	17	28	20	3	22
Evidence factors	78	62	84	93	100	100	79
Facts only the judge knew	7	3	3	4	4	—	5
Disparity of counsel	9	6	9	5	4	—	8
Average number of reasons per case*	1·7	1·6	1·5	1·8	2·0	1·3	1·6
Number of cases	559	142	127	75	25	34	962

*Percentages add to more than 100 because, as indicated in the Average line, some cases have more than one reason, e.g., column one adds to 170 per cent or 1·7 reasons per case.

The last column of Table 10 yields the first over-all measure of the relative roles of the five major reason categories in explaining the judge–jury disagreement. As might more or less be expected, in 79 per cent of all cases, or in four out of every five cases, the disagreement in whole or in part derives from evidence problems. At the other extreme, the over-all roles of disparity of counsel and of differential knowledge to which the judge is privy are low (8 per cent and 5 per cent), a result which in the case of disparity of counsel may cause surprise. A second result that may be unexpected is that in 50 per cent of the cases there is found a jury sentiment at odds with the law.

By way of gaining a preliminary perspective on the broader

sources of disagreement, we see that, apart from evidence difficulties, the primary sources of disagreement are the jury sentiments about the law and about the defendant. Thus, the data in Table 10 give focus to a general theory of judge–jury disagreement.

The data permit another basic observation. The rank order of reasons which we obtained for the Total column, representing all cases of disagreement, remains the same for all six types of disagreements, whether it concerns guilt, charge, or the hung jury, and whether it is in the direction of greater or of lesser jury leniency. But although the rank order remains the same, there is a difference in emphasis: sentiments on the law are most important in respect to disagreements on charge and least important to hung juries: hung juries show a higher level of evidence issues than do the other disagreements on guilt and charge.

Thus far we have counted each reason as one. It is helpful, however, to adjust for multiple reasons and reach a more precise estimate of the roles of the five categories. This is the function of Tables 11, 12, and 13.

Table 11 shows that for roughly half the disagreements there is more than one reason, but in no case were all five reason categories required, and in only 1 per cent of the cases were there four reasons.

Table 11
Frequency of Multiple Reasons

Number of reasons* per case	Per cent	Number of cases
1	47	456
2	41	395
3	11	105
4	1	6
5	—	—
Total disagreements	100%	962

* The term 'reason' refers here only to the five major categories. The multiplicity of reasons *within* one of these categories is ignored. One reason is treated as sufficient to bring the category into play. For example, the defendant may be a mother in one case, and a mother, a widow, and poor in a second case. Yet in each case *Sentiments on the Defendant* would be counted only once as a reason for disagreement.

Next we explore whether the five basic reason categories differ from each other in the degree to which they combine with other reasons as sources of explanation. Table 12 shows how dependent each of the five basic categories is.

Table 12
Frequency with which Major Reasons Appear Alone or with Other Reasons

	Sentiment on law %	Sentiment on defendant %	Issues of evidence %	Facts only judge knew %	Disparity of counsel %
Appears alone	22	8	43	2	8
with other reasons	78	92	57	98	92
Total	100%	100%	100%	100%	100%
Number of cases*	484	213	758	52	78

* The number of cases adds to 1585 although there are actually 962 cases because the same case may appear again in two or more of the five columns.

Each of the reason categories appears more frequently in combination with other reasons than it does alone. Interestingly enough, it is the evidence category that appears alone most frequently, a point on which more will be said later.

The sharing of reasons is particularly interesting with respect to disparity of counsel and jury sentiments about the defendant, both of which combine with other reasons over 90 per cent of the time they operate. This fact has broad implications. Disparity of counsel, for the most part, will not make a difference by itself but will require materials which superior counsel can exploit; the implication is that the cases do not present such material evenly. Again, sentiments about the individual defendant are seldom powerful enough to cause disagreement by themselves; rather, they gain their effectiveness only in partnership with some other factor in the case. The implication again is that for the defendant to be poor and crippled or beautiful and blonde is by itself rarely a sufficient stimulus for the jury to disagree with the judge.

Putting together the sheer frequency with which the reason categories appear in Table 10 and the perspective on multiple reasons gained in Tables 11 and 12, it is possible to show the *power* of each reason category in explaining disagreement. We have adverted earlier to the process by which multiple reasons would be weighed; they are valued inversely to their frequency in the particular case. Making these weighting computations, one obtains the profile presented in Table 13.

Table 13
Summary of Weighted Reasons

	Per cent
Sentiments on the law	29
Sentiments on the defendant	11
Issues of evidence	54
Facts only the judge knew	2
Disparity of counsel	4
Total	100%
Number of cases	*962*

Table 13 permits a major conclusion for a theory of judge–jury disagreement. By giving weights to each of the major reason categories, it states in the large, but with precision, the answer to the question: what causes jury and judge to disagree? Slightly over half the job of explanation falls to the evidence category. Apart from evidence factors, the explanation for disagreements resides principally in jury sentiments on the law or jury sentiments about the defendant. Perhaps the most interesting aspect of Table 13 is the salient role played by jury sentiments on the law in causing disagreements; jury equity looms as a significant factor.

The reason data can be arranged into one further profile. Reducing the categories to two, as in Table 14, by simply placing the evidence category on one side and the other four categories on the other, one gets a crucial image of the jury's performance in terms of *facts* on one hand and *values* on the other.

Table 14
Values and Facts as Causes of Disagreement

Disagree on –	Per cent	
Facts alone	34	
Values and facts	45	Total facts, 79%
Values alone	21	Total values, 66%
Total	100%	
Number of cases	962	

The conventional and official role of the jury, although it is not clear that anyone believes this, is that it is the trier of the facts and nothing else. Table 14 tells us that in only one third of the cases is the jury's fact-finding the sole source of judge–jury disagreement; in the remaining two thirds of the cases the sources of disagreement are to be seen fully only by looking beyond the official role of the jury. On the other hand, only 21 per cent of the disagreements arise from a source having nothing to do with the facts, but purely with values or sentiments. Thus, Table 14 serves to spotlight the peculiar difficulty that attends any effort to isolate the causes of judge–jury disagreement. The difficulty arises because to a considerable extent, or in exactly 45 per cent of the cases, the jury in disagreeing with the judge is neither simply deciding a question of fact nor simply yielding to a sentiment or a value; it is doing both. It is giving expression to values and sentiments under the guise of answering questions of fact. If the factual leeway is not present, the sentiments or values will as a rule have to be particularly strong to move the jury to disagree. Conversely if only ambiguity in the facts is present, and the directionality of the sentiment is absent, the jury will be less likely to disagree with the judge. The decision-making patterns we are pursuing are subtle ones.

In one sense the basic task of this inquiry is now completed. Answers have been given to the question of how often judge and jury disagree and to the question of why they disagree. [...]

Upon our suggestion that it would be of great interest to compare the findings from this study with data on English juries,

Lord Chief Justice Parker of Waddington was kind enough to send us the following communication:

Since your visit to this country I have had the opportunity of consulting all the senior Queen's Bench Judges. As I told you none of us has kept any figures, and accordingly such information as I have obtained is largely a matter of impression. I can I think fairly summarize it as follows:

(1) Cases of 'ordinary crime' in which the Jury reaches a verdict which the Judge sitting alone would not have arrived at.

(a) The cases in which the Judge would have acquitted where the Jury have convicted are very rare.

Such cases as have been specifically referred to comprise sexual cases where the Jury have approached the matter in a common sense way whereas the Judge would have been more influenced by legalistic considerations such as the absence of corroboration.

(b) Cases in which the Judge would have convicted where the Jury have acquitted range from 3 per cent to 10 per cent. These include cases when a Jury convicts of a minor offence rather than the grave offence, for example, convicts of unlawful wounding and not wounding with intent to do grievous bodily harm.

(2) Cases in which the Judge has been unable to say after consideration that the Jury may have been right, that is, where the verdict is perverse, are very rare. The answers received describe them as 'none', 'negligible', 'very rare', or 'hardly ever'.

Those cases that are specifically mentioned include cases where a verdict has clearly been influenced by danger of the death penalty being imposed, in which case the verdict would be one of manslaughter, or where the Jury felt that the complainant and the prisoner were morally both to blame.

I mentioned at the beginning that these views concern 'ordinary crime'. I said that because nearly all the Judges have excluded from their consideration cases of causing death by dangerous driving of motor vehicles.

To translate Lord Parker's letter into the fourfold table used throughout this study, we apply his data to trial statistics published for England and Wales:[2]

2. Home Office Statistics (1952), Table 3, pp. 34–5, give jury acquittals as 2083 and convictions as 19,971. The latter figure includes guilty pleas, which Lord Devlin estimated at 'roughly two thirds' (*Trial by Jury*, 1953 p. 176n). Here we estimate jury convictions at 6657.

Table 15
Estimated Verdict Pattern of English Criminal Juries

	Jury Acquits	Convicts	Total
Judge Acquits	17	1*	18
Convicts	7*	76	82
Total	24	77	100%
Number of cases			8740

*Approximations based on Lord Parker's estimates.

To set up a precise comparison with the American data, it is necessary to adjust also for the fact that English juries deal only with serious offenses. The verdict pattern of American juries for serious crimes then is as follows.

Table 16
Verdict Pattern of American Juries for Serious Crimes

	Jury Acquits	Convicts	Total
Judge Acquits	13	3	16
Convicts	17	67	84
Total	30	70	100%
Number of cases			2418

There seems to be no doubt then that English juries dissent less frequently from the judge than do their American counterparts. Whether this is due to a greater conformity of sentiment or to the greater control of the English judge over the trial process would be a most interesting topic for future investigation.

References
WILLIAMS, G. (1955), The Proof of Guilt: Study of an English Crime Trial, Stevens and Sons.
ZEISEL, H. (1957), Say it with Figures, 4th edn, Routledge.

22 Julius Stone

Computers, Behavioural Science and the Human Judge

Excerpt from Julius Stone, *Social Dimensions of Law and Justice*, Stevens and Sons, 1966, pp. 687–95.

Many issues concerning the possible services of computers and behavioural science in legal tasks have already emerged. Do these sciences express a philosophy irreconcilably alien to the great traditions of law? Is the fear justified that technology demands for its efficient use closed logical systems which would hamstring the growth of a legal order contained within them? Would lawyers' acceptance of these services entail abdication of professional legal skills? Would the precision of concept and language required for the machines make lawyers despise and reject the semantic fertility of legal language? Would the technological ability of machines to handle complex and massive data encourage overrefinement and overcomplexity of legal prescription? When harnessed to expanding governmental powers, would it accelerate the already growing subjection of citizens to centralized, bureaucratic, and technocratic power?

Opposing attitudes fall easily into emotive distortions. Many social scientists working in the area betray undercurrents of hostility to lawyers as men self-centred, defensive and unresponsive to growing knowledge. Even those who try to see both sides sometimes attribute any seeming limits on machine potentialities for legal tasks to accidents of legal history and inadequacies of legal craftsmanship. No less unhelpful are overstated attacks on the newer approaches. No doubt it may be salutary to point out that inquiry on some subjects may disturb essential social processes, that machines tend to focus too much attention on the 'routinizable' or scientific elements in law and justice, and that the capacity of machines within such areas would tend to aggravate the tendency for state intervention to extend itself. But whether these represent actual threats of the still tentative computer developments is another matter. In short, lawyers' anxieties over 'computerization' of their calling should neither be overstated, nor dissolved into mere instinctive cries of alarm or ridicule.

Much of the controversy proceeds from the lawyer's assumption that analysis of appellate decisions proceeding on factorization independent of 'justice' threatens whatever 'justice' may stand for. We are told, for example, that lawyers are hardly prepared to turn the Supreme Court into 'a group of experimental subjects to test the results of factor analysis' (Cowan, 1963). A first point to be made, therefore, is that despite the *apparent* proximity between the explanation of decisions and the making of them, the behaviouralist search for a reliable quantitative analysis (and incidentally a basis of predicting future decisions) may have no designs whatever on the integrity of the judgement of justice. This is precisely, indeed, what Glendon Schubert said in his pioneering *Quantitative Analysis of Judicial Behavior* (1959): 'Scalogram analysis cannot tell us how the Court ought to decide future cases' (p. 320).[1] Nor, probably, do the scholars concerned acknowledge any responsibility for the effects of the search for scientific 'laws' governing decision-making on either the judgement of justice or the judicial institution, any more than nuclear scientists accept responsibility for nuclear war. And the scientific indifference here asserted is twofold: First, as to how the judge *should* now proceed in making his judgement of justice; second, as to the 'feedback' or 'Heisenberg effect' of scientific prediction on future decisions of justice.

This non-concern with justice reminds us that the recent work continues, perhaps with better plans and instruments, some main 'legal realist' challenges of the twenties and thirties.[2] Behaviour-

1. Cf. Schubert (1963a, especially pp. 100, 102–3, 105–8), and Ulmer (1963). When discussing, in his last cited article, why prediction is important, Schubert obviously regards the greater reproducibility and the communicability of his methods of prediction, as compared with those of lawyers, as the significant thing. He says nothing as to the bearing of all this on the doing of justice in future judgements (cf. Sawyer, 1965, pp. 107–8, 203–8).

2. Antecedents in political science are usually seen in C. H. Pritchett (1948). The immediate foundation for the present movement is of course Glendon Schubert's 1959 work referred to above (Schubert, 1964). (See also Schubert, 1960, 1963b [a collection of materials], and 1964 for other acknowledged antecedents.)

alists, too, are seeking to explain judicial decisions in terms of factors going beyond legal propositions formulated in court opinions. What is new is, first, the drive to find factors in *measureable* forms, to allow a *quantitative* analysis of judicial behaviour (Schubert here relies on complementary methods of 'bloc' analysis and 'scalogram' analysis, later to be mentioned). Second, new techniques and instruments of measurement are being tried. Third, this recent work is inspired mainly by political science. This encourages boldness in hypothesis and also, perhaps, draws more indulgence from lawyers than if it came from within the legal fold. But by the same token the new work may often suffer from deficient technical knowledge of both legal processes and the accumulated body of juristic thought.[3] Fourth, behavioural-ists claim to predict future decisions of multi-membered Courts, and even of individual judges whose performance lends itself to scaling with substantial certainty, in such notoriously difficult areas as due process and civil rights.

Yet it would be wrong to think of this work as focused on pre-diction. The aim is rather to see why judges of given backgrounds have made the decisions they have, and to frame verifiable ('scientific') hypotheses for this purpose. Prediction-power is one test (though of course not conclusive) of the validity of the basing hypotheses. Apart altogether from prediction, however, the new approaches must eventually help lawyers to handle the masses of materials now confronting them. Computers can store the flood of past and current legal materials to permit instant retrieval un-der skilled programming of what is relevant to the business at hand. Apart from the promise of *information* retrieval, the mere retrieval of headnotes, extracts, summaries, or full texts of judge-ments, statutes, or legal literature, offers incalculable savings in search time. We are here disposed not to overstress the caveats we laid in *Legal System and Lawyers' Reasonings* (chapter 1, para. 10) as to the dangers of loss during machine processing of emotive components of judicial discourse. The dangers can be

---

3. It is something like witnessing the re-invention of the wheel, for example, to find political scientists in 1964 offering the poles of activism/restraint as a 'dominant variable' for behavioural analysis of judicial decisions. See Spaeth (1962). Cf., over thirty years ago in a mass of *juristic* variations on this theme, Pollock (1929, p. 293).

avoided by storing at full length (as is already being done), and in any case they mainly affect the judgement of justice, later to be considered. Second, even apart from *legal* materials, machines would give lawyers access to vast and otherwise inaccessible bodies of *extra-legal* knowledge, bearing on such increasingly important fields of law as antitrust, tax, public utilities, resources, planning, and criminal and public law. Here machines may not only save time, but also give lawyers more access to non-partisan expertise.

Even prediction of decision, despite its surrounding polemics, holds much promise of relief from ills such as court congestion, backlog, inefficiency and delays. In advising clients, reasonably reliable prediction of future appellate holdings (particularly if behaviouralist claims to accuracy as high as 90 per cent were approached) could encourage settlement of many suits. It would do this, moreover, without thrusting excessive personal responsibility on to the advising lawyer. (We are referring here, of course, to prediction of appellate holdings on the applicable law, in the course of litigation in lower courts.) This might even be resorted to by inferior court judges themselves without serious countervailing risks. For decisions on the applicable law at lower court levels rarely determine the onward movement of the law; and if the margin of error were small few litigants would be prejudiced. Appeal would still be available. Bad legal guessing might be no more serious than it already is today in many inferior courts.

In this respect, however, lower courts occupy a critical borderline position to which we must now turn. On one side of the line, just discussed, is an observer's (including the trial judge's) prediction of how an appellate judge will decide an instant case. On the other, which we now approach, is the appellate judge's own act of judgement as he must make it *here and now* from the judgement seat. The jurist, the political scientist, or the lawyer advising his client or preparing for hearing, are in the position of observers for whom the future behaviour of the hearing judge or appellate judges is properly the subject of prediction. Experienced trial lawyers, for instance, have always regarded such prediction as part of prudent trial preparation, sometimes to the point of manoeuvring to be heard (or not be) before a particular judge. And in lower courts even the trial judge may *as to certain elements to be weighed in his decision* be in the position of an observer. In particular, where the appellate court's rulings on the applicable rule are doubtful in relation to the instant facts, the trial judge is involved (according to what is probably the general view) in some prediction as to how that court will finally decide.

When, however, the appellate judge himself confronts the duty to decide on that applicable rule of law, we are at the other side of our critical border, where lies 'the appellate judgement of justice'. For, first, such a decision (be it a new holding or a reversal) transcends the limits of settled law. It decides *what justice requires that the law should be*. Second, it thus *creates law*; and it is now commonplace that legal stability and movement both depend upon such adequate and regular judicial acts of law-creation. Third, these creative acts *involve more than the perceptive, cognitive, conceptualizing, and reasoning faculties*. Whatever be this 'something more', the judge should perform such acts with integrity on the basis of such experience, insight, and emotion as he has acquired *up to the very moment of performance*.

As already seen, behaviouralist work is not *aimed* to assist or even influence appellate judges in making the judgement of justice. Yet it is pre-eminently data from this area of past judicial activity that have most provoked and inspired them. Schubert's pioneering *Quantitative Analysis of Judicial Behaviour* was focused on classes of decision in the United States Supreme Court where indeterminacies of the constitutional instrument and changing social situations constantly create new problems involving value-choices and their effectuation through law. Behaviouralists seek to identify, delimit, and describe in quantitative terms the extra-legal variables which explain how the judges divided and voted in these past cases. Their 'bloc analysis' concerns itself with relations of stable or changing influence between members of the court, as manifest in concurrences and conflict of decisions; the 'scalogram analysis' with value-attitudes towards specific selected policy issues. Explanation is then sought for decisions of each judge, in terms of the degree of presence of each identified variable by a multivariate analysis. In so far as this shows a degree of concurrence of given variables with given kinds of decisions, not explicable by mere chance, this concurrence is expected to repeat itself in future decisions. In this way, concurrence of given combinations of factors with given kinds of past decisions is used to predict future decisions. Conversely, the degree of accuracy of such predictions is one kind of experimental verification of the adequacy of the factor identification and quantitation.

Values held by the judge are of course among the factors most considered by behaviouralists. They envisage, indeed, ambitious systems of 'recorded notions of justice and social utility, and various natural and social factors, as operative through and by interaction between various policy-makers, policy-appliers and policy-recipients'. The informed lawyer must admire the order and precision of the checklists of possible impact of values thus afforded; yet he is likely to suspect that they contain little, save the claim to systematize and measure, which has not already long been recognized in the best juristic thinking about judicial decision-making. He may also wonder about the predictive power which can really emerge from attempts to work with such disparate variables, some of them vastly oversimplified in formulation. Yet, however all this be, values manifested by each judge both on and off the bench are becoming central in these efforts to predict future decisions, along with other variables of perception, personality, leadership and role among the members of a multi-judge court, as well as *vis-à-vis* other related groups of individuals.

What is significant for us in this focus on the judge's values is the seeming proximity it creates between the behaviouralist concern, and that of the appellate judge himself at the moment of judgement. The semblance, as we have already tried to stress, is not reality. For the behaviouralists' stance is essentially that of interested observers seeking to explain what *has already been done* in judgement. As to the future they do not ask how judges *should* decide, but only how they *will* decide *if they act consistently with past decisions*. If we could assume that this distinction between the behavioural scientist's concern and the appellate judge's concern would always be seen and respected, there would be little problem here.

We cannot, however, assume this, and the risks of over-sanguineness may affect not only political, social and juristic theorists, but also practitioners and judges. We already find a leading Japanese legal scholar, enthusiastic for the predictive power of scalogram analysis in Japanese civil liberty cases, foreseeing with zest that 'the day might come . . . when we lawyers also shall use an electronic machine in predicting judicial behaviour, and when the courts will use one in arriving at their decisions. . . .'[4]

That even Schubert acknowledges a 10 per cent margin of error leaves his enthusiasm undampened. Yet we are concerned in the Japanese Supreme Court, as in that of the United States, with the area *par excellence* of the appellate judge's judgement of justice, where failure to respect the distinction we are making will result in substituting calculations about factors in past decisions for the judge's *present* search for as just a solution as he can *now* find.

In this area lawyers and behaviouralists should be aware that reliance *at the judgement seat* on the new predictive techniques would seriously threaten the judge's central concern with justice. For if the results thus predicted for him did affirmatively[5] guide him in present decisions, each judge would tend to vote somewhat more consistently with his past record. The margin of deviation would accordingly tend to disappear in deference to predicted patterns, aided by the human tendency to follow the less agonizing because already trodden path. Nor can we wholly dismiss such dangers merely in terms of unlikelihood that a judge will resort for counsel to predictions of his own behaviour. For a certain 'feedback' and 'Heisenberg effect' of prediction on future decisions seems unavoidable in any case.

One effect would be to reduce the earnestness of a judge's *review* of his past holdings, related as this is to judicial vacillation, afterthought, new awareness of implications and social settings, sensitivity to emergent cases and the sparking clash of dissent. We plead, here, for recognition of the historical truth that most

4. See the general thesis of Hayakawa (1962, pp. 22–3) (emphasis is added). For a disapproving projection of the use of machine techniques to process legal data, data as to current public value-positions, and factual social data, into 'judicious' decisions, see Becker (1963, pp. 13–14).

5. Negatively, of course, factorization of past holdings may disclose uniformities which are inexplicable save by reasons obviously alien to the duty to do justice; for example uniformity of holdings against the poor, or the rich, whites or negroes, under rules for which these characteristics are legally irrelevant. Such negative guidance is, of course, not only unexceptionable but a most valuable warning of vice in judgement.

legal change springs precisely from deviance, tentativeness, after-thought and even indecision in judgement. On these rest some of the main foundations of the ongoing social good we call 'justice'. Another effect would be to encourage notions that some routin-ized means *based on past performance* is a proper method of search for solutions which are just *now*. We showed twenty years ago that it is those aspects of precedent doctrine which are most problematic in their analytical-logical nature which regularly admit considerations of justice to the judgement seat. It is here, where we cannot *intellectually* control decisional trends in ad-vance, that there often emerge the acts of judgement which give movement and direction to the legal order, making it a means toward justice as *present* men understand it.

Among the vital processes occurring at these intellectually in-tractable points of precedent growth are changes in legal pre-cepts by reference to contemporary social facts and ideals. The agent of these processes is necessarily the *man* in the appellate judgement seat, imbued by his life-span with some of the temper, perplexities, insights, preferences and values of his generation. When we ask how he is to fill this role, the answer is certainly not in the giving of judgements which conform to predictions based on *past* performances. It is rather in deciding what is *now* just in his own present eyes. This is at least part of the reason why appellate judges play a Trojan-horse-like role against existing legal precepts and why this role is so difficult to articulate in cogent intellectual terms. Men, in doing justice, seem always to be transcending the drive, methods, and limits of mere intellect. In so far as this task is left to machines, even by inadvertence, we risk its emasculation to the extent of the incapacity of machines to perform procedures which cannot be intellectualized. Machines can process data for, and *products of*, such procedures; but they cannot perform them. And because there is a tendency to con-fuse these different things we must stress that however great the potentialities of machines, they cannot overleap this *non possumus*. Machines can be programmed to overlook precedents, or even to neglect logic as human judges, often for the sake of justice, are seen to do. Machines cannot, however, be programmed to will to do justice, that is, to choose in each case in the future in which they are consulted, according to the justice *as seen at that future*

263

time by the still unknown standards of unknown men of that future time.

References

BECKER, T. L. (1963), 'On science, political science and law', *American Behavioral Scientist*, vol. 7.

COWAN, T. A. (1963), 'Decision theory in law, science and technology', *Science*, vol. 140, pp. 1065–72; also in *Rutgers Law Review*, 1963, pp. 499–517.

HAYAKAWA, T. (1962), 'Legal science and judicial behaviour', *Kobe University Law Review* (international edition), vol. 1 (2).

POLLOCK, F. (1929), 'Judicial caution and judicial valour', *Law Quarterly Review*, vol. 45.

PRITCHETT, C. H. (1948), *The Roosevelt Court: A Study in Judicial Politics and Values, 1937–47*, Macmillan.

SAWYER, G. (1965), *Law in Society*, Oxford.

SCHUBERT, G. A. (1960), *Constitutional Politics*, Holt, Rinehart and Winston.

SCHUBERT, G. A. (1963a), 'Judicial attitudes and voting behavior', *Law and Contemporary Problems*, vol. 28, pp. 100–42.

SCHUBERT, G. A. (ed.) (1963b), *Judicial Decision-Making*, Free Press of Glencoe.

SCHUBERT, G. A. (1964), *Judicial Behavior*, Rand McNally.

SPAETH, H. J. (1962), 'Judicial power as a variable motivating Supreme Court behavior', *Midwestern Journal of Political Science*, pp. 54–82.

ULMER, S. S. (1963), 'Scientific method and judicial process', *American Behavioral Scientist*, vol. 7.

Part Five The Legal Profession

The opening piece in this section, by Rueschemeyer, deals with the sociological implications of those characteristics of the profession of law which are the most enduring and least changeable. He deals with law as a certain way of thinking about problems and brings out the peculiarities of legal techniques by comparing law with medicine. The main emphasis in this part lies, however, upon the mechanisms by which the legal profession is integrated into, and heavily influenced by, structural features of the larger society. A main theme in the contributions of Carlin, Dahrendorf and Abel-Smith and Stevens, is the relationship between law and the class structure. Since equality is a dominant value in the theory of law, this part represents an effort to confront ideology with social realities. Blumberg and Moriondo are more concerned with social mechanisms internal to the legal institutions. But again it is shown how the realization of ideal demands is deflected by the immediate practical concerns of the professionals.

23 Dietrich Rueschemeyer

Lawyers and Doctors: A Comparison of Two Professions

Abridged from Dietrich Rueschemeyer, 'Doctors and lawyers: a comment on the theory of the professions', *Canadian Review of Sociology and Anthropology*, 1964, pp. 17–30.

The current, predominantly functionalist theory of the professions stresses two characteristics as strategic for the explanation of their position and functioning in society.[1] The professions are conceived of as service occupations that (1) apply a systematic body of knowledge to problems which (2) are highly relevant to central values of the society. Their high degree of learned competence creates special problems of social control: laymen cannot judge the professional performance; in many cases they cannot even set the concrete goals for the professional's work. This means that the two most common forms of social control of work in industrial societies, bureaucratic supervision by virtue of a formal position and judgement by the customer, are of only limited applicability. The need for social control is, on the other hand, especially urgent because of the values and interests that are at stake.

The dilemma is solved by a strong emphasis on individual self-control, which is grounded in a long socialization process designed to build up the required technical competence and to establish a firm commitment to the values and norms central to the tasks of the professional. The values and norms are, furthermore, institutionalized in the structure and culture of the profession. Individual self-control is therefore supplemented by the formal and informal control of the community of colleagues. Accepting the pledge to a self-controlled 'collectivity orientation' as trustworthy, society grants in return privileges and

1. Several articles by Goode (1957, 1960, 1962). Cf., also Merton, Reader, and Kendall (1957). This approach is in many ways an outgrowth of older analyses such as those of A. M. Carr-Saunders and P. A. Wilson, E. C. Hughes, T. Parsons, and T. H. Marshall.

advantages, such as high income and prestige, and protects the profession's autonomy against lay control and interference. Non-professional competitors, customers, mass media, and especially government agencies exert control too, but the autonomy of the profession is sheltered against them by such means as laws against 'quacks', professional referral patterns and norms which restrict certain forms of competition, insistence on exclusive professional competence in judging performance, and professional personnel in and professional advice to government agencies. [. . .]

The legal and medical professions differ significantly in the two respects that form the core of the theoretical model under discussion: the nature of their specific competence and the social values toward which the professional work is oriented.

Apart from borderline cases there exists a near-universal *consensus about the central value* toward which the medical profession is oriented. Physician and patient, the doctor's colleague group and the patient's family, his friends, and his role partners in other contexts, as well as the larger community and its various agencies, agree essentially on the substantive definition of health and on its importance compared with other values.

The situation is far more complex for the legal profession. Justice, like health, ranks high in the societal value hierarchy. In the substantive definition of justice, however, there are considerable ambiguities and wide discrepancies, as well as areas that are clearly understood and largely agreed upon. Certainly, enacted laws and established legal rulings carry the presumption of being accepted as 'just', but the notion of unjust law is by no means uncommon.

These different conceptions of justice are not identical with divergent interests. Interests which stand against a given conception of justice may or may not lay claim to a different conception of justice, and the prevalent ambiguity allows for different shadings between. Divergent interests make for a second difference between the legal and the medical profession that is relevant here. While the interests of the attorney's client may be at odds with what the lawyer considers just, it is rare that the patient's interests stand against the attainment of health.[2]

2. The importance of conflicting interests for the situation of the legal profession is emphasized by Parsons (1954). Parsons' analysis neglects,

Divergent interests and the different more or less articulate conceptions of justice are not randomly distributed in the social structure. They are associated with various subgroups, particularly different socio-economic strata and ethnic and religious groups. A relatively low degree of over-all consensus may contrast with a relatively high degree of consensus within these subgroups. This constellation of societal value dissensus and subgroup value consensus also confronts the religious professional, the minister, priest, or rabbi. However, the diversity of religious commitments is, at least in liberal Western societies, established as legitimate while the diversity of conceptions of justice finds only an indirect legitimate expression in the realm of politics. Moreover, the clergyman's work centers in the context of his subgroup, while the lawyer's activity often cuts across the boundaries of subgroups and his primary loyalty is expected to be to an overarching system of value orientations that represents, beyond a clear-cut core, an ambiguous compromise among several influential conceptions of justice.

It may be argued that people act and think only to a very limited extent with respect to ultimate social values. The norms and values that actually guide men are those incorporated in the more immediate institutional arrangements and role expectations. Therefore, conflicting notions of justice, especially if they are vaguely or ambiguously defined and rarely formulated explicitly, and if they are not anchored in specific institutions and organizations, are of little consequence for the structure and functioning of the legal profession.

It would seem, however, that the argument refers chiefly to those ultimate values that are not fully compatible with the requirements of institutionalized social life and for those that function as integrating mechanisms for concretely divergent notions precisely because they are left vague. It should be noted that the value of health falls into neither of these categories, while the generalized notion of justice in an important sense fits the second. But even ultimate values of this kind are not completely without consequence for behavior. Furthermore, the

---

however, the problem of value dissensus. It is thus implicitly treated as a simple by-product of conflicting interests with no significant consequences of its own.

conflicting conceptions of justice are to some degree associated with interests and anchored in specific groups, organizations, and institutions.

In spite of partial dissensus on the substantive definition of justice, the institutions of the medical and legal professions are similar in a related dimension, and this makes the value dissensus even more consequential. The public exhibits a high degree of concern about the implementation of the central values of both professions. Open neglect or violation of the values of health and of justice, however understood, elicits considerable moral indignation from disinterested third parties.

In this context the emphasis on procedural law that is characteristic of a developed legal profession may be interpreted as a defense against an open clash of emotionally charged conceptions of justice and not solely a safeguard against the emotions, biases, and political violence that grow out of a conflict of interests. However, a strongly procedural conception of justice creates at the same time a new source of alienation between the value orientation of the profession and the substantively defined orientations of the different 'publics' of the profession.

The *technical competence* of the physician rests on a body of systematic scientific theory. In the actual application of this knowledge other elements that are less rationalized and may be called the 'art of medicine' play an important role, for instance, the art of diagnosing on the basis of vague and insufficient clues, certain manual skills, and the use of interpersonal relations in the healing process. All these are, however, intimately connected with the main area of the physician's competence, medical knowledge.

If we compare the technical competence of physician and lawyer, three important differences emerge.

First, the lawyer's knowledge is not scientific. It is concerned not with the prediction and explanation of events on the basis of natural laws, but rather with a body of social norms and with rules for their application. These norms and rules can be systematized for the convenience of teaching or for avoiding inconsistencies and contradictions. But the resulting body of knowledge remains a description of a single normative system, designed for aiding its application and preparing its further development.

This development again requires comment. Legal norms are, in contrast to natural laws, subject to human decisions. Changes in the body of medical knowledge are due to new discoveries; changes in the body of legal knowledge are due to decisions of legislatures and of courts, decisions significantly influenced by members of the legal profession acting as legislators, judges, counsels, legal writers, and law professors. The value orientation of the legal profession, which is subject to patterned social conflict, thus plays a role in the substantive development of the law, while the content of medical knowledge is largely independent of the value orientation of the medical profession.

Second, a good deal of the lawyer's competence is connected with his legal knowledge only indirectly or not at all. Since the law is a generalized mechanism of social control, its application covers a great variety of social situations. Different applications require a grasp of these social contexts as well as of the law. From the good lawyer we may therefore expect a generalized capacity for defining situations and a great variety of 'worldly knowledge'. On the basis of this non-legal knowledge and ability lawyers act often outside their speciality, giving economic advice or providing their clients with organizational 'know-how'. The basic propositions of the theoretical model under discussion do not apply fully to these activities: they are not based on systematic theory, the customer may be in a position to judge them for himself, and society does not imbue them with the same moral significance as strictly legal activities.

Finally, it may be suggested that non-rationalized interpersonal skills play, at least manifestly, a greater role in the lawyer's work than the physician's. His relationship to the client shows significant similarities to the doctor-patient relationship[3] but, in addition, interpersonal skills are of extreme importance in litigation and negotiation, major fields of his professional work.

We have seen, then, that in comparison with the medical profession the lawyer's special technical competence, his legal

3. Cf. Parsons (1954, p. 381 ff.), and (1951, chapter 7 and 10), where the lawyer–client relationship and the physician–patient relationship are each analysed in terms of a paradigm of social control that was originally developed from an analysis of the interaction between psychotherapist and patient.

knowledge, covers less of his work, while generalized intellectual skills, various areas of knowledge outside his specialty, and skills in handling interpersonal relations play a more important role. In these non-legal activities the gap in competence between professional and layman may be considerably reduced. The part of the cultural tradition that is the basis of his learned competence is not a body of scientific knowledge, but a system of legal principles and norms, the application and development of which are substantively influenced by the value orientation of the profession. This value orientation is far from clear-cut and, in addition, is subject to societal value dissensus and to the impact of conflicting interests that may be at odds with any given conception of justice. At the same time, the public's concern with the implementation of these variously conceived values is quite intense.

Up to this point we have compared the legal and medical professions in those characteristics that are the basic independent variables of the theoretical model, technical competence and the social values toward which the professional work is oriented. We should expect corresponding differences between the two professions in those characteristics that are treated as dependent variables, such as their self-control. Several such differences may be found.

Ultimate values are important for the legitimation of more specific and concrete normative patterns. To the degree that within a society there is dissensus and ambiguity about the concrete meaning of the ultimate values underlying the specific norms and orientations of a profession, we should expect these values to be seen by the practitioner as less immediately binding and the specific norms to be more often taken as conventional rules the breach of which is of little consequence if 'one can get away with it'.

Societal dissensus and ambiguity about the central 'reference values' of a profession should also strongly influence how the profession is perceived and evaluated by various more or less distant groups. The public image of the legal profession seems indeed to be characterized by suspicions and ambivalences. These are reinforced if the legal profession is seen as linked to certain social classes or religious and ethnic groups and if the most visible work of the profession is concerned with conflict situations and the defense of morally suspect or already condemned persons. Deprecatory elements in the public image of a profession will probably reduce the identification with the profession and its solidarity as a group, unless it is united by very strong common value orientations and interests. [. . .]

Professional services are extremely costly. Therefore, although nearly every profession holds up the ideal of serving all segments of the population, the middle and upper classes are more strongly represented in the clientele of self-employed professions than the lower classes, unless tax or charity funds supply the professional fees. Compared with the medical profession, this tendency is reinforced in the legal profession by three factors: first, the incidence of problems defined as legal tends to be higher in the middle and upper classes; second, the elasticity of demand for legal services is greater than for medical services; third, tax and charity funds tend to be more generously supplied for medical than for legal problems. This situation structurally shields the legal profession against the full impact of the dissensus about relevant values while associating it more closely with the middle and upper classes.[4]

The clientele of a profession is distributed differentially among its practitioners. In addition to technical specialization, and often connected with it, we find a tendency toward specialization in clients and patients of a particular ethnic and class background. Although the general class range of the legal clientele is narrower than the class range of medical patients, certain factors seem to strengthen the trend toward specialization in terms of client background for the legal profession and to lend special significance to such a differentiation of the clientele. There is, first, a rough connexion between the class position of clients and the

4. In 1938, nearly three-quarters of all families in the United States had annual incomes between 500 and 2500 dollars, with an average of 1500 dollars. These families paid on the average sixty dollars for health and less than one dollar for legal services. 'Plainly, lawyers were getting their paying clients largely from the highest-income groups, including only about 13 per cent of the families in the United States. The mass of the people had practically no contact with the lawyer in a client relationship' (Hurst, 1950, p. 255). This book is of considerable value for general information about the legal profession in the United States; cf. also Blaustein and Porter (1954).

legal character and difficulty of their problems. Furthermore, not all lawyers are trusted with problems the adequate solution of which, in the eyes of the client, not only requires legal competence but a certain set of attitudes and value orientations. Finally, the non-legal competence of the lawyer, especially his interpersonal skills, is highly class specific: for example, skill in negotiating with executives is quite different from competence in handling minor officials in local administration.

Association with clients of a particular social class or ethnic background not only seems to be more characteristic of the legal than of the medical profession; it also has more significant consequences for the lawyer than for the physician. Among the factors that give special significance to this differential association are divergent interests and conflicting conceptions of justice and the fact that, compared with scientific knowledge, 'secular law is considerably looser in its points of reference' which could provide a stable orientation when facing pressures from clients (Parsons, 1954, p. 376). Furthermore, clients will probably attempt to exert such pressures more often than patients, and they are often in a better position to do so: their health is not impaired; their education, to a high degree associated with class position, is better than average; their own occupational competence is often related to the issues at hand, and if the lawyer does not confine himself completely to strictly legal matters the gap in competence between client and lawyer may disappear completely.

One last difference between the medical and the legal profession may be mentioned in this context. The doctor's patients are, with some modifications, individual persons, while the lawyer's clients are very often formal organizations. Organizations provide more recurrent business than the average individual client or patient and they can often, especially if they have their own legal staff, check on the lawyer's performance. They are, in addition, in multiple and complex ways linked to other organizations with similar legal problems. Organizational clients exert, therefore, a more powerful social control over the practitioner than individual clients or patients do. Their large share in the lawyer's business further reduces the importance of the gap in competence between professional and client.

These factors lead to an internal stratification of the bar in terms of income and professional esteem; this is found in other professions too, although probably to a lesser extent. They also expose the various segments of the bar to powerful influences from different client groups with their characteristic interests and value orientations, thus creating pressures to deviate from the traditional orientation of the profession or to emphasize and depreciate selectively certain elements of the professional ethos.

A differentiation of the bar in terms of different client milieux that partially determine the attitudes and value orientations of lawyers will place considerable strain on professional solidarity. It will reduce identification with the profession as a group[5] and severely limit the possibilities of the social control, informal as well as formal, that the profession is supposed to exercise. It also will impede the moral commitment of the profession to values that transcend the lawyer-client relationship and its attendant virtues.

These tendencies could be counterbalanced by a strong internalization of common value orientations in the process of socialization toward the professional role. In the United States the socialization of lawyers shows considerable variation, and this heterogeneity is tied with the societal class structure on the one hand and the internal stratification of the bar on the other. Ethnic origin and class background are varied and show a high correlation with length and quality of pre-law schooling, type and quality of legal education, the incidence of non-legal jobs as part of the work career, and, finally. the type and status of legal practise.[6] The structure of recruitment and socialization is not simply a consequence of the special features of the legal profession which have been discussed. It is largely due to the general structure of higher education in the United States and to the specific time at which formal legal education was institutionalized in the United States. It is, on the other hand, not unrelated to a

5. A factor that may limit this tendency is the ignorance which stems from a near-complete segregation of several segments within the profession. It seems that lawyers in the upper brackets of the stratification system of ten are only dimly aware of the existence and the condition of the lowest strata.

6. Cf. Lortie (1959); Smigel (1960); Carlin (1962); Ladinsky (1963). For a comparison of the American and the German legal professions in this respect, see Rueschemeyer (1961).

professional tradition that is ambiguous to begin with and is subject to divergent influences from clients and other reference groups and to a professional competence that includes a good many non-technical elements which are largely subcultural and class-specific. Once developed, the heterogeneity of professional socialization is reinforced by the heterogeneity of the profession itself.

Although this analysis has been developed on the basis of American materials, the distinctive characteristics of the legal profession presented here are not confined to the United States and its legal, economic, and political system. Their incidence and their implications vary considerably, however, according to different societal conditions.

1. Societies differ in the incidence and intensity of conflicting interests and in subcultural differentiation. To the degree that a society shows less patterned conflict and value dissensus the hypotheses derived from dissensus about justice should apply less.

2. Radical social change upsets legitimate arrangements and requires complex innovations in the legal system. The area of substantive consensus is reduced and the system of legal norms is probably more subject to the impact of contending notions of justice and of conflicting interests than an established legal order of long standing that meets more or less standardized legal problems. The profession or significant parts of it are more subject to divergent pressures, while the cultural reference points are at the same time most fluid and ambiguous.

3. Cultural and political traditions differ in dealing with social conflict and value dissensus. If, for instance, we compare schematically the dominant cultural definitions in nineteenth-century Prussia and nineteenth-century America, we see on the one side a conception of justice and the common good as determined by *a priori* solutions to be found and formulated by experts and a rather low level of tolerance of conflict and dissensus, and on the other a conception of justice and the common good as determined by ordered dispute and compromise and a rather high level of tolerance of conflict and dissensus. These different cultural and political traditions rest, of course, on structural conditions, contemporary and antecedent, among which are the position and structure of the legal profession, as Max Weber has shown. At

any given time, however, they are relatively independent of the legal profession and determine the socio-cultural situation in which the legal profession has to operate. These differences pervade the whole legal system: the system of legal norms, the administration of justice, the political and legal position of government bureaucracy, the role of law professors as quasi-legislators and quasi-judges, as well as the dominant attitudes in major client groups and in major sources of public opinion.

To the degree that the dominant cultural definitions and social institutions shelter the legal profession from the impact of conflict and value dissensus, and create the fiction of law as being derived by scholars, the hypotheses about the consequences of value dissensus and the non-scientific character of legal knowledge would have to be modified considerably.

4. The gap of competence between layman and lawman depends on the relative legal competence of lawyers and their various role partners as well as on the importance of non-legal skills in the lawyers' role performance and the relative skill in these respects of lawyers and their role partners. All the factors involved, such as complexity of the system of legal norms, most prevalent types of client, their legal and non-legal competence, and extension of the lawyer's role performance into non-legal areas, are subject to conditions that vary greatly from society to society; important variations occur even between industrial societies which show considerable similarity in their economic and occupational structure.

References

BLAUSTEIN, A. P., and PORTER, C. O. (1954), *The American Lawyer: A Summary of the Survey of the Legal Profession*, Chicago.

CARLIN, J. E. (1962), *Lawyers on Their Own: A Study of Individual Practitioners in Chicago*, Rutgers University Press.

GOODE, W. J. (1957), 'Community within a community: the professions', *American Sociological Review*, vol. 22, pp. 194–200.

GOODE, W. J. (1960), 'Encroachment, charlatanism, and the emergent profession: psychology, medicine and sociology', *American Sociological Review*, vol. 25, pp. 902–14.

GOODE, W. J. (1962), 'The librarian: from occupation to profession?' in Ph. E. Ennis and H. W. Winger (eds.), *Seven Questions about the Profession of Librarianship*, Chicago, pp. 8–22.

HURST, J. W. (1950), *The Growth of American Law*, Boston.

LADINSKY, J. (1963), 'Careers of lawyers, law practise and legal institutions', *American Sociological Review*, vol. 28, pp. 47–54.

LORTIE, D. C. (1959), 'Laymen to lawmen: law schools, careers and professional socialization', *Harvard Educational Review*, vol. 29.

MERTON, R. K., READER, G. G., and KENDALL, P. L. (eds.) (1957), *The Student-Physician: Introductory Studies in the Sociology of Medical Education*, Cambridge, Mass.

PARSONS, T. (1951), *The Social System*, Glencoe, Ill.

PARSONS, T. (1954), 'A Sociologist looks at the Legal Profession', *Essays in Sociological Theory*, Free Press of Glencoe, pp. 370–85.

RUESCHEMEYER, D. (1961), 'Rekrutierung, Ausbildung und Berufsstruktur: Zur Soziologie der Anwaltschaft in den Vereinigten Staaten und in Deutschland', Sonderheft 5 der *Koelner Zeitschrift fuer Soziologie und Sozialpsychologie*, pp. 122–44.

SMIGEL, E. O. (1960), 'The impact of recruitment on the organization of the large law firm', *American Sociological Review*, vol. 25.

24 Brian Abel-Smith and Robert Stevens

Lawyers and the Courts

Excerpts from Brian Abel-Smith and Robert Stevens, *Lawyers and the Courts: A Sociological Study of the English Legal System 1750–1965*, Heinemann, 1967, pp. 1–3, 459–68.

In England 'the law' plays a less important role than in almost any other western country. As many have observed, the British constitution is unwritten; and it is largely based on conventions rather than legal rules. If possible, constitutional issues in England are settled outside the courts as political or social, rather than legal questions. Until recently, for instance, there was little administrative law in England: complaints against the Executive were registered in Parliament rather than the courts. Even civil liberties, traditionally thought of in connexion with the common law, in so far as they are protected, are protected primarily by political and social pressures rather than by any activities of the courts.

This attitude permeates much of English life. The very nature of English society permits many things to be settled by custom or convention, political or social pressure, which in other countries would be settled by some enactment or judicial decision. The government, for instance, exerts its power over the economy not so much by exercising any specific legal powers over the banking community as by a process of discussion and negotiation. In this way changes in the bank rate or exchange control regulations can normally be arranged without any need to resort to legal powers. Control over the stock market is exerted not by a Securities and Exchange Commission, with strong legal powers, as in the U.S.A., but rather through political pressures and the 'sense of responsibility' on the part of the Council of the Stock Exchange. Control over insurance is effected in a similar way rather than through a State Insurance Commissioner. The normal method of enforcing Monopolies Commission reports is through a process of negotiation with industry rather than by reliance on the legal

279

powers which do in fact exist to handle such situations. A similar moral rather than legal pressure controls drug research in the United Kingdom; while most aspects of labour relations are outside the purview of the courts.

The centralization of power in England has meant that there has been less need for legal controls; and this in turn has meant there has been less need for 'lawyers'.[1] But even within this context English lawyers have restricted their own horizons. In many countries, all aspects of 'law' – whether emanating from the legislature, custom or the courts – are regarded as within the legitimate purview of lawyers. With the growth of government powers, represented by increased legislation and administrative activity, the majority of countries in the last few years have seen increasing power pass to a legal profession deeply involved in all aspects of the modern social service state. This has not happened in England for, in general, English lawyers have not regarded themselves as concerned with 'the law' as a whole, but only that part of the law which is dealt with in the courts. This, of course, does raise many questions of statutory law; but the courts are chiefly concerned with non-statutory matters – that is with actions involving breaches of contract or claims for personal injuries where negligence is alleged, or actions concerning property. While English lawyers are conversant with the statutory changes which have been grafted on to the two principal streams of English substantive law – common law and equity – they have remained remarkably ignorant of those many other areas of statutory law which have come to be the basis of modern England.

Social and political pressures, therefore, have made the concept of 'law' in England a narrow one; and lawyers themselves have restricted their interests primarily to the 'law' which is concerned with the courts. But the scope of the lawyer has been restricted still further in this century by the relative decline in the importance of the courts. At the turn of the century it seemed to many that the English courts and English lawyers were at the heart of affairs; but as the Welfare State expanded most new and

1. The functions performed by lawyers in other countries have to be performed by others in England. For an interesting analysis of the distribution of 'law-jobs', from an anthropological stand-point, see Llewellyn and Hoebel (1941, chapter 11).

vital issues were left either completely in the hands of the increasingly powerful Civil Service, or if some adversary procedure were deemed necessary, governments came to prefer flexible policy-conscious administrative tribunals to the more cumbrous and formalistic courts of law. While the courts still perform a vital service in criminal law, in civil law matters they handle for the most part only the same issues as they did at the turn of the century. As the Franks Committee on Administrative Tribunals explained: 'What is judicial has been worked out and given expression by generations of judges.'[2] Common lawyers who, for instance, had sneered at the French *droit administratif*, did nothing to develop a coherent body of English law to supervise executive procedures. Meanwhile even former patrons of the courts, such as the commercial and industrial interests, gradually turned to arbitration rather than settle their disputes in the courts.

The result was that a relatively smaller number of the major problems of modern society were coming before the courts of law. This, in turn, meant that most of the really important issues of modern society were not getting into solicitors' offices and barristers' chambers. [. . .]

Why do courts and lawyers play the role they do in modern England? Do English businessmen often settle their differences without resort to the courts because they are more honest and more willing to compromise than their counterparts in other nations? Is the wide decision-making function given to the English Civil Service entirely due to its quality and the respect it enjoys from the public? Why have administrative tribunals and arbitration tribunals evolved alongside the ordinary courts? Why has the ordinary man in the street so few problems which he regards as matters of law? Why do lawyers appear to serve a relatively narrow segment of society? Why is legal education so narrow in scope? How did the Legal Aid and Advice scheme achieve the structure it has today?

Some part of the relatively minor role accorded by society to

2. Its distinction from what is administrative recalls great constitutional victories and marks the essential difference in the nature of the decisions of the judiciary and of the executive. *Report of the Committee on Administrative Tribunals and Enquiries*, 1957, H.M.S.O., Cmnd 218, para. 28.

courts and lawyers may be due to the quality of civil servants and businessmen; some part may be due to trends in the welfare services. But this is far from being the whole story. There has been an almost continuous dissatisfaction with the courts as a means of settling disputes, registered by businessmen over a period of more than a century. The costs, delays, formalities and publicity of court proceedings, and also the personal antagonisms engendered by the English approach to litigation, have led a large segment of the industrial and commercial community to abandon the courts and establish their own tribunals for settling disputes.

It has been seen that successive governments have deliberately avoided giving new responsibilities to the courts. In relatively simple matters, where swift decisions were needed in accordance with established precedents, the judicial function has been assumed nominally by Ministers and in practice by their civil servants. Where not only speedy action was needed but also a public hearing comprehensible to the ordinary citizen and available without charge, specialist administrative tribunals have been established. This has become the pattern for the administration of the 'welfare state'; the legislature apparently lacking confidence in the judges as arbiters of the public interest in such matters.

The fact that the courts have failed to adjust to the needs of the modern state and the modern economy is relatively easily established. What is of greater importance is to establish why this has occurred. Other ancient institutions have been radically reformed and adapted to serve changing social needs during the last century. Almost alone, courts and lawyers have been left with many eighteenth-century practices and institutions, and in many respects with an eighteenth-century outlook. Some tentative explanations can be offered.

Part of the explanation lies in the weighty representation which lawyers have long enjoyed in both Houses of Parliament and in virtually all governments. The law has always been one of the few demanding occupations which could be readily combined with politics. Lawyers trained by the conservative method of apprenticeship have always resisted changes in the methods by which their successors are introduced to the mysteries of the law. They have also, on the whole, irrespective of party, opposed changes in the High Court – the most sacred temple where the law's mysteries are practised. Moreover, individual lawyers in Parliament have been discouraged from espousing radical reforms of the legal system by the extensive and centralized patronage system controlled by successive Lord Chancellors.

But this is not the whole explanation. A heavy representation of lawyers is also to be found in the legislatures of many other countries, yet many of them have a much more flexible system of courts. Part of the explanation may lie in the tremendous respect and position which Britain has over the years accorded to its judges. By convincing influential opinion of each generation that they were the champions of English liberties, they have been able to ward off attempts to dilute their quality, reorganize their deployment, or alter their responsibilities as dangerous challenges to the liberties of individual Englishmen. The judges have long had a vested interest in the *status quo*, as well as possessing more than one forum for expressing their opposition to change. Politicians may well have feared that any tampering with the judicature would, in the short run, incur public odium on a scale equivalent to tampering with the monarchy.

The most significant difference between the profession in England and many other countries is in its division. As the Evershed Committee recognized, the separation of the legal profession into two parts is closely associated with the distribution of responsibilities between the various courts. The effect of this separation has been to maintain an effective and continuing alliance between leading barristers who have had, like the judges, a clear vested interest not only in the system of centralized courts but also in the complex procedure of the High Court which provides a living to their junior members. In its cohesion the Bar, with its close association with the judiciary, and its effective trade union (the Bar Council), has been a mighty force for resisting changes which would be damaging to its pecuniary interests.

Over the years the junior branch of the profession has also obtained a cohesion and a powerful spokesman in the form of the Law Society, and the latter has pressed for many years for more powerful local courts. Lacking the right of representation in the superior courts, solicitors have not generally pressed for permanent branches of the High Court in the provinces, as this would effectively result in a reduction of the audience rights which they already enjoyed. Instead their contention has always been that the jurisdiction of the County Courts should be greatly extended. The senior branch has, however, been able to persuade the legislature that this would not be desirable. It has been regularly claimed that if County Courts were given wider jurisdiction they would pay less attention to the 'small' cases which should be their principal responsibility. As a result important cases would be handled by an inferior tribunal. Such a reform would reduce the work of the High Court and lead eventually to a reduction in the number of barristers. As judges are exclusively drawn from the latter, it would narrow the field for recruitment of the judiciary and thus, it is always said, have the damaging long-term consequence of lowering the quality of judges.

The divided legal profession has had other important effects upon the administration of justice. Local civil courts were only accepted by the Bar and particularly by barristers in Parliament, when it was conceded that the judges of the County Courts should be chosen exclusively from the Bar. A similar factor may well explain why, quantitatively, the major share of work that concerns the civil liberties of individuals has always been in the hands of lay Justices of the Peace. If, as was always assumed, judges could only be drawn from barristers, it would clearly be impossible to find over 500 stipendiary magistrates to undertake this work from a Bar which had only about 2,000 practising members. Thus the Bar, which had railed against the dangers of appointing solicitors to the County Court bench, have enthused over the work of lay justices with their extensive criminal jurisdiction and not inconsiderable civil jurisdiction. The divided legal profession has thus been one important reason why England has never had a professional criminal judiciary.

For all these reasons Britain's system of courts has escaped radical reform over the past century. The centralized High Court and the assize system have remained despite the evident need for a swifter and cheaper legal machine. So has a judiciary with remarkably little preparation for the responsibilities entrusted to it. After a narrow professional examination and a brief apprenticeship, the future judge devoted years to a busy practice, often of a specialist kind, and during this time, he was carefully prevented from enjoying any close contact with his client. Only an exceptional man could emerge from this experience with the wide knowledge of human nature and ability to recognize and respond to social, economic and political changes which are required of the most senior judges.

The failings of the judiciary and the failings of the formal courts has led to the creation of a variety of specialist tribunals to perform judicial functions. Most important has been the establishment of over 2,000 administrative tribunals which between them hear more cases than the High and County Courts combined. Nor are the matters dealt with by tribunals all trivial. The total value to the individual of awards of social security benefits or of reductions in rents can greatly exceed the common law jurisdiction of County Courts; while decisions on compulsory purchase, a road haulage licence or permanent disability may alter a man's whole future. Lacking the traditions of courts, some tribunals have developed features which could prove valuable for consideration in any reform of the Courts. No fees are payable for using their machinery. They normally work on an appointment system. Applicants can appear in person or be represented by barristers, solicitors or non-lawyers. The procedure is far less formal than that of a court. The bench normally consists of lawyers, laymen and experts, sitting in a variety of combinations.

It therefore seemed in the mid-1960s that England's courts and lawyers were never likely to play as large a role as in some other countries. There were, however, some signs that major reforms of some kind might yet be made. For the first time for a hundred years there were a number of lawyers who were wondering whether their tasks in connexion with tort, contract, property and criminal law were really as important as was suggested by the somewhat extravagant boasts of their leaders. Increasingly it was recognized that power and influence in the modern state had ebbed away from both lawyers and judges. In public affairs it had moved toward the Civil Service, in business matters toward businessmen themselves and their advisers ranging from accountants to business consultants, and even in matters of private law the lawyers found themselves regarded as alien by the working class and, with some exceptions, as parasitic by the middle class. The decline in role, power, image and importance had become obvious to all who were prepared to face the facts. But an appreciation of the facts did not provide a means of changing them. Any effort to increase the relevance of the law and the legal system was faced with innumerable obstacles.

Quite apart from all the political and professional reasons for opposing change the lawyers were still reluctant to regard themselves as providing a service to consumers, let alone a *social* service *for* consumers. The law had remained the last citadel in a capitalist economy where the concept of consumer sovereignty had failed to penetrate. Moreover, the idea that the courts were public services like hospitals, Assistance Board offices or fire stations was not one that lawyers felt readily able to accept. In matters of civil litigation there was still a general feeling that things in England were healthy because litigation *per capita* was lower than in many other countries. Self-medication was still thought of as the ideal in legal disputes. But such general assumptions exhibited a reluctance to examine the rationale of litigation, to see whether society would be better served by encouraging rather than discouraging litigation, and whether the reluctance to litigate was not induced more by the expense, publicity and formality of the courts than by a peculiar English facility at obtaining justice by negotiation and compromise. Nor had the analysis of the role of the criminal courts, or their relationship to civil courts, engaged the serious attention of the profession.

This same reluctance to re-examine basic assumptions was reflected in the absence of any clear direction in that other aspect of the provision of legal services – legal advice. The divided profession made specialization by subject-matter difficult among solicitors, while even the Bar found some intellectual obstacles to specialization although justifying its own existence in terms of specialization of function. Meanwhile it was left to solicitors to mark out the limits of legal advice and the limits had, with few exceptions, been set a hundred years before. Perhaps as much as three-quarters of their income was derived from conveyancing and probate; and for many solicitors these and related subjects formed almost 100 per cent of their work. For most solicitors litigation was an unremunerative inconvenience. Only a minority undertook litigation in a modern and efficient way. Again, only a minority made a genuine effort either to provide proper services to industry or to offer to the more humble elements in society a service through which they might understand and cope with their rights and obligations in the modern state.

This reluctance to examine themselves either as a commercial service or as a part of the 'welfare state' was reflected in the Legal Aid and Advice Act. Once again the legal profession had avoided having itself judged by utilitarian standards. Left to run the scheme itself, it provided an important service well. But the whole outlook reflected nineteenth-century concepts of charity. The lawyer could not conceive of society existing without his services; yet the idea of allowing citizens to obtain legal services as of right was almost inconceivable. What had the makings of an example to the world was in danger of becoming a stringently restricted service as the lawyers undermined the provisions for making legal advice widely available and the Treasury encouraged the profession in its charitable outlook towards the granting of legal aid for civil litigation. Moreover, it almost went without saying, that while legal aid in criminal cases had helped to bring unprecedented prosperity to the Bar, its availability to accused persons was still limited and the tardiness of its granting often fatal to the latter's interests.

The lack of analysis of role or function was perhaps nowhere more obvious than among the judges. It was partly a question of numbers. The implications of the vast number of administrative tribunals were not yet fully appreciated. Some 16,000 magistrates had for generations administered criminal law and parts of the civil law on the cheap. What criminal cases they could not handle were mainly dealt with by members of the Bar acting as part-time judges at Sessions. Small civil work on the other hand, with the exception of that given to J.P.s, was all handled by lawyers – mainly the registrars and judges of the County Courts. But the most important civil and criminal work was left to a High Court Bench of some sixty judges; lawyers, chosen for their success as advocates, untrained as judges, reflecting a narrow social outlook, and accorded an enviable and, by tradition largely uncriticized, position in the social hierarchy.

In general the High Court judges lived by certain self-evident truths. They remained as blissfully ignorant of developments in the psychology of decision-making as they did of other aspects of the social sciences. Despite the advent of democracy they still accepted the mythology of Coke and regarded themselves as protectors of civil liberties, especially those relating to personal property. They still saw themselves as men of power and independence, curbing in their wisdom the excesses of an ignorant Parliament and over-efficient Civil Service – preserving a democratic state by occasionally defying its intentions. For this reason they were deeply jealous of their political position. It was not easy to suggest that they might handle new issues since it was revealed to the judges alone which issues were judicial and which were not. To suggest they might deal with this or that area of government power, or to suggest that many of the decisions they took were very similar to those taken by relatively humble civil servants, who had no security of tenure or independence, were major heresies.

There was an equal lack of serious analysis of the role of the appeal judges. While they were of necessity left with a discretion in deciding appeals it was never clearly articulated whether in exercising that discretion they should seek to adhere faithfully to the internal logic of the common law, or whether they should allow themselves to consider 'non-legal' factors in reaching a decision, which in practice changed the law. But even if they chose the latter it was still far from settled whether they should seek to develop the law by applying policies which appealed to 'right-thinking men' (i.e. the judges) or to seek to apply the policies which might be expected to be followed by the elected branch of government. What was clear was that for Parliament to attempt to overrule even their most absurd decisions was liable to be branded as a breach of the 'Rule of Law'. Only the judges understood the mystique of the law; and the preservation of the mystique required a clear dividing line between the functions, role and (preferably) the salary of the judges and even the most important of the civil servants and legislators.

But even if the judges were anxious to insist that their role as judicial decision-makers was inherently and fundamentally different from any other type of government decision-maker, there were growing pressures during the 1960s which seemed to spell an end to the privileged position of the judges. The historical accident that the courts were originally a part of the royal prerogative, coupled with the fact that appointment to a judgeship was treated as the natural reward from a grateful State to a private practitioner for years of service to largely private clients, often meant that many of the superior judges, when appointed, showed less concern for the interests and convenience of the public than might have been desirable. But the position was changing. Fixed dates, retirement ages and a growing feeling on the part of the younger judges that they were in fact providing a service all helped. There were also other straws in the wind. The pressure of criminal work on Quarter Sessions and of both criminal and civil work at Assizes suggested that the High Court might yet yield to decentralization. The reforms following the Streatfield Report were the first step. There were still arguments about the dangers faced by judges in the County and Crown Courts, cut off as they were from the intellectual stimulation of the Inns of Court; but these arguments began to be taken less seriously as scepticism about the broadening effects of social life at the Inns grew rather than receded. Just as the National Health Service had been an important factor in decentralizing medical services and thereby improving their quality in the provinces, the availabilty of legal aid was putting the assize system under greater pressure and criticism than it had been subject to for a hundred years.

If the senior judges ultimately agreed to decentralization, the work of the courts at all levels might be speeded. It might also raise innumerable possibilities for reform. It might make possible a merging of civil and criminal jurisdiction, and provide for the first time a professional judiciary to hear criminal cases and thus provide greater protection for the freedom of the individual, and not limit this luxury to civil litigants. An expanded judiciary might well acquire recruits from the solicitors' branch of the profession and this change might also lead to the introduction of formal training for judicial responsibilities. Moreover, the expansion of the judiciary would make possible reforms in the hearing of cases, so that those who wished to use the courts or even those who were brought before the courts, or even those who practised before the courts, wasted a minimum of their time. Such a system clearly involved some 'waste' of judicial time; but such time might always be spent in preparing for the hearing of later cases or even keeping up with professional writings – obligations which the judiciary had not always had time to undertake.

If the judges could be threatened with reform, no branch of the profession might remain immune. As the possibilities of home ownership had spread to a much larger section of the population, the basic monopoly of solicitors – conveyancing – was increasingly the subject of attack by critics; especially as the Law Society, in its role as a trade union, had, during the 1950s, provided for even more effective exploitation of that monopoly. It was clear that if the monopoly itself did not fall, increasing public pressure would ultimately ensure that major reforms in the law or conveyancing procedure would be undertaken, so that the fees charged to the public would be reduced. There was even a possibility that the scale fee itself might disappear; and in the long run there was the awful ogre (for the profession) that developments in land registration and computer science might make the sale or leasing of land no more difficult than the sale or hiring of a car – a legal transaction from which the solicitor was conspicuous by his absence. At no time had the Law Society been more sensitive about its public image.

With their restrictive practices under attack in the press, solicitors attempted to turn the spotlight on to restrictive practices at the Bar. Under pressure, the circuit rules were relaxed and, by 1965, the two branches of the profession were locked in combat over many aspects of the barrister–solicitor relationship. But talk of fusion had largely evaporated. The quasi-judicial function of the Bar, by which counsel's opinion might encourage an opposing party or a tax inspector to abandon a claim, was too important to be frittered away. Moreover, fusion would have been a catastrophe for the vast majority of solicitors who practised on their own or in small partnerships. But the Law Society was anxious to see the Bar modernize itself so that solicitors might take the maximum and most economical advantage of specialization at the Bar through the much-vaunted 'cab rank' principle. In achieving this, however, there were those who would not have been averse to solicitors having their audience rights extended, particularly with respect to undefended divorce cases. To the purist, at any event, this presented some difficulty. Since both branches of the profession were proud of the fact that the majority of the Evershed Committee had apparently been convinced that the high cost of litigation had nothing to do with the profession in general or the absence of fusion in particular, the rationale for division in the profession would seem to have lain in specialization of function. But specialization of function would seem to have pointed towards taking away the solicitor's right of audience even in the lower courts – a prospect unlikely to appeal even to the leaders of the Law Society, who were at the same time publicly so opposed to fusion.

But if such logical thoughts delighted the Bar Council, there were more practical and more threatening ideas in the air. An increasing number of responsible persons were doubting the wisdom of keeping compensation cases – that is road and factory accidents – in the courts. The subsidy to the Bar by way of undefended divorce actions also seemed in danger. Even a major crime wave could not come close to compensating the Bar for the loss of all this work. Before the end of the 1960s there might be a real danger of unemployment at the Bar.

The intensive warfare between barristers and solicitors helped to crystallize the power structure in the two branches of the profession. In the case of the Bar, while the Inns of Court still controlled the vital issues of admission, discipline and education, they were increasingly feeble institutions. Their behaviour towards the influx of colonial students after the war, their reluctance to publish accounts even to their members or to discuss publicly their responsibilities under their trusts (if they existed), increasingly helped to consign their activities to the level of the City Livery companies. While the Inns showed little sense of responsibility, the Bar Council, although it achieved power through its effectiveness as a trade union, showed increasing responsibility and sensed its obligations to the public. Similarly, the Law Society, uncomfortably balancing its highly effective trade union activities with its public responsibilities, managed to retain the respect of most of the profession, and even partially to curb the reactionary views of local law societies, although the British Legal Association presented the Law Society with its most important 'ginger group' for some decades.

If the lawyers of the 1950s were complacent about their role and those of the 1960s incapable of offering rationalizations of the legal system, some at least of the blame had to be attributed to legal education and training. Until well into the twentieth century both branches of the legal profession relied basically on apprenticeship, and, subject to acquiring the 'right type' of entrant, were unconcerned with legal education. Law was learnt in chambers or the office just as judging was learnt on the bench. If the universities chose to teach law, this might be useful, so the argument ran, especially for those who were not going to be lawyers. Eventually, however, both the Law Society and the Inns of Court felt the need to provide some more formal type of education, although both had in fact provided some nominal educational institutions since the middle of the nineteenth century. In the case of the Law Society serious efforts were made to develop a proper school of law; and rather more languid efforts were made by the Inns of Court. The Law Society was also toying with the idea of radically altering its apprenticeship system. While both wished to develop more effective schools of law, these were both to be geared to the narrow techniques of the law.

The urge by academic lawyers in the universities, particularly those who had discovered the existence of the social sciences, to develop an approach to academic law which would involve analysis of the policies embodied in the law and the way law operated in practice (in addition to the traditional functions of teaching doctrinal analysis and techniques) met with little encouragement from the profession. University law teaching, which had been grafted on to the legal system only in the nineteenth century, still seemed to have no practical role to play in a profession which was basically eighteenth-century in its orientation. The development of graduate Schools of Business along the lines of the Harvard School of Business Administration did not generate any demand for graduate legal education along the lines of the Harvard Law School. The concern about the narrowness of medical education, which led to the appointment of a Royal Commission in 1965, had no parallel in the law.

Thus in many areas there was little encouragement for the reformer; but everywhere there was more hope than in previous decades. Some element of social conscience was being awakened within the profession, if not spontaneously at least by well-informed pressure from outside. Investigation of social phenomena was becoming acceptable, if not in the law at least in many areas of national life; and there seemed little doubt that the legal system was about to enter a period of reform and re-analysis. Courts, judges, legal aid and advice, the profession and legal education had all avoided a major investigation for nearly a hundred years. The time for such an investigation was at hand.

References

LLEWELLYN, K. N. and HOEBEL, E. A. (1941), *The Cheyenne Way: Conflict and Case Law in Primitive Jurisprudence*, University of Oklahoma Press.

25 Ralf Dahrendorf

Law Faculties and the German Upper Class

Ralf Dahrendorf, 'The education of an elite: law faculties and the German upper class', *Transactions of the Fifth World Congress of Sociology*, International Sociological Association, Louvain, Belgium, 1964, vol. 3, pp. 259–74.

In a sense, German society as a whole has never had an identifiable and reasonably homogeneous upper class. German history since the foundation of the Empire in 1871 may in fact be described as a continuous process of decomposition and displacement of the old Prussian aristocracy of civil servants, soldiers, *Junker*, and diplomats. Even as an intact elite this group could never be called the upper class of the whole of German society: Bavaria had her own aristocracy, Württemberg and the Hanseatic Towns had their patriciate; other distinct elites prevailed in other parts of the country. As it is, however, the traditional and authoritarian elite of Prussia was already, in 1871, no longer an intact upper class. Even in Prussia herself, other groups had begun to compete with the *Junker* elite for economic and political power. In the industrializing society of late nineteenth-century Germany, the feudal upper class of Prussia was an elite in retreat.

However, the displacement of this elite in the decades after 1871 was neither as rapid nor as complete as the corresponding process in England half a century earlier. This is why the upper class of German society remained extremely heterogeneous throughout the last century. Aristocrats and *homines novi*, Prussians and Bavarians, Protestants and Catholics, civil service groups and entrepeneurs, National Conservatives and National Liberals competed and continue to compete for social acceptance, economic position and political power. Even the two German societies of the present could be described in terms of the varying fortunes of one or the other of these elites; this is certainly true for the inter-War years.

Of course, analysis must be pushed further than stating that numerous groups were competing for upper-class status. Some of these groups obviously stood a better chance than others; in fact, some were successful in their claims, and others not. In a formula, the development of German elites presents the picture of a pre-industrial upper class holding on to its position despite a rapid and radical process of industrialization. The incongruities of German economic development on the one hand, and social and political structure on the other, have been noticed by many analysts before and after Veblen's study of *Imperial Germany and the Industrial Revolution*. Contrary to what, in the nineteenth century, was still considered the English 'model', industrialization strengthened rather than weakened the traditionalism of German values and the authoritarianism of German politics. At the same time it did produce new claimants for power – as did the unification of Germany under Prussian hegemony. Although, in the early years of the Empire, most of these groups strove to be accepted by the established upper class rather than to assert their own interests (and although, therefore, industrialization in Germany did not produce a tradition of representative government), the years of the Weimar Republic bear witness to the fierce competition between the old Prussian elite (DNVP – German National People's Party), South and West German Catholics (Z – Centre Party, and BVP – Bavarian People's Party), a more or less liberal bourgeoisie (DDP – German Democratic Party, DVP – German People's Party, and several other groups), and the more radical groups of the Right and the Left. When, in the final years of Weimar, German society once again called upon the 'proven' aristocratic and military elites of the past (in the persons of Hindenburg, Schleicher, von Papen, and many others), this was the last appearance – apart from the tragic revolt of 20 July 1944 – of the Prussian tradition of leadership in German politics.

This context has to be seen in order to understand a distinction which lies at the basis of the following analysis of the recruitment of German elites. There are upper classes of an almost tangible reality, easily identifiable, visible to most people in a society, with well-defined borders and conditions of entry. I shall call them elites of the *establishment type* or *established elites* (thereby alluding to the English case which is perhaps unique among industrial societies). Here, most incumbents of top positions in politics, in the civil service, in the economy, the military, the educational system, and elsewhere, are connected by numerous important links: more often than not, they are – however distantly – related; many of them have been either to the same, or the same kind of school; if they went to universities at all, only a few were in question; there are often sustained personal relations between the members of such a class, including memberships in the same or similar organizations of many kinds. By contrast, there are elites of an extremely *abstract type*, or *abstract elites*, and it can be shown that for these, German society is a case in point. Members of abstract elites have nothing but their elite position in common: there are few if any family relations between them; they did not attend significantly similar schools; they have no personal relations to speak of; in fact, their subjects of conversation are limited to the 'shop talk' emerging from their common incumbency of positions of leadership.

Without doubt, historical conditions could be specified under which the upper class of a society tends toward either the established or the abstract type. So far as the latter is concerned the brief sketch of the development of German elites above may contain a few hints. But here, as elsewhere, it would be wrong to confuse our pure and neat concepts with reality. By simply describing the British upper class as an established elite, one would miss out all the important changes which have taken place in the last decades. Similarly, German elites are in fact neither quite as heterogeneous nor quite as abstract as implied by the definition offered. There are certain ties which apart from social position, if they do not define elite membership in German society, certainly facilitate it. Among these, the most important one has been throughout the last century and continues to be training in the law faculties of German universities. A significant section of the German elite has been trained in law faculties. Some discussion of the extent of this training, its specific features, and its consequences for elite membership may help to elucidate further both the distinction introduced above and the peculiarities of German social structure.

For purposes of this analysis, the terms 'elite' and 'upper class' (used interchangeably) will be applied only to incumbents of indubitable top positions in the institutional orders of politics, economy, education, law, the military, religion, and cultural institutions. Moreover, I shall here confine myself largely to political and economic elites. That is, directors of the largest industrial and commercial enterprises, members of parliament and the cabinet, the highest civil servants and comparable groups in some other spheres. Of these it can be shown that throughout the last decades, and more particularly in contemporary German society, a significant proportion has been trained in the law faculties of German universities. There is considerable evidence to support this claim.

1. Cabinet Members: In his study of *The German Executive 1890–1933*, M. E. Knight reports that 40·7 per cent of all members of Imperial Cabinets between 1890 and 1918 had come from 'non-political occupations' classifiable as 'law'.[1] In the Weimar Republic, this proportion had dropped to 31·1 per cent, the decrease continuing in the Nazi period to 15·2 per cent. These figures are likely to be incomplete since many of those included in the categories of 'civil service' and 'business' are probably also lawyers by training. The estimate would seem conservative that throughout the period in question (with the possible exception of the Hitler governments[2]) about half of all cabinet members had been trained in law faculties.

This estimate is confirmed by an analysis of the four cabinets of the Federal Republic since 1949, where more precise data are available.[3] Thirty-five of the forty-four members of Chancellor Adenauer's four cabinets have university degrees; of these, eighteen have law degrees, and a further six degrees in economics involving at least some legal training. Furthermore, it is instructive to look at the Cabinet offices most frequently occupied by lawyers since 1949. The Chancellor is a lawyer; both Foreign Ministers, all four Ministers of Interior, all three Ministers of Finance, all five Ministers of Justice have been lawyers; the Ministers for Family Affairs and for Health are both lawyers;

1. Knight (1952, p. 41). The classification used here is not very clear.

2. However, 56 per cent of a random sample of Nazi leaders studied by D. Lerner were graduates of law. Cf. Lerner (1951, p. 47).

3. The following data about Federal Cabinets have been collected by a student of mine, Miss Hannelore Schmidt (1963).

two out of three Ministers for Economic Property of the State, two out of four Ministers of Housing, one out of three Ministers for Refugee Affairs, and one out of two Ministers for Affairs of the Federal Council have been lawyers. Among important offices, only those of Economy and of Defence have been occupied by non-lawyers; and in both cases this is a matter of personality rather than principle.[4]

2. *Highest Civil Servants:* With respect to our problem, no detailed statistical analysis of this group is needed, since a law degree is a condition of entry to most positions in the higher civil service in Germany. This *Juristenmonopol* has only recently been broken by the formal admission of graduates of economics, political science and sociology, but it seems safe to predict that this extension of qualifications will have no noticeable effect on the composition of the higher civil service in the foreseeable future. The only realistic exception to the rule of legal degrees as conditions of entry to the higher civil service is at the level of secretaries of state (*Staatssekretäre*), that is, the highest civil service positions in the various ministries, filled not necessarily by career civil servants but on political grounds. Even here the number of non-lawyers is however very small.

3. *Members of Parliament:* Surprisingly, there is little difference between the proportions of legally trained members of parliament in Germany and a number of other countries. Some comparative figures about the proportion of lawyers in various parliaments are given by G. Franz (1957, p. 98n). According to these, the proportions are 7 per cent in Germany, 13 per cent in France, 19 per cent in Britain, 26 per cent in Italy; but 56 per cent in the United States House of Representatives, and as much as 68 per cent in the Senate. The German and French figures are, however, considerably too low, since they do not include those legally trained members who are not actually barristers. In fact 21·9 per cent of all members of the fourth *Bundestag* (elected in 1961) have law degrees,[5] so that we may describe a proportion of

4. The persons involved are, of course, Ludwig Erhard (graduate in economics) and Franz-Josef Strauss (graduate in classics).

5. This and all following data about German parliaments have been compiled by myself from the following sources: *Reichstags-Handbuch, VII, Wahlperiode,* Berlin, 1933: *Amtliches Handbuch des Deutschen Bundestages,*

about one-fifth as the normal rate of lawyers in European parliaments.

Although their explanation is difficult and cannot be attempted here, a few further facts about lawyers in German parliaments are worth considering. It is striking that the last freely elected *Reichstag* of the Weimar Republic (Seventh Period, 1932) only had fifty-four lawyer members among a total of 584. Could this be a sign of the decreasing legitimacy of the system? Among the 466 members of the East German *Volkskammer*, there are but fifteen members with a law degree, seven of whom have recently acquired this degree in correspondence courses.[6] It is clear from this fact that a deliberate attempt has been made, in East German society, to destroy the very structures under discussion in this paper; an attempt, moreover, which – in so far as one can tell from an analysis of the *Volkskammer* delegates – appears to have been successful.

Of the 114 lawyers in the fourth West German *Bundestag*, seven are judges or public prosecutors, forty-four barristers, twenty-one higher civil servants, and the remainder in a variety of political and business occupations. The proportion of lawyer members is highest in the FDP (Free Democratic Party), twenty-one of the sixty-seven members of which are lawyers, and lowest in the Social Democratic parliamentary party with a mere 14 per cent (twenty-eight of 203) members.

4. Entrepreneurs and Managers: In 1954, H. Hartmann conducted a study of the education of 2·018 top-level entrepreneurs and managers in Germany who had university degrees. Of these, the highest proportion (36 per cent) had engineering degrees, but the second largest group (19 per cent) consisted of lawyers, followed by economists (17 per cent). It would seem probable that a portion of those graduates whose professional field could not be identified (18 per cent) as well as of those members of top management who, from the sources used by Hartmann, could not be identified as university graduates because they had no

---

4. *Wahlperiode*, Bonn, 1962; *Handbuch der Volkskammer der Deutschen Demokratischen Republik 3. Wahlperiode*, Berlin, 1959.

6. Of the remaining eight, no fewer than four are Cabinet Ministers or Deputy Ministers, so that the *Volkskammer* is almost entirely deprived of legal skill.

academic title, are in fact also trained lawyers. Probably almost 10 per cent of all entrepreneurs and managers of the highest level are, in present day Germany, graduates in law.[7]

In addition it would seem that, by and large, lawyers have a considerably greater chance to reach the very highest positions than, say, engineers. There are few chairmen of the boards of large enterprises who are engineers, but many who are lawyers. Some of the evidence pointing to this conclusion is presented by Hartmann, who summarizes his analysis as follows:

Our results show that graduates of a law faculty have a greater chance to be promoted to top management positions at a comparatively young age than graduates in other fields.... Moreover, among all entrepreneurs with academic training, lawyers have the relatively best chance to be called into one or more supervisory boards (Aufsichtsräte). More than half of all LL.D.s are members of both board of directors and supervisory board.... In addition, the group of LL.D.s includes the relatively largest number of members, who sit in one or two boards of directors and four or more supervisory boards at the same time (Hartmann, 1956, p. 161 sq.).

5. Other Elite Positions: Needless to say, the legal institutions themselves are borne exclusively by trained lawyers. But another point is worth mentioning, since it distinguishes German society from some others. By tradition, or rather, by the absence of a liberal tradition, a large number of activities in Germany are more or less directly controlled by the State. The administration of schools and universities, of many cultural activities including State Opera Houses and museums, of church funds, of the Federal Railways and many other State-owned enterprises, and of numerous other activities is carried on entirely or partly by public bureaucracies, that is, by civil servants. Since most higher civil servants are trained lawyers, many of the elite positions in the spheres mentioned are occupied by graduates of law faculties.

The numerical importance of lawyers in the German upper class is not, perhaps in every respect, surprising or unusual. There are elite positions which are filled by lawyers as often, or even more

7. Cf. Hartmann (1959, p. 165). The 2018 graduates were taken from a total of 6578 entrepreneurs, but it would seem that Hartmann missed some of those whose degrees are not associated with titles. This group includes lawyers.

often in other countries. In any case too little comparative evidence has been presented to justify dogmatic conclusions. But it may be said that legal training is certainly a considerable advantage, in some cases a condition for entering leading positions in important spheres of German society. In this there is also considerable continuity throughout the last century or so. Looked at from a different angle, this means that many members of the German upper class, however abstract an elite it may be, have at least one experience in common: they attended the law faculty of one of the German universities. This conclusion is further strengthened by the findings of studies showing that a large proportion of incumbents of elite positions in Germany come from families of lawyers. Probably, one out of five university students in Germany has a father who was trained in law: the proportion is certainly very much higher among law students.[8] The question is, then, what does it mean for German law faculties, for the German elite, and for German society that a common experience of legal training connects so many members of the upper class?

If we interpret our findings in terms of the English experience, the point I am trying to make in this paper is that, for German society, law faculties are the 'functional equivalent' of the Public Schools in English society. As the British elite is educated in the Public Schools, the education of the German elite takes place in the university faculties of law. In view of the evidence presented this is, as far as Germany is concerned, clearly an exaggeration. But it is a useful exaggeration since its very statement suggests a number of questions. The first of these will be discussed in this section: How can German law faculties act as 'functional equivalent' to English Public Schools when there are no restrictions on entry? Obviously Public Schools can serve as an agent of social selection by admitting some and rejecting others; but in German law faculties there is no formal admission procedure and, above all, no possibility of rejecting any qualified applicant. I shall suggest that we encounter, within German universities, a subtle system of selection and stratification in a framework of formal openness.

Ever since the Humboldt reforms of the early nineteenth

8. Some of the evidence on the social origin of various elite groups in German society is presented in the essay 'Deutsche Richter', included in Dahrendorf (1961). Cf. especially p. 185.

century, anybody with the necessary qualification (which means today the *Abitur*, or School Final Certificate) may register for any subject at any German university. There is no entrance examination of any kind, nor any control of a student's movements from subject to subject, faculty to faculty, university to university in the course of his career.[9] Yet the analysis of the social origin of students in various faculties shows remarkable differences. In general, the proportion of university students from working class homes is still extremely small in Germany (5·0 per cent in 1958). But it is much smaller in some fields than in others, the extremes being medicine with as few as 1·9 per cent, and theology (both Catholic and Protestant) with as many as 12·2 per cent students of working class origin (Dahrendorf, 1961, p. 187). Probably law is close to medicine, but exact figures are not available since in the official statistics students of law and economics are always combined, although they presumably display rather different social characteristics. There are, of course, some obvious explanations of such differences, including above all the length of study required in various fields, that is, the cost of different degrees. But even allowing for this economic argument, the differences in the social stratification of faculties without any differentiation of formal access remain surprising. As far as law faculties are concerned a few suggestions may be made.

It is clear that those who make their choice of subjects of study – that is, the secondary school leavers – have some notion (correct or not) of what would expect them in various fields. Of all faculties that of law probably presents, in Germany, the least specific 'image'. In fact, it is a standing joke among older schoolboys (very few girls study law) that those who do not know what they want will take up law. Whereas fairly clear professional careers may be associated with almost all other fields of study, that of law opens up a wide and unspecific range of positions. However, it may well be that there is a profound mistake in the schoolboy's jest about those who do not know what they want, in that they are in fact (more or less consciously) those who want to get to the top, and who therefore reject all those professional fields which lead very

9. There are today a number of exceptions to these general rules in subjects where students need training equipment (medicine, science) but these need not concern us here.

nearly, but not quite, to the top. It seems a general feature of modern social structure that specific professional qualifications are in fact a barrier for those who aspire to positions in that small layer of real power where interchangeability is the first condition of entry. Thus a combination of high calibre and unspecific aspirations in the individual is the appropriate motivation for leadership positions; and in Germany it is the law faculties which seem to attract this kind of person.

No systematic study has yet been made of the motives for abandoning law and switching to other subjects of study, although it is well known that the number of students who do so is fairly large. Again, it may be suggested that one of the main complaints of those who change their field of study is lack of specificity and, quite often, lack of intrinsic interest which really amounts to the desire for professionally useful information. Ex-law students often switch to economics, more rarely to subjects leading to secondary school teaching, sometimes to disciplines without a clear professional image such as philosophy, or sociology. In all these cases, however, one contributing factor for giving up law may well be a lack of motivation to achieve positions of extreme power rather than of specific skill.

Apart from such complex (and, for the individual concerned, evidently at best subconscious) motivations, the obvious social attributes of the study of law must of course not be underestimated (although frequently they require an explanation themselves). Thus, it is an often-confirmed observation that students of law are generally much better dressed than students in other faculties. It would not be surprising to find that there are more cars among law students than among others. The proportion of students organized in fraternities (*Korporationen*), duelling and non-duelling is higher in law faculties than in others. Generally speaking the mixture of hard work (or the appearance of it), artistic interests, and a certain sloppiness of personal appearance which characterizes so many university students is rare among law students, who seem more interested in politics than in art, and in social life than in hard work. Since these differences are easily noticeable it seems plausible to assume that they work as a system of selection.

One further observation may be added. Many law students

sincerely believe that as such they are engaged in something special, if not 'better'. This feeling of belonging to an elite is systematically fostered by at least some professors who continue to tell their students that the lawyer has a special responsibility 'for the whole' (of society, presumably) in a manner in which other professionals do not. What is meant as a demand for responsible behaviour is understood by many as a promise of exceptional status which reinforces the other motivations mentioned.

Evidently, many of these suggestions are of a rather unsystematic kind. Even if they hold they do not, moreover, fully explain the surprising social stratification of equally accessible university faculties and the exceptional role of law faculties. Suggestions of this kind may, however, indicate how subtle a system of social selection is required where the crude principles of restricting access to elite schools are absent. Possibly such invisible mechanisms of elite formation are of much greater interest to the sociologist than the traditional caste-like systems which are so often described. In any case, the subtlety of the mechanisms of selection inherent in the law faculties of German universities confirms the description of the resulting upper class as an 'abstract elite', that is, an elite which is ignorant of its status and limits.

In many societies it would be misleading, if not incomprehensible, to distinguish training in law from training for other professional occupations. Law, of course, is a profession, and there is little reason why legal training should be less specific than, say, medical training. But I am trying to suggest that in Germany the distinction between law on the one hand and the professions on the other does in fact hold – at least in so far as the students of law are concerned. A professional training and ethos for more narrowly legal positions is only part of what characterizes training in German law faculties. The subject matter taught and, even more, the ways in which students learn and spend their time generally, are subtly affected by the place occupied by law faculties in German social structure. In this process the teaching of law loses in professional specificity.

This effect is often not recognized because most professors of law belong to the atypical group of professional lawyers. Contrary to their students they (or most of them) have a specific scholarly interest in their subject matter. While unconsciously furthering the elite function of law faculties by insisting on the unique place of law and the study of law in society, most professors of law would resent the suggestion that they are using their subject matter almost as a chance instrument for educating the elite of their country. Yet from the point of view of the student this is exactly what happens (and for this reason the gulf between professors and students is nowhere quite as pronounced as in law faculties). Law is probably the only field of study in which students try to outdo each other in their confessions of disinterest in the subject. Some, of course, begin to take a professional interest in law either shortly before or, more often, after the first state examination. But the majority never cease to ridicule the substance of what they hear and learn, and to assert how boring it all is. For most students of law in Germany the acquisition of specific professional knowledge is clearly a consideration of secondary importance. What matters is to pass the examinations, and – significantly – to pass them with average marks, for it is distinctly 'not done' to get the equivalent of a 'First' or 'Upper Second' in law (nor is it particularly useful in one's later career). In most German universities 'cramming' is the accepted method of acquiring the necessary knowledge, and experienced 'crammers' manage to impart this knowledge to even their laziest customers in less than one year. Thus, what is learned and assimilated by law students in the four or more years of study at the university is clearly something other than specific skills; the subject of law merely functions as an occasion for a more important social process.

This conclusion – speculative as it is – requires one important reservation. It would clearly be wrong to describe the choice of law faculties as places of selection and education of the German elite as purely accidental. It is unlikely that faculties of medicine or of engineering could function in the same way. The reason for this might easily be that the legal system has in fact a special place in any social structure; a place, moreover, which under all conditions connects it very closely with the more general system of values by which a person's social worth in a given society is measured. At the same time, elites are almost by definition the embodiment of such prevailing values in that they control the sanctions with which the conformist is rewarded and the deviant

305

punished. Thus, the norms of a society and its ruling groups are intertwined to the extent of being inseparable – whether one chooses to express this fact by saying that the ruling elites are the groups who 'lay down the law', or, more conservatively, that there is some kind of prestabilized structural harmony between the reasonable and the real, that is, society's values and the interests of its elites. If any subject of specific professional training (rather than, say, the kind of general education imparted by secondary schools) has to be chosen as an instrument of selection and preparation for positions of power, none is more suited to this purpose than law. The study of law is always both specific and general, both technical and almost philosophical, both professional and educational; and perhaps societies differ merely in the extent they emphasize one or the other aspect of legal training. While in Britain there is considerable emphasis on the technical and professional side of legal training, Germany tends to the other extreme. The future members of the German upper class learn the values of their society at the same time as the allure and technique of elite status.

Many general analyses of German social structure could take off from the thesis that, in Germany, law faculties function as an equivalent of the Public Schools in England, and other more or less explicit institutions for elite formation in other countries. Here, I shall confine myself to explore two more general consequences of this thesis. The first of these follows directly from the discussion of the social motives for choosing faculties of law rather than medicine or engineering as agents of elite selection. Evidently, the social function of faculties of law has ramifications both for the legal system and for the characteristic attitudes of German elites. As far as the legal system is concerned, the main consequence is a depreciation of its institutions, and of the legal profession in the technical sense, which becomes especially visible in the comparatively low status of the position of judge. Since the technical aspects of legal training occupy but a secondary place in the minds of many students and since a majority do not enter the legal profession after their training, there is no distinct professional group which might be described as a guardian of the legal institutions. What is more, for many students of law the professional side of their training is not only secondary in importance but also in value. Since studying law offers many more attractive prospects of status, there seems for many no point in aspiring to a place in the legal profession. There are without doubt many other reasons for the comparatively low status of judges, the widespread tendency to denounce the quality of professional lawyers, and a generally low level of confidence in the legal system in Germany, but the present analysis suggests a further contributing cause.

For German social structure in general, however, the other side of the picture is even more important. An elite educated in law faculties is bound to think and act differently from an elite educated in Public Schools or more comprehensive university courses in the humanities. This difference is accentuated by the difference between legal systems of Roman and of common-law tradition. If the present analysis is at all plausible, it is clearly no accident that many decisions made by leaders of politics, business, and other spheres of German society are inspired by a kind of authoritarian legalism: Those in power believe themselves to be experts for almost all decisions, and they often justify such presumed expertise by reference to the 'letter of the law'. The widespread distrust of common sense follows directly from the confidence of German society in an upper class reared in the tradition of Roman Law. In the interest of a spreading of liberal ideas, almost any other subject would be a better medium of elite education than law.

A second general consequence of the analysis presented in this paper leads us back to our point of departure. Even accepting the attempt to compare German law faculties in their social function with English Public Schools, there are a number of obvious differences between the two which are bound to affect their social context. One of these differences has been mentioned before; it is the simple fact that fewer members of the German upper class have studied law than there are Old Boys of the accepted Public Schools in the British elite. There is clearly much less homogeneity in the German elite than in that of Britain and of many other countries. The factor singled out for discussion in this paper is the only one creating some kind of common experience, if not coherence, for a large proportion of the German upper class.

Another difference between law faculties and Public Schools is equally evident: boys enter law faculties eight to ten years later than Public Schools. By the time they begin their university career they are much more finished already than at the age of eleven. Thus most members of the German elites in question have received their most effective education and training in their families and at one of the numerous State secondary schools among which there is, in most areas, no hierarchy of social or scholastic status. The additional influence of training in the law faculties must, of course, not be discounted, but it is not likely to change the ways of grown-up students.

This limitation is further emphasized by the peculiarities of German university structure. To speak of any formal training in many faculties, including that of law, is at best a euphemism. There is no supervision of what students are doing: they may go to courses and seminars or not; in view of the large numbers it is not infrequent that they meet their professors for the first time in the examination room. Under such conditions it is surprising that faculties of law or any other field of study should continue to exert any influence on their students at all, to say nothing of an influence strong enough to mould a homogeneous social elite.

What these differences prove is that, despite the considerable unifying impact of law faculties, the German upper class is still an elite tending towards the abstract type. There have been remarkable changes in the composition of the German elite, especially in recent years. New groups have risen to political prominence; for the first time in German history there is a really strong representation of business in other spheres of power. Throughout these changes the avenues leading to prominence have remained remarkably stable. Today, as in Imperial Germany, the safest way to the top leads through the law faculties of German universities. But the combination of changes in composition and continuities in education has not as yet sufficed to weld the German upper class into an established elite. Recently, the Bonn correspondent of *The Times* remarked in an article: 'Certainly, one would be hard put to discover any real "society" in Bonn, in the rather esoteric sense of that word' (*The Times*, 22 February, 1962). The absence of a 'society' is usually a clear indication that there is no elite in the established sense, that is, no group of top people connected by more than the abstract fact of incumbency of similar positions. By many, this lack of a 'society' and of an established elite will not be regarded as a terrible loss to a country. But the resentment of many may be too quick. It is just possible that where there is no established elite and no 'society' in the esoteric sense there is also no real society in the exoteric sense, no reliable structure of social relations.

References

DAHRENDORF, R. (1961), 'Deutsche Richter', *Gesellschaft und Freiheit*, München.

FRANZ, G. (1957), 'Der Parlamentarismus', *Führungsschicht und Eliteproblem*, Jahrbuch der Ranke-Gesellschaft, Nr. 3, Frankfurt.

HARTMANN H. (1956), 'Der zahlenmässige Beitrag der deutschen Hochschulen zur Gruppe der industriellen Führungskrafte', *Zeitschrift für die Gesamte Staatswissenschaft*, vol. 112 (1).

HARTMANN, H. (1959), *Authority and Organization in German Management*, Princeton.

KNIGHT, M. E. (1952), *The German Executive 1890–1933*, T.23, Stanford.

LERNER, D. (1951), *The Nazi Elite*, T.39, Stanford.

SCHMIDT, H. (1963), 'Die deutsche Exekutive 1949–62', *European Journal of Sociology*.

26 Ezio Moriondo

The Value-System and Professional Organization of
Italian Judges

Abridged from Ezio Moriondo, 'The value-system of Italian judges', paper
given at the Sixth World Congress of Sociology, Evian. The International Sociological Association, 1966.

Until 1961 almost all Italian judges were members of one professional association, the *Associazione nazionale magistrati*. [. . .]

In 1961, as a result of harsh internal disputes arisen a few years
before, the *Associazione magistrati* split in two and a second
Unione dei magistrati was established by a dissenting group of
Supreme Court judges. After this event, of course, the conflict
grew more violent and nowadays the Italian judiciary is broken up
into two main associations and a number of minor factions,
dissenting on almost every issue of judicial life. This kind of
situation is dissimilar from that existing in other countries of the
world and is probably unique in recorded judicial history. [. . .]

As frequently occurs in large-scale organizations, ideological
conflict stems largely from social change. The Italian judicial
system is faced by rapid changes in the social environment, and the
rising 'cohorts' of younger judges are themselves the carriers of
new attitudes toward the professional values handed down to them
by older generations of judges. While Supreme Court justices
(about 400) join, with few exceptions, the conservative-minded
Unione dei magistrati that stubbornly resists innovation and
considers itself the defender of orthodoxy, the overwhelming
majority of trial and appellate judges uphold the radical reforms
proposed by the *Associazione magistrati*. [. . .]

For the analysis of the ideological change brought into the
judiciary by the normal process of organizational recruitment, I
have examined the bulletins issued by the two aforementioned
associations from 1945 to 1965. [. . .] My study is divided into
two main sections: a static part, on the one hand, concerning the
collective value-system shared by Italian judges after the collapse
of fascism, and, on the other hand, a dynamic part focusing on the

way that value-system has been applied in the years after 1948 and on the change it underwent in the same period. [...]

The Value-System of Italian Judges after the Collapse of Fascism

The structure of the system of values expressed by the *Associazione magistrati* in 1945–7, and scattered in a great number of articles and official documents, turned out to be based on a means–ends chain that was at the same time a deductive system into which fitted the logical interrelations linking together the various values and ideas. First, let us examine this value-system as a means–ends chain.

The ultimate ends that oriented the system were *freedom* and *democracy*, as opposite to the fascist emphasis on dictatorial power and imperialism. The judges' conception of freedom and democracy enhanced the importance of the role of the judiciary in maintaining them. To attain these goals the judges claimed full *independence* from the political powers, and this 'penultimate end' could be called their 'master ideal', reaffirmed at every moment in speeches and writings. Independence of justice had formerly been protected by the principle of life-long tenure (*inamovibilità*) of the judge, but the *Associazione magistrati* maintained that tenure failed to secure a full independence as long as the selection and promotion of the magistrates were controlled by the government. Even if reassured by irremovability, the judge might be induced to trade off his sense of independence for a higher post in the professional hierarchy. To avoid this danger the *Associazione* claimed that tenure be supplemented by *autonomy* (self-government) as a means to bring about the collective independence of the judiciary. According to this principle, the competence over the appointment, promotion and good behaviour of the judges should be delivered from governmental control and bestowed upon the judges themselves by means of an elective body, the High Council of the Magistrature.

The fascist régime had fractioned the jurisdiction by creating a number of special courts staffed with men chosen for their allegiance to the regime. *Unity of jurisdiction* ranked high in the value-system of the judges after 1945, as a major means to secure independence of justice. The *Associazione magistrati* was so

311

uncompromising in this issue as to ask for a suppression of special courts and agencies of administrative jurisdiction. Also for the sake of the same principle they asked that the constitutional jurisdiction would be assigned to the Supreme Court of cassation.

Independence, autonomy, and unity of jurisdiction were the basic tenets around which were arranged a number of more specific, instrumental requests, among which can be mentioned: the extension to the *public prosecutor* of all legal guarantees granted to the judge, to avoid the risk that the benefits of an independent Bench would be made void by political manipulation of criminal cases, the creation of a specialized body of *judicial police* under the direct command of the public prosecutors, to speed up crime-detection and to prevent political encroachments on the field of penal justice, a suitable economic remuneration for the judge, modern *technical facilities.*

The ideology expressed by the *Associazione magistrati* after 1945 addressed no criticism against the internal structure of court organization, except for minor remarks concerning the re-apportionment of court districts, the limits of economic competence, the professional training, juries, etc. The court hierarchy and the supremacy of the court of cassation were not criticized, and even less the criteria regulating the relationship between the judge and the law, such as the principles of legal positivism, the doctrine of certainty of law, judicial formalism, and so on. The judges just wanted to loosen the links with the political powers and to remove the distortions those links had caused to the genuine working of the judicial model created by the classic legal ideologies of continental Europe. Even the career system, once cleared of political interference, was highly thought of as a good technique for a proper selection of candidates to the upper courts.

As already mentioned, the pattern of values and ideas that I have sketchily summarized in terms of a means – ends chain may also be viewed as a deductive system. Those same values were linked together in a set of deductions that started from the basic assumption of the sovereignty of judicial power and went, through the intermediate principles of independence and autonomy, down to more specific conclusions, such as the independence of the public prosecutor, the necessity of a specialized body of judicial police, a good economic remuneration.

This scholastic way of reasoning, even if it was unconscious to individual minds and has been brought to light by a comparative analysis of a great number of speeches and writings, suggests that a high degree of rationalization had been reached by the ideology of the judges. This was due to their professional skills and habits, to a long doctrinal tradition, and to the great significance of fascist experience that was often recalled as a negative proof to test the validity of the various values and to demonstrate the necessity of reshaping the relationship between law and politics.

The Borders of a Value-System

The high level of ideological rationalization was also demonstrated by the existence of precise, clear-cut limits to the value-system in question. These limits were marked by two general values, which I have termed '*valori-limite*' (border-values) in order to specify their function, while the judges called them '*apolicità*' (non-politicalness, i.e. unconcern for politics, or lack of political character) and '*a-sindacalità*' (non-trade unionism, or limited concern for economic interests). Both these values entailed collective and individual norms of behaviour. On the collective level they forbade the *Associazione magistrati* to have any connexion with political movements or to make use of the pressure techniques, usually employed by trade unions, for the solution of the economic and institutional issues of the judicial profession. On the individual level the two 'border-values' forbade the single judges to join political parties and trade unions.

The value of 'non-politicalness' was, in a sense, reciprocal with the values of independence, the latter disapproving of the politicians' encroachments of the sphere of justice while the former banned any commitment of the judge to the political world. The idea of non-politicalness was also closely connected with the prevailing conception that the judge, in the exercise of his duties, takes no political decision or choice but only applies the statute law in an impartial, impersonal way.

The value-system that we have just reconstructed enjoyed general consensus among the Italian magistracy in post-war years. To put this into figures: a referendum organized in 1946 by the *Associazione* among its members to test their attitudes toward 'non-politicalness' ascertained that a majority of 1318 stood up for a legal prohibition for the judge to join political parties, and only 180 rejected this proposal.

A great part of the value-system expressed by the *Associazione magistrati* was institutionalized into the Italian constitution (1948), except for minor corrections and a few restrictions. Let's have a look at them. As to 'autonomy', in the High Council of the magistrature the number of judges is limited to a majority of two thirds, plus two members ex-officio (the Supreme Court president and public prosecutor). One third of the members are lawyers appointed by the parliament, and the chairman is the president of the republic. The minister of justice is excluded from the council, and his competence is restricted to the administration of technical and bureaucratic services of the judiciary. As to 'unity of jurisdiction', the special courts of administrative justice were not suppressed. The 'economic independence' of the judiciary was not proclaimed by the framers of the constitution, and the possibility to enforce 'non-politicalness' (i.e. to forbid the judges' joining political parties) was left open to the legislators.

The Application of the Value-System of Italian Judges

From a perusal of the bulletin of the *Associazione* in the years after 1948 it emerges that the judges applied their value-system in a two-fold way. On the one hand, they used it as a framework for evaluating the events of external reality, by means of a constant flow of value-judgements concerning what the government did, what the legislators or the journalists said, and, sometimes, how the judges themselves behaved. On the other hand, the judges tried to embody their value-system into their own collective action, in the endeavour to change the state of judicial affairs and bring about the *attuazione costituzionale*. Among the ends that we have examined a major role was assumed by autonomy. Most efforts of the *Associazione* were directed toward its attainment, but met with a polite, yet strong resistance from the government that disguised its own unwillingness to renounce the controls over the judges' career under the pretext of the 'extreme complexity' of the reform. Once the constitution had been set up as a stately crowning of the existing legal system, the political forces showed a reluctant face to the task of deriving from the supreme law more specific provisions. The resistance met by the judges was a little softer on the economic ground. In 1951 a law was passed that fixed a good economic income for the judges and redefined their legal status as separated from, and superior to, that of the civil servants, among which they had been enrolled by the fascist régime. The controls over the career of the judges, however, still rested in the hands of the minister of justice. The *Associazione magistrati* did not appease itself with the economic satisfaction and went on with pressures on the parliament and on the executive to get the High Council established. In fact, as we saw before, in the value-system of the *Associazione* autonomy went first, and economy had only an instrumental significance.

It was only in 1958 that the High Council was enacted. The Council was provided with all the decision-making powers stated by the constitution, except the power of initiative; that was restricted by the fact that the council could operate only if a matter had been submitted to it by the minister of justice. Even with this restriction a foreign observer, A. Wagner, stated in 1959 that 'in Italy the influence of the minister of justice over the appointment of judges is minimal and the self-administration of judges is greater than in any other country of continental Europe'. The judges, however, reacted bitterly against the law of 1958 for its restrictions of the full initiative powers of the Council. At last a decision of the Constitutional court in 1963 repealed those restrictions as unconstitutional. Hence the political dispute between the judiciary and the executive, having been settled in favour of the former, has slowly calmed down. To make up for it a new conflict has been started, this time amidst the judges themselves. To understand this conflict we must trace the process of ideological change that has obtained inside the Italian judiciary after 1948.

The Ideological Change of the Judiciary

The Italian judicial organization may be divided into three main organizational units that I have distinguished for the purpose of analysing the objects and trends of ideological change. The ideology of a profession, of course, is both conditioned by, and oriented to, the problems of the organizational structure. The main units of Italian judicial structure are: the court system, headed by the Supreme Court of cassation; the professional system of the judges, headed by the High Council of the magistrature which controls the selection, promotion and discipline of the judges; the administrative system, headed by the minister of justice, that purveys the technical and bureaucratic resources to the courts. As we have just seen, the shift of powers from the minister of justice to the high council required ten full years of political tension.

For the study of the ideological change of the magistrature we can confine our analysis to the problems of the court system and of the professional organization of the judges. The technico-bureaucratic system, in fact, hasn't been involved in the process of ideological change, even though its shortcomings and in-effectiveness may have fostered the judges' discontent, thus quickening the phenomena of disadaptation out of which ideo-logical change often arises. But, as a matter of fact, the protest of the magistrature against the evil plight of technical services has not changed since 1945.

The first organizational unit to be invested by ideological change was the professional system. As early as 1950 it became clear that most peripheral sections of the *Associazione* opposed the promotion methods then employed, based on a competition in which the candidates exhibited their most 'learned' judicial decisions to prove their own fitness for higher posts. Of course 'learning', in that case, largely coincided with compliance with the doctrines sustained by the Supreme Court. The commissions deciding over the promotions were appointed by the minister of justice who chose the members among Supreme Court justices. This sharing of the organizational power may account for the fact that members of the Supreme Court never criticized the selection methods they employed, and gave but epidermic sup-port to the *Associazione*'s efforts to bring about the High Council. This would have forced them to share their ruling power over the judges' career with members elected by lower courts.

Anyhow, the competition method, according to its opponents,

did not select the best candidates, troubled the professional activities, and gave way to more or less unintentional favouritism for the benefit of recommended judges. Until 1957 these grievances, despite their prevalence in the whole body of trial and appellate magistracy, did not give rise to a reform movement because the leaders of the *Associazione*, that professed the principle of 'non-politicalness', tried to soothe the potential conflict between Supreme Court and lower judges. At the same time, all attempts to modernize and streamline the promotion methods were frustrated by the government's listlessness.

The Marxian view that ideological change is often fostered by economic factors is once again corroborated by what happened to the Italian judges in the crucial years 1956–7, even though their ideology disregarded economic factors as shabby interests or, at worst, as a trouble for the olympian calmness of justice. In 1956 the government planned a reform of the bureaucratic careers to improve the economic conditions of civil servants. Of course the judges, who had been separated from the civil servants in 1951, were not considered by the reform, so that their economic supremacy over the bureaucracy was virtually destroyed. The threat to the 'prestige of justice' stirred up a great deal of anxiety among the judges and it soon became clear that the 'border-value' of non-trade unionism would be strained by a rising storm. The upper spheres of the magistracy, that affected a lofty indifference toward the economic difficulties, opposed any kind of protest while the younger generations of judges, who were less socialized and had a lower income, were reluctant to throw themselves to the politicians' mercy, and proposed that the judges would go on a sort of strike disguised under the label of '*non collaborazione* with the government'. Instead of striking they proposed to paralyse the judicial work by carefully applying all the provisions of the codes of civil and criminal procedure. However, after a whole year of disputes inside the *Asociaziones* the view upheld by the upper spheres of the judiciary prevailed, and the judges' remuneration lost its supremacy over the bureaucracy.

The events of 1956 began to polarize the ideological trends of the magistracy around two opposite positions, mainly because the frustration that prevailed among younger judges induced them to change the traditional value-system of the profession. The same radical group that had proposed the disguised strike of *non collaborazione* attacked again the ruling elite of the profession in a congress held in Naples in 1957, claiming that the career system should be abolished because it was inefficient and violated the principle of equality among judges. The same obnoxious effects that had formerly been ascribed to the particular methods of promotion were now imputed to the more general principle of the career system, that justified the necessity of promotions. In other terms, the process of ideological change moved up from the technicalities to more general principles. At first the radicals rejected the general principles of hierarchy within the judicial profession: all judges are equal because each of them applies the law according to their individual conscience alone, and not to hierarchical orders. As a consequence they introduced, in subsequent years, the new general requirement of 'internal independence', thus modifying the traditional conception of independence. In the value-system prevailing in the first post-war years, this conception concerned only the relationship between the judiciary and the executive. Now the internal relations among the judges were discussed, and the 'equalitarians' claimed an equal share of organizational power for all judges in the field of selection, training and professional discipline, without any discriminating barriers between 'lower' and 'upper' justices. Once full autonomy from the government became a matter of fact, the debate shifted to the internal question of how to allocate the autonomous power inside the professional organization.

The Supreme Court of cassation itself reacted officially to these ideological changes in the lower strata of the judicial profession and organization by reasserting that the career system was the best for a proper selection. Because of their experience and authority the Supreme Court judges are entitled to a larger amount of power in the profession's organization, that is, in the field of promotion and discipline.

Since 1957 the rift between the younger, more 'left-wing' judges and the top hierarchy of the court of cassation has become a yawning gap. In the meantime the area of the dispute has widened beyond the problems of the career. The career-system was established as a subsidiary organization to supply professionally trained human resources to the higher courts, and the ends and criteria governing the court system oriented also the technical working and structure of the career system. As the technical problems of the career were not solved, the judges in the years after 1960, started criticizing the higher level of the organizational system (the court structure) and of the professional ideology that inspired the system. The supremacy of the court of cassation, that passes over the logical correctness of the decisions delivered by lower courts and does not touch the merits of the decisions, had been established in the Italian legal system to secure the attainment of 'legal certainty', or uniformity and consistency of adjudicative constructions all over the nation. Legal certainty is, of course, the main principle of the ideology of the enlightenment that inspired most legal systems of continental Europe. In present-day Italy, however, there is a strong feeling, especially among radical lawyers, that the same criteria applied for its attainment (such as the separation between the letter of the norm from the investigation of social reality by the legal interpreter, or the predominance of the cassation over local courts) lead also to the bad consequences of formalism and legal technicism. The fact that even the basic and most general tenets of legal doctrines, and the organizational norms and structures derived from them, are now criticized, and that many judges request a deep-going reform of the cassation and the abolition of its supremacy, suggest that the process of ideological change has reached the highest level of the ideological system. This process (that in Marxist language would be termed 'revision') proceeded in a direction opposite to the process of ideological application. While the judges applied their value-system in a deductive way, starting from ultimate ends and general ideas, the revision process went the upward way from particular, economic and technical problems to more general levels of the ideological and organizational system. 'Revision' somehow coincided with a sort of 'inductive' process, which again demonstrates the high level of rationalization inborn in the mind of the judicial profession. The empirical experience which formed the basis of the old value-system of post-war years derived largely from the events of the fascist period, characterized by a strong influence of political power over the judiciary. Thus, the ideology focused on relations between the judiciary and the executive. When the process of ideological application introduced a full autonomy of the judiciary, the ideology shifted to another problem, that of the internal relations between the judges themselves, and many of them felt for the first time the need of 'internal' independence. This Italian experience is important from the comparative standpoint, because the Italian system tried to implement judicial autonomy to an extent that is hardly equalled in other countries. In other legal systems, as for instance those of the U.S.A., England and the U.S.S.R., the nomination of the judges at any level of the court system is a competence of political powers (either the citizens or the government). We may hypothesize that in such systems the tensions that may arise inside the judicial profession tend to be solved by, or to discharge themselves on, the political powers, as it was the case in Italy before 1958, when the judges put lots of pressure on the government to get enacted the rule of autonomy.

27 Abraham S. Blumberg

The Practise of Law as Confidence Game

Abridged from Abraham S. Blumberg, 'The practise of law as confidence game: organizational co-optation of a profession', *Law and Society Review*, vol. 1 (1967), pp. 15–39.

The *Gideon*,[1] *Escobedo*,[2] and *Miranda*[3] cases pose interesting general questions. In all three decisions the Supreme Court reiterates the traditional legal conception of a defense lawyer based on the ideological perception of a criminal case as an *adversary*, *combative* proceeding, in which counsel for the defense assiduously musters all the admittedly limited resources at his command to *defend* the accused.[4] The fundamental question remains to be answered: Does the Supreme Court's conception of the role of counsel in a criminal case square with social reality?

The task of this paper is to furnish some preliminary evidence toward the illumination of that question. Little empirical understanding of the function of defense counsel exists; only some ideologically oriented generalizations and commitments. This paper is based upon observations made by the writer during many years of legal practise in the criminal courts of a large metropolitan area. No claim is made as to its methodological rigor, although it does reflect a conscious and sustained effort for participant observation.

Court Structure Defines Role of Defense Lawyer

The overwhelming majority of convictions in criminal cases (usually over 90 per cent) are not the product of a combative, trial-by-jury process at all, but instead merely involve the

1. *Gideon* v. *Wainwright*, 372 U.S. 335 (1963).
2. *Escobedo* v. *Illinois*, 378 U.S. 478 (1964).
3. *Miranda* v. *Arizona*, 384 U.S. 436 (1966).
4. Even under optimal circumstances a criminal case is a very much one-sided affair, the parties to the 'contest' being decidedly unequal in strength and resources. See Goldstein (1960).

sentencing of the individual after a negotiated, bargained-for plea of guilty has been entered.[5] [. . .]

The institutional setting of the court defines a role for the defense counsel in a criminal case radically different from the one traditionally depicted. Sociologists and others have focused their attention on the deprivations and social disabilities of such variables as race, ethnicity, and social class as being the source of an accused person's defeat in a criminal court. Largely overlooked is the variable of the court organization itself, which possesses a thrust, purpose, and direction of its own. It is grounded in pragmatic values, bureaucratic priorities, and administrative instruments. These exalt maximum production and the particularistic career designs of organizational incumbents, whose occupational and career commitments tend to generate a set of priorities. These priorities exert a higher claim than the stated ideological goals of 'due process of law', and are often inconsistent with them.

Organizational goals and discipline impose a set of demands and conditions of practise on the respective professions in the criminal court, to which they respond by abandoning their ideological and professional commitments to the accused client, in the service of these higher claims of the court organization. All court personnel, including the accused's own lawyer, tend to be co-opted to become agent-mediators[7] who help the accused redefine his situation and restructure his perceptions concomitant with a plea of guilty.

Of all the occupational roles in the court the only private individual who is officially recognized as having a special status and concomitant obligations is the lawyer. His legal status is that of

5. F. J. Davis, *et al.* (1962, p. 301); Orfield (1947, p. 29). The criminal court as a social system, an analysis of 'bargaining' and its functions in the criminal court's organizational structure are examined in my forthcoming book, *The Criminal Court: A Sociological Perspective*, to be published by Quadrangle Books, Chicago.

6. For a concise statement of the constitutional and economic aspects of the right to legal assistance, see Paulsen (1964); for a brief traditional description of the legal profession, see Freund (1963).

7. I use the concept in the general sense that Erving Goffman employed in his *Asylums: Essays on the Social Situation of Mental Patients and Other Inmates*, 1961.

'an officer of the court' and he is held to a standard of ethical performance and duty to his client as well as to the court. This obligation is thought to be far higher than that expected of ordinary individuals occupying the various occupational statuses in the court community. However, lawyers, whether privately retained or of the legal-aid, public defender variety, have close and continuing relations with the prosecuting office and the court itself through discreet relations with the judges via their law secretaries or 'confidential' assistants. Indeed, lines of communication, influence and contact with those offices, as well as with the Office of the Clerk of the court, Probation Division, and with the press, are essential to present and prospective requirements of criminal law practise. Similarly, the subtle involvement of the press and other mass media in the court's organizational network is not readily discernible to the casual observer. Accused persons come and go in the court system *schema*, but the structure and its occupational incumbents remain to carry on their respective career, occupational and organizational enterprises. The individual stridencies, tensions, and conflicts a given accused person's case may present to all the participants are overcome because the formal and informal relations of all the groups in the court setting require it. The probability of continued future relations and interaction must be preserved at all costs.

This is particularly true of the 'lawyer regulars' i.e., those defense lawyers who, by virtue of their continuous appearances in behalf of defendants, tend to represent the bulk of a criminal court's non-indigent case workload, and those lawyers who are not 'regulars', who appear almost casually in behalf of an occasional client. Some of the 'lawyer regulars' are highly visible as one moves about the major urban centres of the nation, their offices line the back streets of the courthouses, at times sharing space with bondsmen. Their political 'visibility' in terms of local club house ties, reaching into the judge's chambers and prosecutor's office, are also deemed essential to successful practitioners. Previous research has indicated that the 'lawyer regulars' make no effort to conceal their dependence upon police, bondsmen, jail personnel. Nor do they conceal the necessity for maintaining intimate relations with all levels of personnel in the court setting as a means of obtaining, maintaining, and building their practise.

323

These informal relations are the *sine qua non* not only of retaining a practsie, but also in the negotiation of pleas and sentences.[8]

The client, then, is a secondary figure in the court system as in certain other bureaucratic settings. He becomes a means to other ends of the organization's incumbents. He may present doubts, contingencies, and pressures which challenge existing informal arrangements or disrupt them; but these tend to be resolved in favor of the continuance of the organization and its relations as before. There is a greater community of interest among all the principal organizational structures and their incumbents than exists elsewhere in other settings. The accused's lawyer has far greater professional, economic, intellectual and other ties to the various elements of the court system than he does to his own client. In short, the court is a closed community.

This is more than just the case of the usual 'secrets' of bureaucracy which are fanatically defended from an outside view. Even all elements of the press are zealously determined to report on that which will not offend the board of judges, the prosecutor, probation, legal-aid, or other officials, in return for privileges and courtesies granted in the past and to be granted in the future. Rather than any view of the matter in terms of some variation of a 'conspiracy' hypothesis, the simple explanation is one of an ongoing system handling delicate tensions, managing the trauma produced by law enforcement and administration, and requiring almost pathological distrust of 'outsiders' bordering on group paranoia.

The hostile attitude toward 'outsiders' is in large measure engendered by a defensiveness itself produced by the inherent deficiencies of assembly-line justice, so characteristic of our major criminal courts. Intolerably large caseloads of defendants which must be disposed of in an organizational context of limited resources and personnel, potentially subject the participants in the court community to harsh scrutiny from appellate courts, and other public and private sources of condemnation. As a consequence an almost irreconcilable conflict is posed in terms of

8. Wood (1956); Carlin (1962, pp. 105–9); Goldfarb (1965, pp. 114-15). In connexion with relatively recent data as to recruitment to the legal profession, and variables involved in the type of practise engaged in, will be found in Ladinsky (1963). See also Warkov and Zelan (1965).

intense pressures to process large numbers of cases on the one hand, and the stringent ideological and legal requirements of 'due process of law,' on the other hand. A rather tenuous resolution of the dilemma has emerged in the shape of a large variety of bureaucratically ordained and controlled 'work crimes', short cuts, deviations, and outright rule violations adopted as court practise in order to meet production norms. Fearfully anticipating criticism on ethical as well as legal grounds, all the significant participants in the court's social structure are bound into an organized system of complicity. This consists of a work arrangement in which the patterned, covert, informal breaches, and evasions of 'due process' are institutionalized, but are, nevertheless, denied to exist.

These institutionalized evasions will be found to occur to some degree in all criminal courts. Their nature, scope and complexity are largely determined by the size of the court and the character of the community in which it is located, e.g., whether it is a large urban institution, or a relatively small rural county court. In addition, idiosyncratic, local conditions may contribute to a unique flavor in the character and quality of the criminal law's administration in a particular community. However, in most instances a variety of stratagems are employed – some subtle, some crude – in effectively disposing of what are often too large caseloads. A wide variety of coercive devices are employed against an accused client, couched in a depersonalized, instrumental, bureaucratic version of due process of law, and which are in reality a perfunctory obeisance to the ideology of due process. These include some very explicit pressures which are exerted in some measure by all court personnel, including judges, to plead guilty and avoid trial. In many instances the sanction of a potentially harsh sentence is utilized as the visible alternative to pleading guilty, in the case of recalcitrants. Probation and psychiatric reports are 'tailored' to organizational needs, or are at least responsive to the court organization's requirements for the refurbishment of a defendant's social biography, consonant with his new status. A resourceful judge can, through his subtle domination of the proceedings, impose his will on the final outcome of a trial. Stenographers and clerks, in their function as record keepers, are on occasion pressed into service in support of

325

a judicial need to 'rewrite' the record of a courtroom event. Bail practises are usually employed for purposes other than simply assuring a defendant's presence on the date of a hearing in connexion with his case. Too often the discretionary power as to bail is part of the arsenal of weapons available to collapse the resistance of an accused person. The foregoing is a most cursory examination of some of the more prominent 'short cuts' available to any court organization. There are numerous other procedural strategies constituting due process deviations, which tend to become the work style artifacts of a court's personnel. Thus, only court 'regulars' who are 'bound in' are really accepted; others are treated routinely and in almost a coldly correct manner.

The defense attorneys, therefore, whether of the legal-aid, public defender variety, or privately retained, although operating in terms of pressures specific to their respective role and organizational obligations, ultimately are concerned with strategies which tend to lead to a plea. It is the rational, impersonal elements involving economies of time, labor, expense and a superior commitment of the defense counsel to these rationalistic values of maximum production of court organization that prevail, in his relationship with a client. The lawyer 'regulars' are frequently former staff members of the prosecutor's office and utilize the prestige, know-how and contacts of their former affiliation as part of their stock in trade. Close and continuing relations between the lawyer 'regular' and his former colleagues in the prosecutor's office generally overshadow the relationship between the regular and his client. The continuing colleagueship of supposedly adversary counsel rests on real professional and organizational needs of a *quid pro quo*, which goes beyond the limits of an accommodation or *modus vivendi* one might ordinarily expect under the circumstances of an otherwise seemingly adversary relationship. Indeed, the adversary features which are manifest are for the most part muted and exist even in their attenuated form largely for external consumption. The principals, lawyer and assistant district attorney, rely upon one another's cooperation for their continued professional existence, and so the bargaining between them tends usually to be 'reasonable' rather than fierce.

Fee Collection and Fixing

The real key to understanding the role of defense counsel in a criminal case is to be found in the area of the fixing of the fee to be charged and its collection. The problem of fixing and collecting the fee tends to influence to a significant degree the criminal court process itself, and not just the relationship of the lawyer and his client. In essence, a lawyer-client 'confidence game' is played. [. . .] In a genuine confidence game the perpetrator manipulates the basic dishonesty of his partner, the victim or mark, toward his own (the confidence operator's) ends. [. . .]

Legal service lends itself particularly well to confidence games. Usually, a plumber will be able to demonstrate empirically that he has performed a service by clearing up the stuffed drain, repairing the leaky faucet or pipe – and therefore merits his fee. He has rendered, when summoned, a visible, tangible boon for his client in return for the requested fee. [. . .]

In the practise of law there is a special problem in this regard, no matter what the level of the practitioner or his place in the hierarchy of prestige. Much legal work is intangible either because it is simply a few words of advice, some preventive action, a telephone call, negotiation of some kind, a form filled out and filed, a hurried conference with another attorney or an official of a government agency, a letter or opinion written, or a countless variety of seemingly innocuous, and even prosaic procedures and actions. These are the basic activities, apart from any possible court appearance, of almost all lawyers at all levels of practise. Much of the activity is not in the nature of the exercise of the traditional, precise professional skills of the attorney such as library research and oral argument in connexion with appellate briefs, court motions, trial work, drafting of opinions, memoranda contracts, and other complex documents and agreements. Instead, much legal activity, whether it is at the lowest or highest 'white shoe' law firm levels, is of the brokerage, agent, sales representative, lobbyist type of activity, in which the lawyer acts for someone else in pursuing the latter's interests and designs. The service is intangible (Mills, 1951, pp. 121–9; Carlin, 1962). [. . .]

The lack of visible end product offers a special complication in the course of the professional life of the criminal court lawyer with respect to his fee and in his relations with his client. The plain fact is that an accused in a criminal case always 'loses' even when he has been exonerated by an acquittal, discharge, or dismissal of his case. The hostility of an accused which follows as a consequence of his arrest, incarceration, possible loss of job, expense and other traumas connected with his case is directed, by means of displacement, toward his lawyer. It is in this sense that it may be said that a criminal lawyer never really 'wins' a case. The really satisfied client is rare, since in the very nature of the situation even an accused's vindication leaves him with some degree of dissatisfaction and hostility. It is this state of affairs that makes for a lawyer-client relationship in the criminal court which tends to be a somewhat exaggerated version of the usual lawyer-client confidence game. [. . .]

Defense Lawyer as Double Agent

The lawyer has often been accused of stirring up unnecessary litigation, especially in the field of negligence. He is said to acquire a vested interest in a cause of action or claim which was initially his client's. The strong incentive of possible fee motivates the lawyer to promote litigation which would otherwise never have developed. However, the criminal lawyer develops a vested interest of an entirely different nature in his client's case: to limit its scope and duration rather than do battle. Only in this way can a case be 'profitable'. Thus, he enlists the aid of relatives not only to assure payment of his fee, but he will also rely on these persons to help him in his agent-mediator role of convincing the accused to plead guilty, and ultimately to help in 'cooling out' the accused if necessary.

It is at this point that an accused-defendant may experience his first sense of 'betrayal'. While he had perhaps perceived the police and prosecutor to be adversaries, or possibly even the judge, the accused is wholly unprepared for his counsel's role performance as an agent-mediator. In the same vein, it is even less likely to occur to an accused that members of his own family or other kin may become agents, albeit at the behest and urging of other agents or mediators, acting on the principle that they are in reality helping an accused negotiate the best possible plea arrangement under the circumstances. Usually, it will be the lawyer who will activate next of kin in this role, his ostensible motive being to arrange for his fee. But soon latent and unstated motives will assert themselves, with entreaties by counsel to the accused's next of kin, to appeal to the accused to 'help himself' by pleading. *Gemeinschaft* sentiments are to this extent exploited by a defense lawyer (or even at times by a district attorney) to achieve specific secular ends, that is, of concluding a particular matter with all possible dispatch. [. . .]

In effect, in his role as double agent, the criminal lawyer performs an extremely vital and delicate mission for the court organization and the accused. Both principals are anxious to terminate the litigation with a minimum of expense and damage to each other. There is no other personage or role incumbent in the total court structure more strategically located, who by training and in terms of his own requirements is more ideally suited to do so than the lawyer. In recognition of this, judges will co-operate with attorneys in many important ways. For example, they will adjourn the case of an accused in jail awaiting plea or sentence if the attorney requests such action. While explicitly this may be done for some innocuous and seemingly valid reason, the tacit purpose is that pressure is being applied by the attorney for the collection of his fee, which he knows will probably not be forthcoming if the case is concluded. Judges are aware of this tactic on the part of lawyers who, by requesting an adjournment, keep an accused incarcerated a while longer as a not too subtle method of dunning a client for payment. However, the judges will go along with this on the ground that important ends are being served. Often, the only end served is to protect a lawyer's fee.

The judge will help an accused's lawyer in still another way. He will lend the official aura of his office and courtroom so that a lawyer can stage manage an impression of an 'all out' performance for the accused in justification of his fee. The judge and other court personnel will serve as a backdrop for a scene charged with dramatic fire, in which the accused's lawyer makes a stirring appeal in his behalf. With a show of restrained passion the lawyer will intone the virtues of the accused and recite the social deprivations which have reduced him to his present state. The speech varies somewhat, depending on whether the accused has been convicted after trial or has pleaded guilty. In the main, however, the incongruity, superficiality, and ritualistic character of the total performance is underscored by a visibly impassive, almost bored reaction on the part of the judge and other members of the court retinue.

Afterward, there is a hearty exchange of pleasantries between the lawyer and district attorney, wholly out of context in terms of the supposed adversary nature of the preceding events. The fiery passion in defense of his client is gone, and the lawyers for both sides resume their offstage relations, chatting amiably and perhaps including the judge in their restrained banter. No other aspect of their visible conduct so effectively serves to put even a casual observer on notice that these individuals have claims upon each other. These seemingly innocuous actions are indicative of continuing organizational and informal relations, which in their intricacy and depth, range far beyond any priorities or claims a particular defendant may have.[9]

Criminal law practise is a unique form of private law practise since it really only appears to be private practise.[10] Actually it is bureaucratic practise, because of the legal practitioner's enmeshment in the authority, discipline, and perspectives of the court organization. Private practise, supposedly, in a professional sense, involves the maintenance of an organized, disciplined body of knowledge and learning; the individual practitioners are imbued with a spirit of autonomy and service, the earning of a livelihood being incidental. In the sense that the lawyer in the criminal court serves as a double agent, serving higher organizational rather than professional ends, he may be deemed to be engaged in bureaucratic rather than private practise. To some extent the lawyer-client 'confidence game', in addition to its other functions, serves to conceal this fact.

9. For a conventional summary statement of some of the inevitable conflicting loyalties encountered in the practise of law, see Cheatham (1955, pp. 70–79).

10. Some lawyers at either end of the continuum of law practise appear to have grave doubts as to whether it is indeed a profession at all (Carlin, 1962, p. 192; Smigel, 1964, pp. 304–5). Increasingly, it is perceived as a business with widespread evasion of the Canons of Ethics, duplicity and chicanery being practised in an effort to get and keep business.

References

CARLIN, J. E. (1962), *Lawyers on Their Own: A Study of Individual Practitioners in Chicago*, Rutgers University Press.

CHEATHAM, E. E. (1955), *Cases and Materials on the Legal Profession*, 2nd edn.

DAVIS, F. J. *et al.* (1962), *Society and the Law: New Meanings for an old Profession*, Free Press of Glencoe.

FREUND, P. A. (1963), 'The legal professions', *Daedalus*, pp. 689–700.

GOLDFARB, R. (1965), *Ransom – A Critique of the American Bail System*.

GOLDSTEIN, A. S. (1960), 'The state and the accused: balance of advantage in criminal procedure', *Yale Law Journal*, vol. 69, pp. 1149–99.

LADINSKY, J. (1963), 'Careers of lawyers, law practise, and legal institutions', *American Sociological Review*, vol. 28, pp. 47–54.

MILLS, C. W. (1951), *White Collar: American Middle Classes*, Oxford University Press, pp. 121–9.

ORFIELD, L. B. (1947), *Criminal Procedure from Arrest to Appeal*, Oxford University Press.

PAULSEN, M. G. (1964), *Equal Justice for the Poor Man*.

SMIGEL, E. O. (1964). *The Wall Street Lawyer: Professional Organization Man?*, Free Press of Glencoe.

WARKOV, S., and ZELAN, J. (1965), *Lawyers in the Making*, Aldine Publishing Co.

WOOD, A. L. (1956), 'Informal relations in the practise of criminal law', *American Journal of Sociology*, vol. 62, pp. 48–55.

28 Jerome E. Carlin and Jan Howard

Legal Representation and Class Justice

Abridged from Jerome E. Carlin and Jan Howard, 'Legal representation and class justice', *U.C.L.A. Law Review*, vol. 12 (1965), pp. 381–431.

Half a century ago Reginald Heber Smith delivered the following indictment of our legal system:

The administration of American justice is not impartial, the rich and the poor do not stand on an equality before the law, the traditional method of providing justice has operated to close the doors of the courts to the poor, and has caused a gross denial of justice in all parts of the country to millions of persons (Smith, 1919, p. 8).

Smith saw this denial of justice as arising from the very nature of our legal system which requires the services of trained lawyers for its effective use but prices such services beyond the means of large numbers of individuals:

The machinery of justice can be operated only through attorneys ... attorneys must be paid for such services. This is the great, the inherent and fundamental difficulty, inherent because our legal institutions were framed with the intention that trained advocates should be employed, and fundamental in the sense that no amount of reorganization or simplification, short of a complete overturn of the whole structure, can entirely remove the necessity for the attorney (1919, p. 241).

He also proposed a solution: an expansion of the newly emerging Legal Aid organizations:

They are, indeed, the key to the solution of the whole problem, for if we can speedily give them resources which they need and deserve, they will move forward and become the instrument through which we can attain the desired end (1919, p. 240).

The administration of justice in the United States still results in a radically different quality for the rich and the poor. This class system of justice rests very largely, as Smith saw, on differences in availability and quality of legal representation. We do not believe, however, that inequality in legal representation is simply a function of differential income or that the situation can be effectively remedied by Legal Aid organization.

1. Class Differences in Legal Representation

(a) Use of private lawyers

The use of lawyers is considerably less prevalent among lower than upper classes in the United States. Surveys of laymen in

Table 1

Relationship Between Social Class and Use of Private Lawyers (Findings from Five Studies)

California study[a] (1940)		Iowa study[b] (1949)			
Income groups	% who have ever employed a lawyer	Income groups	% who have ever hired a lawyer	Selected occupational groups	% who have ever hired a lawyer
Upper	76 (207)*	High	69 (176)	Manager	66 (110)
Upper middle	63 (579)			Professional	54 (69)
				Clerical	48 (156)
				Skilled	42 (78)
Lower middle	52 (734)	Middle	(No Information)	Semi-skilled	30 (110)
				Unskilled	37 (39)
Lower	36 (582)	Low	37 (234)	Farm laborer	22 (18)

Koos study[c] (1949)				Texas study[d] (1952)		Missouri study[e] (1963)	
In the five Cities Studied		In the City of Akron					
Socio-economic class	% who have ever hired a lawyer	Socio-economic class	% who have ever hired a lawyer	Socio-economic class	% who have ever hired a lawyer	Income groups	% who have ever gone to a lawyer
				Upper and upper middle	49 (394)	10,000 to 19,999	77
						6,000 to 9,999	67
Middle class	60 (843)	Middle class	77 (133)				
				Lower middle	38 (324)	4,000 to 5,999	61
						2,000 to 3,999	64
Working class	44 (730)	Working class	38 (87)	Lower	31 (282)	and Under	57

* Number in parenthesis indicates the number of respondents.

a *Public Opinion Poll for the State Bar of California*, Lord and Thomas, 1940. No indication given as to selection of sample or definition of income groups. Percentages reported here are based on the number of respondents experiencing one or more problems listed in the questionnaire.

b *Lay Opinion of Iowa Lawyers, Courts and Laws*, Iowa State Bar Association, 1949. 'This Survey was conducted on the same cross-section used by the Iowa Poll, designed and kept current by Dr Norman C. Meier of the State University of Iowa. The "quota sampling" method was used, the regular Iowa Poll Practise.' The sample con-

several states over the past years indicate that about two-thirds of lower-class families have *never* employed a lawyer, compared to about one-third of upper-class families (see Table 1).

A recent study of lawyers in private practise in New York

---

sisted of 978 persons. No indication given as to how income groups were defined.

[c] *The Family and the Law*, Earl Loman Koos, National Legal Aid Association, Rochester, 1949. 4,150 questionnaires were mailed to middle-class families in the six cities and 2,027 responses were received. 'These [mailed] questionnaires were matched for each city with an approximately equal number of interviews with working class families,' 2,050 in all. No indication given as to how the socio-economic status of the families was determined. Figures for the middle class appear to be based on use of lawyers within the 12 months prior to the study, whereas, the figures for the working class refer to use of a lawyer *ever*, with no limitation on the time.

[d] *What Texans Think of Lawyers*, Joe Belden and Associates, 1952. The sample of 1,000 was designed to be representative of the adult population of the State. Less than 1 per cent refused to start the interview and even fewer quit in the middle. 'Each interviewer received an assignment that told him the exact quotas of different types of people to interview. These quotas ... impart to the total sample the proper proportions of people by section of the state, by size of city, by urban-rural residence, ... by sex, by age, by socio-economic level, and by race.... The socio-economic level classification was made by the interviewer for every respondent, on the basis of apparent social position, financial well-being, education, appearance of the home, occupation and the like.' The 'upper and upper middle' class represents about 40 per cent of the Texas population, and the 'lower and lower middle' the remaining 60 per cent.

[e] *Prentice-Hall Missouri Bar Study*, Missouri State Bar Association, 1963. 2,500 laymen were chosen as a layman sample. Seven geographic regions covering all of Missouri were used as the basis for selecting the sample. Interview quotas by occupation, sex and socio-economic status were established on the basis of the U.S. Census of Population, 1960. This is the only one of the five studies in which the proportion using lawyers does not refer to those who have employed or hired a lawyer. Therefore, those who have gone to Legal Aid offices could be included, and this might account for the larger percentage of lower class use of lawyers than shown in the other studies.

City corroborates the findings from these surveys of laymen. Thus it was found that less than 5 per cent of the lawyers report that the median income of their clients was under $5,000 a year, although half the families and unrelated individuals in New York City have incomes under this amount. Conversely, 70 per cent of the lawyers report that the median income of their clients was in excess of $10.000, though less than 10 per cent of New York's families and unrelated individuals receive incomes that high.[1]

(b) Quality of representation

Lawyers representing lower-class persons tend to be the least competent members of the bar, and those least likely to employ a high level or wide range of technical skills.

In the highly stratified professional community of the metropolitan bar, for example, the large firms serving wealthy individuals and large corporations claim a lion's share of the best legal talent (Smigel, 1964, chapter 3). Lawyers available to lower-class clients, on the other hand, practise almost exclusively in the smaller firms,[2] and consequently are at the lower end of the

1. See Carlin (1966). This study is based on interviews conducted in 1960 with a random sample of 800 lawyers in private practise in Manhattan and the Bronx.

2. The median income of clients by size of firm in New York City (1960) is as follows:*

Median income of clients	Individual practitioner	Size of firm Small firm (2–4 lawyers)	Middle firm (5–14 lawyers)	Large firm (15+ lawyers)
Under $5.000	11	12	1	0
$5.000–$9.999	36	25	11	1
$10.000–$20.000	32	28	23	19
Over $20.000	23	36	64	80
Total	100%	100%	100%	100%
No. of cases	(329)	(138)	(116)	(49)

*From Carlin (1966). Lawyers in individual practise and small firms represent 64 per cent of the lawyers in private practise in New York City.

bar in terms of quality of training and academic achievement.[3]

Lawyers available to lower-class clients are not only less competent, but whatever legal talents they have are less likely to be employed in handling matters for their poorer clients. In part this is in direct consequence of the fee. Thus, Hubert O'Gorman reports that among matrimonial lawyers in New York City (practically all of whom are individual practitioners or in small firms) the size of the fee has considerable impact on the quality of service provided. Not only is the amount of time spent on legal research conditioned by the anticipated compensation, but fees may also 'dictate the strategy and tactics employed in legal representation'.

In particular:

In giving advice about types of actions, places of jurisdiction, gathering of evidence, negotiation and litigation, a lawyer must consider carefully his client's finances. Sound professional guidance is useless if the client cannot pay the costs involved (O'Gorman, 1963, p. 61).

The quality of service rendered poorer clients is also affected by the non-repeating character of the matters they typically

3. The following table (from Carlin, 1966, p. 178) shows that, in New York City, the smaller the firm a lawyer is in the less likely he is to have had a full four years of undergraduate training, to have attended a top quality law school, or to have attained a high academic standing in law school:

Proportion of Lawyers with Specified Characteristics in Each Size of Firm

Training characteristics	Individual practitioners	Size of firm		
		Small	Middle	Large
A four-year college degree	47	52	56	77
Attended a full-time university law school	19	22	43	77
Attained high academic standing in law school (*Law Review*)	9	13	27	32
No. of cases	(376)	(161)	(204)	(60)

Data from this study indicate that it is primarily the younger and hence the least experienced lawyers who are most likely to represent low-status clients.

bring to lawyers (such as divorce, criminal, personal injury) this combined with the small fees encourages a mass processing of cases. As a result, only a limited amount of time and interest is usually expended on any one case – there is little or no incentive to treat it except as an isolated piece of legal business. Moreover, there is ordinarily no desire to go much beyond the case as the client presents it and such cases are only accepted when there is a clear-cut cause of action; that is, when they fit into convenient legal categories and promise a fairly certain return (see Carlin 1962, chapter 2).

A final significant fact about quality of representation is that lower-class clients are most likely to be provided with remedial service only. If a poor person gets to a lawyer it is generally after the fact – after he has been arrested, after his wages have been garnished, or after his property has been repossessed.

The quality of legal service provided the poor, of course, is a far cry from that available to the well-to-do client. In representing these clients lawyers provide a much wider range of services and they are of a more continuous and preventive nature. Such services include: (1) planning and setting up legal arrangements by establishing contractual relationships to effectuate the client's wishes and to insure certain legal advantages, and (2) clarifying and fashioning the law to provide maximum protection of the client's interests by means of lobbying in legislative and administrative agencies, and by presenting carefully worked out legal arguments before various official bodies, including appellate tribunals.

(c) Integrity of representation

In addition to the foregoing, the lawyers available to lower-class clients (those in smaller firms) are less likely to conform to the minimal ethical standards of the bar; which means, among other things, that they are most likely to take advantage of their clients.[4] A study of individual practitioners in Chicago has shown, for example that lawyers with lower-status clients who become dependent on intermediaries to supply them with a large number of 'one-shot' matters often consider their clients

4. This includes such infractions as: conversion of clients' funds, over-reaching, abuse of confidential information. See Carlin (1966).

expendable and are apt to exploit them.[5] Data from a study of the New York City Bar also show that lawyers with a low-status, high-turnover clientele are most likely to succumb to temptations to exploit clients (see Carlin, 1966).

2 Denial of Justice to the Poor

Class differences in legal representation need not necessarily constitute a denial of justice to the poor. To the extent that there is exploitation by lawyers, there is, of course, a denial of justice; but with respect to class differences in the use and quality of private representation one could maintain that inequality is not tantamount to injustice. It could be argued that:

1. The poor are less likely to use lawyers because they are less likely to need lawyers, the contention being that they have fewer problems requiring legal representation. Proponents of this view may go even further and claim that the problems of the poor are inherently non-legal – that they are essentially economic, social or psychological in character.

2. Although private counsel may be inaccessible to the poor, adequate substitutes for such representation are provided in the form of Legal Aid, court-assigned counsel, public defenders and special tribunals.

Let us now carefully consider the validity of these arguments.

(a) The poor have fewer legal problems

The thrust of this argument is as follows. Since the poor are, by definition, less likely to have the kinds of property or business interest that require legal services, they quite naturally have less need for legal representation. Data from the layman surveys

5. 'In the case of those lawyers specializing in personal injury, local tax, collections, criminal, and to some extent divorce work, the relationship with the client, as we have seen, is generally mediated by a broker or business supplier who may be either another lawyer or a layman. In these fields of practise the lawyer is principally concerned with pleasing the broker or of winning his approval, more so than he is with satisfying the individual client. The source of business generally counts for more than the client, especially where the client is unlikely to return or to send in other clients. The client is then expendable; he can be exploited to the full' (Carlin, 1962, pp. 161–2).

referred to above seem to support this contention. For example, as shown in Table 2, the California survey indicates that lower-class families are less likely to make wills, to enter into contracts or into lease and deed agreements, and to sue or be sued.

Table 2
Relationship Between Social Class and Various Events

% Reporting	Lower	Lower-middle	Upper-middle	Upper
		Social class		
Made a will	7	14	25	46
Entered into a contract	14	20	32	44
Made a lease or deed	15	26	37	50
Sued another	7	13	18	26
Sued by another	6	8	12	19
No. of cases	207	579	734	582

* Public Opinion Poll for the State Bar of California.

Furthermore, this survey shows that among those who do make wills, enter into contracts, etc., lower-class persons are as likely as the upper class to use lawyers. Upon further reflection, however, it appears that these findings do not necessarily indicate that the poor have fewer legal problems. Although the events represented in Table 2 are legal acts, they hardly exhaust the list of such acts.

Further, the bases for this line of argument appear to be unsound. In the first place, the different rates of making wills, contracts, etc., do not necessarily represent different *needs* for legal services. They represent differences in legal *faits accomplis*. The actions presented in Table 2 reflect problems that have been translated into legal events. One who makes a will or enters into a contract or files a suit obviously has already defined his problem as one that calls for some kind of legal action. There need not be, however, a one-to-one relationship between the *existence* of a legal problem on the one hand and the recognition and the exercise of legal rights on the other.

Furthermore, those who pursue this particular argument to show that the poor have fewer legal problems generally adopt a quite narrow and somewhat unrealistic definition of property.

It is undoubtedly true that lower-class persons are less likely to own or to be involved in transactions concerning the more traditional forms of property such as real estate or corporate securities. These traditional forms of property, however, do not necessarily exhaust the full range of economic interests that already have or may well deserve to be given the protection of property. Job rights, social security, unemployment compensation, public assistance, health insurance, retirement funds, and a host of similar interests tend to be the characteristic forms of economic wealth for the poor. The fact that these interests may not always be recognized as property may well be the result of the failure of the poor to establish or pursue their legal rights in these areas. Indeed, Charles Reich argues that to insure the dignity of the individual these benefits must be recognized as property and protected as a matter of right:

> The concept of rights is most urgently needed with respect to benefits like unemployment compensation, public assistance, and old age insurance. These benefits are based upon a recognition that misfortune and deprivation are often caused by forces far beyond the control of the individual, such as technological change, variations in demand for goods, depressions, or wars. The aim of these benefits is to preserve the selfsufficiency of the individual, to rehabilitate him where necessary, and to allow him to be a valuable member of a family and a community; in theory they represent part of the individual's rightful share in the commonwealth. Only by making such benefits into rights can the welfare state achieve its goal of providing a secure minimum basis for individual well-being and dignity in a society where each man cannot be wholly the master of his own destiny (Reich, 1964, pp. 733, 785–6).

If one now considers the whole range of problems that might call for legal representation, there appear to be a number of areas in which the poor encounter at least as many legal problems as the rich.[...]

As suggested above, the argument that the poor have fewer legal problems than the rich and therefore less need for lawyers, often merges into the welfare-oriented idea that the problems of the poor are inherently non-legal. This view entails the risk of misconceiving the individual in such a way as to rob him of the dignity of citizenship.

Those who argue that the problems of the poor are essentially social or psychological rather than legal tend to conceive of the poor as incapable of comprehending, let alone altering, their predicament. The poor are thus seen as 'human material that will be worked on, helped, and hopefully transformed' (Matza, 1964, p. 2), as objects to be manipulated or treated by those who claim to know what is good for them – that is, social workers, psychiatrists, probation officers or marriage counsellors.

Although advanced as an empirical fact, this conception of the poor is essentially a value judgement that tends to stigmatize them and reinforce their impotency. In a discussion of the limitations of the New Haven programme for combating poverty, it was pointed out:

A service program fills a need, but experts, not recipients, designate the need to be filled and establish the criteria for eligibility for aid. Typically, there is no effective means of challenging the basic criteria or for obtaining review of particular decisions applying those criteria. The pattern of aid is one of a donee's unquestioning acceptance, of an expert's dictation of what is 'good for the client', and of an administrator's unchecked and unreviewable authority to terminate assistance. That power defines a status of subserviency and evokes fear, resentment and resignation on the part of the donee (Cahn and Cahn, 1964, pp. 1317, 1321–2).

We propose that a distinctive characteristic of the poor, and an essential condition of their predicament, is their lack of participation in the legal and governmental process. Thus the answer to the question of whether the poor have legal problems and need lawyers turns ultimately on the strength of our commitment to the extension of citizenship, for enfranchisement necessarily rests on the capacity to participate in and make effective use of the legal order – in our legal system, this means access to competent legal representation.

Finally, the contention that the problems of the poor are inherently non-legal is based on an extremely narrow view of the law and of the lawyer's role. What is needed is a wider view:

The lawyer's function is essentially that of presenting a grievance so that those aspects of the complaint which entitle a person to a remedy can be communicated effectively and properly to a person with power to provide a remedy. Slum dwellers have many grievances not thought of as calling for lawyer's skills. Yet the justiciability of such grievances should not be prejudged; they require the scrutiny of a skilled advocate, for it is altogether possible that for many a remedy is available if the grievance is properly presented – even though the decision-maker may be a school board, principal, welfare review board, board of police commissioners, or urban renewal agency (Cahn and Cahn, 1964, p. 1336).

(b) There are adequate substitutes for private legal representation

Whatever class differences exist in legal representation have also been defined on the ground that the poor are provided with adequate substitutes for private lawyers in the form of Legal Aid, assigned counsel, public defenders, and special tribunals which have been purposely designed to obviate the necessity of counsel. In order to evaluate this contention it is necessary to examine each of these traditional substitutes.

Legal aid. Much can and should be said in praise of those who have contributed so much time and energy to the cause of providing legal services to the needy. Although there is tangible evidence of their labors, it is our opinion – shared by a number of Legal Aid workers themselves – that Legal Aid is seriously handicapped both in meeting the vast potential need for legal representation and in dealing with cases that are actually handled. Moreover, we suggest that the effectiveness of Legal Aid is undermined by the way it is organized and financed and the way it conceives of its task. [...]

3 Causes of Inequality in Legal Representation

(a) Factors involved in the unequal use of lawyers

Lack of economic resources is undeniably a factor limiting the use of lawyers. However, this represents only one element in a complex social process leading an individual to seek out and obtain legal representation. At least four steps are involved: (1) awareness or recognition of a problem as a legal problem; (2) willingness to take legal action for solution of the problem; (3) getting to a lawyer; and (4) actually hiring a lawyer.

1. Awareness of a problem as a legal problem. Certain situations or actions may objectively give rise to legal problems, but the individuals experiencing such events may not perceive them as

343

generating problems of a legal nature. They may be ignorant of the rights at stake and unaware of the possibility of legal remedies. We suspect this is particularly true of lower-income persons. Precisely what their legal rights and remedies are as tenants, as recipients of welfare benefits, or as creditors, may not be known or clearly understood by those with limited formal education. For example, David Caplovitz has noted that in the consumer area lower-income families have little understanding of their legal rights or of how to exercise them:

Many consumers have almost no idea of the complex set of legal conditions embodied in the contracts they sign. The penalties that can be brought to bear on them, such as the loss of possessions already paid for, the payment of interest on money owed, the payment of lawyer and court fees, are matters that some families become rudely aware of only when – for whatever reasons – they miss their payments (Caplovitz, 1963, p. 155).

Awareness of rights may also be attenuated by the attitude of many welfare agencies and legal aid offices that the poor have 'problems' not 'grievances'.

2. Willingness to take legal action. Awareness of legal problems does not itself result in seeking a lawyer's help. The person must be willing to take legal action, and this presumably means he accepts the appropriateness, efficacy, and fairness of legal solutions to his problems. The indications are that lower-class individuals are much more reluctant to take any legal action even when they recognize they have a legal problem. Thus, in a study of persons who had been mildly injured in auto accidents in New York City, it was found that the lower the socio-economic status of the injured person the less likely he was to take any action to recover: 27 per cent of the lower-class respondents did nothing, compared to only 2 per cent of the higher-class respondents.[6] Similarly, a study in Newark disclosed that close to 90 per cent of the Negroes interviewed who reported alleged acts of discrimination took no action at all in such cases. When

6. Carlin (1959, p. 8). Based on interviews conducted in 1957 with 155 persons collected at random from official records. We recognize that part of the class difference noted above could be explained by a difference in awareness.

asked, 'Who would you turn to if you ran into discrimination?' close to 40 per cent who answered the question said they didn't know or that they would do nothing. The researcher concluded, 'that there is an awareness, for a majority at least, of their problems is clear, but what is equally clear is the profound inertia gripping our sample'.[7]

Two factors seem to be involved in the reluctance of lower-class individuals to take legal action: (1) prior contact or experience with the 'law', resulting in alienation from the legal process, and (2) a general condition of dependency and insecurity leading to fear of reprisal if legal remedies were to be pursued.

Most contacts of lower-class individuals with the law are with police, probation and parole officers, inferior courts, and the like. As to the police, it is concluded from interviews with lower-class Negroes that 'The police are seen, at least in their active roles, as antipathetic (at best) to the interests of the Negro. Mention of the police brought forth a deluge of complaints ranging from callousness and apathy through brutality and extortions.'[7] Contact with courts appears to be equally alienating. Thus, a study[8] of auto accident victims in New York City found that the more often respondents had come in contact with

7. This is taken from an unpublished manuscript by Zeitz and Blumrosen in Rutgers School of Law.

8. The relationship between prior court contact and taking some action (on their own or through a lawyer) to recover for losses arising out of the accident, for low and high socio-economic groups, is as follows:*

Per Cent who Do Nothing† to Recover for Injuries

	Socio-economic status	
	Low	High
No. of times in court		
2 or more	42 (12)	15 (13)
Once	24 (17)	5 (20)
Never	13 (46)	4 (47)

*Source: Carlin (1959). Number in parenthesis indicates the number of respondents.

† I.e., neither filed a claim themselves with an insurance company nor sought help from a lawyer.

courts the less likely they were to take any action to recover for their injuries. And this was especially true of lower-class respondents.

Many actions and decisions of the legal system with respect to the poor tend to degrade and stigmatize them. The following observations regarding the effect on the poor of the process of proving and maintaining eligibility before an administrative agency are clearly in point:

An applicant becomes eligible for assistance when he exhausts his money, gives a lien of his property to the welfare department, turns in the license plates of his car and takes legal action against his legally responsible relatives. When he is stripped of all material resources, when he 'proves' his dependency, then and then only is he eligible. Welfare policies tend to cast the recipient in the role of the propertyless shiftless pauper. This implies he is incompetent and inadequate to meet the demands of competitive life. He is then regarded as if he had little or no feelings, aspirations or normal sensibilities. This process of proving and maintaining eligibility in combination with the literal adherence to regulations and procedures tends to produce a self-perpetuating system of dependency and dehumanization (*Report to the Moreland Commission on Welfare*, 1962, p. 78).[9]

Consequently, the law is frequently viewed by the poor person as something that works against his interest, as his enemy,[10] and as a device that can only be effectively employed through pull and connexions. As Zeitz notes:

Political and legal redress for wrongs is viewed as being part of a patronage system, rather than as a culturally approved part of a system of legal institutions. Thus, the Negro, seeking restitution or redress of wrongs, would prefer to deal on an individual level with a powerful patron, than to deal with the more formal ... legal institutions (see footnote 7 above).

In so far as the poor have contact with lawyers, it is mainly with prosecuting attorneys or lawyers representing collection

9. The use of first names or the term 'boy' in referring to Negroes in southern courts has a similar degrading effect. See *Hamilton* v. *Alabama*, 376 U.S. 650 (1964).

10. 'The poor man looks upon the law as an enemy, not as a friend. For him the law is always taking something away.' From Attorney General Robert F. Kennedy's address on Law Day, 1 May 1964, at the University of Chicago Law School.

agencies, landlords, etc. Furthermore, those who consult lawyers often come too late to get any effective help. They may also be treated with indifference (as part of a volume clientele) or with condescension (as in Legal Aid), and at worst they may be exploited. It is little wonder that many poor persons have a negative image of the law and of lawyers and hesitate to turn to them for help.

Alienation from the legal process is heightened by fear of reprisal from those interests against whom effective action would have to be taken – landlords, employers, local merchants, suppliers of public assistance, police – in short, all those in positions of power *vis à vis* the poor. The poor person is naturally reluctant to challenge these people.

3. Getting to the lawyer. Awareness of legal problems and willingness to take legal action are still not sufficient to put the person in the hands of a lawyer; he must also have access to a lawyer and believe it possible to obtain his services. Lower-class individuals have less access to lawyers; they are less likely, compared to the upper class, to be acquainted with or related to lawyers, and are less likely to know someone who can refer them to lawyers both comparatively and absolutely. A California survey, for example, found that less than 30 per cent of lower-income individuals have either a friend or relative who is a lawyer, compared to 75 per cent of upper-income individuals (*Public Opinion Poll for the State Bar of California*; see Table 1 above). Caplovitz reports, moreover, that in answer to the question, 'Where would you now go for help if you were being cheated by a merchant or salesman?' Sixty-four per cent of the respondents replied that they didn't know, and of those who knew of some source of help, only 8 per cent mentioned a private lawyer (Caplovitz, 1963, p. 175).

The poor are not only out of touch with private attorneys, but they lack knowledge of the availability of free or low-cost legal services. An Iowa study, for example, shows that over 80 per cent of lower-class persons interviewed had no knowledge of where free or low-cost legal services could be obtained (*Lay Opinion of Iowa Lawyers*, p. 34; see Table 1 above). And, as we have seen, the legal aid societies are generally not eager to advertise their services.

Lack of geographical proximity to a law office is a further impediment to use of lawyers by lower-class individuals. Private attorneys, and even legal aid lawyers, tend to be located in the business centres of the city, and this means that considerable time and expense may be involved merely in travelling to the lawyer's office. The extent to which this constitutes a real obstacle to employment of lawyers is suggested by the fact that over 40 per cent of lower-class individuals interviewed in the California study reported they would consult a lawyer more frequently if the law office were near their home (*Public Opinion Poll for the State Bar of California*; see Table 1 above).

Apprehension over costs of legal service may also prevent a poor person from seeking a lawyer's help. There appears to be widespread ignorance as to how much lawyers charge,[11] and fear that whatever the charge, it would be more than he could afford.[12]

4. *Hiring a lawyer*. Assuming a potential client has actually contacted a lawyer, there is a final obstacle in the possible refusal of the lawyer to represent him. And here again, class seems to make a big difference. The indications are that lower-class persons are more likely to be screened out by lawyers. Thus, in a study of individual practitioners in Chicago it was found that most lawyers interviewed had turned away clients and mainly for economic reasons.[13] Moreover, other reasons given for turning away clients (dislike of the client or of the case, lack of legal merit) possibly mask economic or class considerations. Dislike of the client (because he is 'obnoxious', 'mentally unbalanced', 'drunk', of 'low moral character', a 'sponger', etc.) may reflect the cultural distance between the lower-class client and the middle-class lawyer. Dislike of the problem (e.g. criminal, divorce) suggests that it is precisely those cases that are most distinctive

11. Two out of three lower-class respondents in a Texas study did not know how much lawyers charge for giving advice, compared to half of upper class respondents. See Table 1 above.

12. In the California study 55 per cent of lower-class respondents said they would not consult a lawyer for simple advice because of the expense (*Public Opinion Poll for the State Bar of California*; see Table 1 above).

13. These findings are based on further analysis of interview data from the study reported in Carlin (1962).

of lower-class clients that are being rejected. These cases may not be accepted because they often involve lawyers in unethical practises or simply because they are brought by lower-status clients. Lack of legal merit is indeed a legitimate reason for turning down a case. However, lawyers who reject clients on this basis may be unwilling (given the small fee) to put in the time and effort to find a legal solution.

It would appear, then, that lawyers systematically exclude lower-class clients, and that this is based mainly on the following considerations: low expectation of financial gain, a desire to avoid a less prestigeful type of practise and clientele, and perhaps, also, conceptions of what merits consideration in the legal arena. Further, lawyers act as gatekeepers not only by selectively excluding cases and clients, but also by selectively soliciting clients. And here, too, with the exception of personal injury cases (handled primarily on a contingent fee basis), lawyers are unlikely to be looking for legal business from lower-class clients.[14]

At every step of the way, lower-class persons are handicapped by a lack of organizational support. The poor are characterized by a relatively low level of organizational participation; they belong to few if any voluntary organizations, and they are ordinarily not even members of unions.[15] As a result there are few organized groups to alert them to their legal rights, to encourage them to take legal action, or to provide them either with lawyers or with the resources for obtaining lawyers.

(b) Factors affecting class differences in quality and integrity of legal representation

Class differences in the quality of legal service obtained and the integrity of lawyers providing the service are related to the system of stratification of the legal profession. As we have seen previously, individual practitioners and lawyers in smaller firms (particularly in the large metropolitan centres) are least competent, least

14. To quote Wickenden: 'You will have to admit that not many lawyers have been brought before bar associations for unethical behavior in aggressively seeking welfare cases' (From a Paper presented at the Conference on the Extension of Legal Services to the Poor).

15. See Harrington (1964, pp. 18, 26–7).

likely to exercise a high level of technical skill, and least responsible. The question is: why are lower-class persons almost exclusively represented by lower-status lawyers? The answer is that lower-class persons are least able to afford higher-status lawyers, and they generally have access only to those informal referral networks that are tied into lower-status lawyers (Carlin, 1962, chapter 3). Finally, the small fees and high-turnover clientele characteristic of lower-status lawyers lead not only to a low level of technical skill (because of the standardization of practises in handling a volume clientele), but also to a weakening of the lawyer's capacity to resist opportunities for exploiting clients.

References

CAHN and CAHN (1964), 'The war on poverty: a civilian perspective', *Yale Law Journal*, vol. 73.

CAPLOVITZ, D. (1963), *The Poor Pay More*, London.

CARLIN, J. E. (1959), 'How accident victims get to lawyers: summary of findings', mimeographed paper on file at Columbia University's Bureau of Applied Social Research.

CARLIN, J. E. (1962), *Lawyers on Their Own: A Study of Individual Practitioners in Chicago*, Rutgers University Press.

CARLIN, J. E. (1966), *Lawyers' Ethics*, New York.

HARRINGTON, M., (1964) *The Other America: Poverty in the United States*, Macmillan.

MATZA, D. (1964), 'Unmovables', *Stratification Systems: The Disreputable Poor*, unpublished paper prepared for the S.S.R.C. Conference on Social Structure and Social Mobility.

O'GORMAN, H. (1963), *Lawyers and Matrimonial Cases*, Free Press of Glencoe.

REICH, C. (1964), 'The new property', *Yale Law Journal*, vol. 73. *Report to the Moreland Commission on Welfare, Findings of the Study of the Public Assistance Programs and Operations of the State of New York*, no. 78, Greenleigh Associates Inc.

SMIGEL, E. O. (1964), *The Wall Street Lawyer: Professional Organization Man?*, Free Press of Glencoe.

SMITH, R. H. (1919), *Justice and the Poor*.

Further Reading

General

ECKHOFF, T., 'Sociology of Law in Scandinavia', *Scandinavian Studies in Law*, 1960.

EHRLICH, E., *Fundamental Principles of the Sociology of Law*, Harvard University Press, 1936, Russell & Russell, 1962.

SAWER, G., *Law in Society*, Oxford, 1965.

SELZNIK, P., 'The Sociology of Law', *International Encyclopedia of the Social Sciences*, Macmillan and the Free Press, 1968, pp. 50–9.

SKOLNICK, J. H., 'The sociology of law in America: overview and trends', *Law and Society: A Supplement to the Summer Issue of Social Problems*, 1965, pp. 4–39.

TIMASHEFF, N. S., *An Introduction to the Sociology of Law*, Harvard University Committee on Research in the Social Sciences, 1939.

Law and social structure

AUBERT, V., 'White collar crime and social structure', *American Journal of Sociology*, vol. 58, (1952), pp. 263–71.

HOEBEL, E. A., *The Law of Primitive Man*, Harvard University Press, 1954.

PARSONS, T., 'The law and social control', in W. M. Evan, *Law and Sociology*, The Free Press of Glencoe, 1962, pp. 56–72.

POSPISIL, L., 'Legal levels and multiplicity of legal systems in human societies', *Journal of Conflict Resolution*, vol. 11 (1967), pp. 2–26.

REHBINDER, M., 'Wandlungen der Rechtsstruktur im Sozialstaat', *Studien und Materialen zur Rechtssoziologie. Sonderheft 11, Kölner Zeitschrift für Soziologie und Sozialpsychologie*, 1967, pp. 197–222.

SCHWARTZ, R. D., and MILLER, J. C., 'Legal evolution and societal complexity', *American Journal of Sociology*, vol. 70 (1964), pp. 159–69.

SOROKIN, P. A., *Social and Cultural Dynamics. Vol. II: Fluctuations of Systems of Truth, Ethics and Law*, American Book Company, 1937, pp. 523–61.

Legislation, law enforcement and the public.

GOLDSCHMIDT, V., 'Primary sanction behaviour', *Acta Sociologica*, vol. 10, (1966), pp. 173–90.

KUTSCHINSKY, B., 'Law and education: some aspects of Scandinavian studies into "The general sense of justice"', *Acta Sociologica*, vol. 10, (1966), pp. 21–41.

MEAD, G. H., 'The psychology of punitive justice', *American Journal of Sociology*, vol. 23, (1917–18), pp. 577–602.

MOORE, U., and CALLAHAN, C. C., *Law and Learning Theory: A Study in Legal Control*, Yale Law Journal Company Inc., 1943.

SCHMIDT, F., GRÄNTZE, L., and ROOS, K., 'Legal working hours in Swedish Agriculture', *Theoria*, 1946.

SKOLNICK, J. H., *Justice Without Trial: Law Enforcement in Democratic Society*, Wiley, 1966.

Law and conflict resolution

AUBERT, V., 'Competition and dissensus: two types of conflict and of conflict resolution', *Journal of Conflict Resolution*, vol. 7 (1963), pp. 26–42.

AUBERT, V., 'Courts and conflict resolution', *Journal of Conflict Resolution*, vol. 11 (1967), pp. 40–50.

BOHANNAN, P., (ed), *Law and Warfare*, Natural History Press, 1962.

FRANK J., *Courts on Trial: Myths and Reality in American Justice*, Princeton, 1949.

GALTUNG, J., 'Institutionalized conflict resolution', *Journal of Peace Research*, vol. 2 (1965), pp. 348 ff.

LLEWELLYN, K. N., and HOEBEL, E. A., *The Cheyenne Way: Conflict and Case Law in Primitive Jurisprudence*, University of Oklahoma Press, 1941.

SKOLNICK, J. H., 'Social control in the adversary system', *Journal of Conflict Resolution*, vol. 11 (1967), pp. 52–70.

Judicial behaviour

GAUDET, F. J., 'Individual differences in the sentencing tendencies of judges', *Archives of Psychology*, vol. 32 (1938).

GREEN, E., *Judicial Attitudes in Sentencing: A Study of the Factors Underlying the Sentencing Practice of the Criminal Court of Philadelphia*, Macmillan; St Martins Press, 1961.

LASSWELL, H. D., *Power and Personality*, 1948, pp. 65–88.

NAGEL, S. S., 'Political party affiliations and judges' decisions', *American Political Science Review*, 1961, pp. 843 ff.

PRITCHETT, C. H., *The Roosevelt Court: A Study in Judicial Politics and Values, 1937–47*, Macmillan, 1948; Octagon Books, 1963.

SCHUBERT, G. A. (ed.), *Judicial Decision-Making*, Free Press, 1963.

The legal profession

CARLIN, J., *Lawyers on Their Own: A Study of Individual Practitioners in Chicago*, Rutgers University Press, 1962.

LADINSKY, J., 'Careers of lawyers, law practice, and legal institutions', *American Sociological Review*, vol. 28 (1963), pp. 47–54.

PARSONS, T., 'A sociologist looks at the legal profession', *Essays in Sociological Theory*, Free Press of Glencoe, 1954, pp. 370–85.

RIESMAN, D., 'Toward an anthropological science of law and the legal profession', *American Journal of Sociology*, vol. 57 (1951), pp. 121–35.

SMIGEL, E. O., *The Wall Street Lawyer: Professional Organization Man*, Free Press of Glencoe, 1964.

Acknowledgements

Permission to use Readings in this selection is acknowledged
from the following sources:

Reading 1   Free Press of Glencoe
Reading 2   J. M. Dent and Sons Ltd and E. P. Dutton and Company
            Inc.
Reading 3   Routledge and Kegan Paul Ltd
Reading 4   Routledge and Kegan Paul Ltd
Reading 5   Thurman W. Arnold
Reading 6   Free Press of Glencoe
Reading 7   Macmillan and Company Ltd and The Macmillan Com-
            pany of Canada Ltd
Reading 8   The London School of Economics
Reading 9   Tulane Law Review Association
Reading 10 *Acta Sociologica*
Reading 11 *Acta Sociologica*
Reading 12 Tavistock Publications Ltd and Basic Books Inc
Reading 13 *Polish Sociological Bulletin*
Reading 14 Harvard University Press
Reading 15 Manchester University Press
Reading 16 *Acta Sociologica*
Reading 17 Harvard University Press
Reading 18 American Sociological Association and Stewart Macaulay
Reading 19 Scott, Foresman and Company
Reading 20 Tavistock Publications Ltd
Reading 21 Little, Brown and Company Inc
Reading 22 Maitland Publications Pty Ltd
Reading 23 *The Canadian Review of Sociology and Anthropology* and
            Dietrich Rueschemeyer
Reading 24 Heinemann Educational Books Ltd
Reading 25 International Sociological Association
Reading 26 International Sociological Association
Reading 27 Law and Society Association and Abraham S. Blumberg
Reading 28 *U.C.L.A. Law Review* and Jerome E. Carlin

Author Index

357

Subject Index